The Vanity Girl

Compton MacKenzie

Alpha Editions

This edition published in 2024

ISBN : 9789362926029

Design and Setting By
Alpha Editions
www.alphaedis.com
Email - info@alphaedis.com

Contents

CHAPTER I

I

WEST KENSINGTON relies for romance more upon the eccentricities of individual residents than upon any variety or suggestiveness in the scenery of its streets, which indeed are mostly mere lines of uniform gray or red houses drearily elongated by constriction. Yet the suburb is too near to London for some relics of a former rusticity not to have survived; and it is refreshing for the casual observer of a city's growth to find here and there a row of old cottages, here and there a Georgian house rising from sooty flower-gardens and shadowed by rusty cedars, occasionally even an open space of building land, among the weeds of which ragged hedgerows and patches of degenerate oats still endure.

How Lonsdale Road, where the Caffyns lived, should have come to obtrude itself upon the flimsy architecture of the neighborhood is not so obvious. Situated near what used to be the western terminus of the old brown-and-blue horse-omnibuses, it is a comparatively wide road of detached, double-fronted, three-storied, square houses (so square that after the rows of emaciated residences close by they seem positively squat), built at least thirty years before anybody thought of following the District Railway out here. Each front door is overhung by a heavy portico, the stout pillars of which, painted over and over again according to the purse and fancy of the owner, vary in color from shades of glossy blue and green to drabs and buffs and dingy ivories. The steps, set some ten yards back from the pavement, are flanked by well-grown shrubs; the ground floor is partially below the level of the street, but there are no areas, and only a side entrance marked "Tradesmen" seems to acknowledge the existence of a more humble world.

There are thirty-six houses in Lonsdale Road, not one of which makes any sharper claim for distinction than is conferred by the number plainly marked upon the gas-lamp suspended from the ceiling of its portico. Here are no "Bellevues" or "Ben Lomonds" to set the neighborhood off upon the follies of competitive nomenclature; and although at the back of each house a large oblong garden contains a much better selection of trees and flowering shrubs than the average suburban garden, not even the mild pretentiousness of an appropriate arboreal name is tolerated. Away from the traffic of the main street with its toy dairies and dolls' shops, its omnibuses and helter-skelter of insignificant pedestrians, Lonsdale Road comes to an abrupt end before a tumble-down tarred fence that guards some allotments beside the railway, on the other side of which a high rampart with the outline of cumulus marks the reverse of the panoramic boundary of Earl's Court Exhibition. The road is a thoroughfare for hawkers, policemen, and lovers, because a narrow lane follows the line of the tumble-down fence, leading on one side to the hinterland of West Kensington railway station and on the other gradually widening into a terrace of small red-brick houses, the outworks of similar terraces beyond. Why anybody at least fifty years ago should have built in what must then have been open country or nursery gardens along the North End Road these thirty-six porticoed houses remains inexplicable. Whoever it was may fairly be honored as one of the founders of West Kensington, perhaps second only to the one who divined that by getting it called West Kensington instead of East Fulham or South Hammersmith, and so maintaining in the minds of the professional classes a consciousness of their gentility, he was doing as much for the British Empire as if he had exploited their physique in a new colony.

With whatever romance one might be tempted to embellish the origin of Lonsdale Road on account of an architectural superiority to the streets around, it would be fanciful merely for that to endow it with any influence upon the character of the people who live there. Apart from a house where the drains are bad, that has achieved the reputation of being haunted, because the landlord prefers to let it stay empty rather than spend money on putting the drains in order, Lonsdale Road possesses as unromantic a lot of residences as the most banal of West Kensington streets. The nearest approach to a scandal is the way human beings and cats go courting in the lane at the end; but since the former do not live in Lonsdale Road and the latter are not amenable to any ethical code administered by the police, the residents do not feel the burden of a moral responsibility for their behavior.

Such a dignified road within seven minutes of the railway station had in the year 1881 made a strong appeal to Mr. Gilbert Caffyn, who, having just been appointed assistant secretary to the Church of England Purity Society at the early age of twenty-six, with a salary of £150 a year, was emboldened by his father's death and the inheritance of another £200 a year in brewery shares to persuade Miss Charlotte Doyle that their marriage was immediately feasible. Mr. Caffyn had been all the more anxious to press for a happy conclusion of a two years' engagement because Mrs. Doyle was showing every sign of imminent decease, an event which would eliminate a traditionally unsatisfactory relationship and enrich her daughter with £300 a year of her own. Mr. Caffyn therefore sold a quarter of his shares, purchased a ninety-nine years' lease of 17 Lonsdale Road, the last house on the right-hand side away from the growing traffic of West Kensington, and got married. If No. 17 was nearest the railway, it was also rather larger than the other houses, an important consideration for the assistant secretary of the Church of England Purity Society, who was bound to expect at least as many children as a clergyman. Still, for all its extra windows, it was not a very large house; and when in the year 1902 Mr. Caffyn, now secretary of the Church of England Purity Society, with a salary of £400 a year, looked at his wife, his nine children, his two servants, and himself, he wondered how they all managed to squeeze in. He hoped that his wife, who had been mercifully fallow for seven years, would not have any more children, though it might almost be easier to have more children than to provide for the rapid growing up of those he had already. Why, his eldest son Roland was twenty. The question of his moving into cheap rooms to suit his position as the earner of a guinea a week at a branch bank had been mooted several times already, and Mr. Caffyn had been compelled to turn his study (which he never used) into a bedroom for him and his brother Cecil, now a lanky schoolboy of fifteen, rather than expose himself to the likelihood of having to supplement the bank clerk's salary from his own. Then there was Norah, who was eighteen ... but at this moment Mr. Caffyn realized that he had only eight minutes to catch his train up to Blackfriars, and the problem of Norah was put aside. It was a hot morning in late September, and he had long ceased to enjoy running to catch a train.

The departure of the head of the house shortly after his eldest son was followed by Cecil's hulking off to St. James's with half a dozen books under his arm, then by Agnes's and Edna's chattering down the road like a pair of wagtails to their school, and last of all by Vincent's apprehensive scamper to his school. In comparison with the noise during breakfast, the house was quiet; but Dorothy, the second girl, was fussing in the pantry, and Mrs. Caffyn was fussing in the dining-room, while Gladys and Marjorie, two very pretty children of eight and seven, were reiterating appeals to be allowed to play in the front garden. All these noises, added to the noises made by the servants about their household duties, seemed an indication to Norah Caffyn that she ought to take advantage of such glorious weather to wash her hair. She withdrew to the room shared with Dorothy and, having promised her mother to keep an eye on the children, devoted all her attention to herself. She set about the business of washing her hair with the efficiency she applied to everything personal; it used to annoy her second sister that, while she showed herself so practical in self-adornment, she would always be so wantonly obtuse about household affairs.

"I believe you make muddles on purpose," her sister used to declare.

"I don't want to be domestic, if that's what you mean," Norah would reply.

"Wasting your time always in front of a glass!"

"Sour grapes, my dear! If your hair waved like mine you'd look at yourself often enough."

But this morning Dorothy was making a cake, and Norah was able to linger affectionately over the shampoo, safe from her jealous sneers. When she had dried away with a towel enough of the unbecoming lankness she went over to the open window to recapture from the rich September sun the gold that should flash among her fawn-soft hair. Down below among the laurels and privets of the front garden her two youngest sisters were engaged upon some grubby and laborious task which, though they looked like two fat white rabbits, did not involve, so far as Norah could see, without leaning out of the window, any actual burrowing; and she was much too pleasantly occupied with her own thoughts to take the risk of having to interfere. She had propped against the frame of the wide-open window a looking-glass in which she was admiring herself; but the mirror was not enough, and she often glanced over with a toss of her head to the houses opposite, whence the retired colonel in No. 18 or the young heir of No. 16 might perhaps be able to admire her, too. But Norah was not only occupied in contemplating the beauty of her light-brown hair; she was equally engaged with her heart's desire. For the ninth time in two years she was deep in love, this time so deep indeed that she was trying to bring her mind to bear seriously upon the future and the problem of convincing her father that the affection she had for Wilfred Curlew was something far beyond the capacity of a schoolgirl presented itself anew for urgent solution. Yesterday, when her suitor had joined the family in the dining-room after supper, her father had looked at him with an expression of most discouraging surprise; if he should visit them again to-night, as he probably would, her father might pass from discouraging glances to disagreeable remarks, and might even attempt, when Wilfred was gone, to declare positively that he visited Lonsdale Road too often. Intolerable though it was that she at eighteen should still be exposed to the caprice of paternal taboos, it was obvious that until she made the effort to cut herself free from these antiquated leading-strings she should remain in subjection.

Norah regarded the not very costly engagement-ring of intertwined pansies bedewed with diminutive diamonds. In her own room this ring always adorned the third finger of her left hand, and while she was about the house during the day the third finger of her right hand; but when her father came back from the city it had to be concealed, with old letters and dance programs and moldering flowers, in a basket of girlish keepsakes, the key of which was continually being left on her dressing-table and causing her moments of acute anxiety in the middle of supper. If it was not a valuable ring, it was much the prettiest she had ever possessed, and it seemed to Norah monstrous that a father should have the power to banish such a token of seniority from the admiration of the world. What would happen if after supper to-night she announced her engagement? Some time or other in the future of family events one of the daughters would have to announce her engagement, and who more suitable than herself, the eldest daughter? Was there, after all, so much to be afraid of in her father? Was not this tradition of his fierceness sedulously maintained by her mother for her own protection? When she looked back at the past, Norah could see plainly enough how all these years the mother had hoodwinked her children into respecting the head of the family. He might not be conspicuously less worthy of reverence than the fathers of many other families she knew, but he was certainly not conspicuously more worthy of it. The romantic devotion their mother exacted for him might have been accorded to a parent who resembled George Alexander or Lewis Waller! But as he was—rather short than tall (he was the same height as herself), fussy (the daily paper must remain folded all day while he was at the office, so that he could be helped first to the news as he was helped first to everything else), mean (how could she possibly dress herself on an allowance of £6 5s. a quarter?)—such a parent was not entitled to dispose of his daughter; a daughter was not a newspaper to be kept folded up for his gratification.

"For I am beautiful," she assured her reflection. "It's not conceit on my part. Even my girl friends admit that I'm beautiful—yes, beautiful, not just pretty. Father ought to be jolly grateful to have such a beautiful daughter. I'm sure *he* has no right to expect beautiful children."

A figure moved like a shadow in the depths of one of the rooms in the house opposite, and Norah leaned a little farther out of the window to catch more sunbeams for her hair; but when the figure came into full view she was disgusted to find it was only the servant, who flapped a duster and withdrew without a glance at herself. "If father persists in keeping me hidden away in West Kensington," she grumbled, "he can't expect me to marry a duke. No, I'm eighteen, and I'll marry Wilfred—at least I'll marry him when he can afford to be married, but meanwhile I *will* be engaged. I'm tired of all this deception." Norah was pondering the virtue of frankness, when she heard a step behind her and, turning round, saw her mother's wonted expression of anxiety and mild disapproval.

"Oh well," said Norah, quickly, to anticipate the reproach on her lips, "this is the only place I can dry my hair. And, mother, I can't wait any longer to be engaged to Wilfred. I'm going to have it out with father to-night."

Mrs. Caffyn looked frightened, which was what Norah intended, for she felt in no mood to argue the propriety of sitting at an open window with her hair down, and had deliberately introduced the larger issue.

"My dear child, I hope you will do nothing of the kind. Father has been very worried during the last month by that horrid theater advertisement which upset Canon Wilbraham so much, and he won't be at all in the right mood."

Norah sighed patiently, avoided pouting, because she had been warned by a girl friend whose opinion she valued against spoiling the shape of her mouth, and with a shrug of her shoulders turned away and went on brushing her hair.

"My dear child," Mrs. Caffyn began, deprecatingly.

"Oh well, I can't sit in any other room! Besides, the kids are playing down below, and I can't keep an eye on them from anywhere else as well as I can from here."

"Playing in the front garden?" repeated Mrs. Caffyn, anxiously. Anything positive done by any of her children always made her anxious, and she hurried across to the window to call down to them. The two little girls had managed to smear themselves from head to foot with grimy garden-mold, and most unreasonably Mrs. Caffyn could not see that their grubbiness was of no importance compared with the question of whether Norah's hair was not always exactly the color of mignonette buds. She began to admonish them from the window, and they defended themselves against her reproaches by calling upon their eldest sister to testify that what they had done they had done with her acquiescence, since she had not uttered a word against their behavior. Norah declared that she could not possibly go down-stairs without undoing all the good of her shampoo, and in the end Mrs. Caffyn, after ringing ineffectually for her second daughter or one of the servants, had to go down herself and rescue Gladys and Marjorie from the temptations of the front garden.

"Thank Heaven for a little peace," sighed Norah to herself. She sat there in a delicious paradise of self-esteem and, looking at herself in the glass, was so much thrilled in the contemplation of her own beauty that she forgot all about her engagement, all about the lack of spectators, all about everything except the way her features conformed to what in women she most admired. She thought compassionately of her mother's faded fairness, and wondered with a frown of esthetic concern why her mother's face was so downy. If her own chin began to show signs of fluffing over like that, she would spend her last halfpenny on removing hairs that actually in some lights glistened like a smear of honey; luckily there was nothing in her own face that she wanted to change. Her mother must have been pretty once, but never more than pretty, because she had blue eyes. How glad she was that with her light hair went deep brown eyes instead of commonplace blue eyes, and that her mouth instead of being rather full and indefinite was a firm bow the beauty of which did not depend upon the freshness of youth. Not that she need fear even the far-off formidable thirties with such a complexion and such teeth. Apart from superfluous hairs her mother's complexion was still good, and even her father had white teeth. Her own nose, straight and small, was neither so straight nor so small as to be insipid, and her chin, tapering exquisitely, was cleft, not dimpled. Dimples seemed to Norah vulgar, and she could not imagine why they were ever considered worthy of admiration. No, with all her perfection of color and form she was mercifully free from the least suggestion of "dolliness"; she was too tall, and had much too good a figure ever to run any risk of that.

"I'm really more beautiful even than I thought, now that I'm looking at myself very critically. And, of course, I shall get more beautiful, especially when I've found out what way my hair suits me best. I shall make all sorts of experiments with it. There's bound to be one way that suits me better than others, if only it isn't too unfashionable. I suppose father hopes secretly that I shall make a brilliant marriage, because even he must realize that I am exceptionally beautiful."

She played condescendingly with the notion of being able to announce that she was engaged to a viscount, and imagined with what awe the family would receive the news.

"However, that's my affair," she decided. "It's not likely father will bring back a viscount to supper. Besides, I'm not mercenary, and if I choose to love a poor man I will. My looks were given to me, not to father, and if he thinks he's going to get the benefit of them he's made a great mistake."

Norah's meditations were suddenly interrupted by the entrance of her sister Dorothy, a dark, pleasant, practical girl of sixteen, who was already so much interested in household affairs that Norah feared her indifference to dress was due to something more than immaturity, was indeed the outcome of an ineradicable propensity toward dowdiness.

"I wish you wouldn't burst into rooms like that," she protested, crossly.

But Dorothy only hummed round the room in search of what she was looking for, and paid no more attention to her elder sister than a bee would have done.

"And if you've got to come up-stairs to our room when you're in the middle of cooking," Norah went on, "you might at least wipe your hands and your arms first. You're covering everything with flour," she grumbled.

"That's better than covering it with powder," retorted Dorothy.

"What a silly remark!"

"Is it, my dear? Sorry the cap fits so well."

Norah turned away from this obtrusive sister in disdain, asking herself for perhaps the thousandth time what purpose in life she was possibly intended to serve. Apart from the fact that she was dark and distinctly not even good-looking, there seemed no excuse for Dorothy's existence, and Norah made up her mind that she would not bother any more about trying to make her dress with good taste; it simply was not worth while.

"Eureka!" cried Dorothy, triumphantly waving an egg-beater.

"What a disgusting thing to leave in a bedroom!" Norah exclaimed.

Her sister courtesied exasperatingly in the doorway for answer, and before Norah could say another word was charging down the stairs three at a time in a series of diminishing thuds.

Norah turned back, with a shudder for her sister's savagery, to the contemplation of her own hair. In a revulsion against the indecency of family life she resolved firmly that, whatever the fuss, she would be engaged to Wilfred Curlew immediately, and that Wilfred himself must at all costs quickly accumulate enough money to enable her to marry him and escape from this den of sisters and brothers and parents.

"If father had only one child, or perhaps two, he might be entitled to interference with our private lives; but when he's got nine, he must expect us to look after ourselves. It's bad enough now when Cecil, Agnes, Edna, and Vincent are all at school and out of the way, at any rate for some of the time, but what will it be like in a few years?"

Norah shrank from the prospect of that overpopulated future for which the temporary emptiness of Lonsdale Road was no consolation, and, removing the mirror from the window-sill, she sat down at her dressing-table and devoted herself to the adjustment of the arcuated pad of mock hair that was an indispensable adjunct to the pompadour style then in vogue.

Norah had just succeeded in achieving what was hitherto her most successful effort with the pompadour when she heard somebody whistling for her from the pavement; going to the window, she saw that it was her friend, Lily Haden, whom she had known and hated at school two years ago, but whom now, by one of those unaccountably abrupt changes of feminine predilection, she liked very much. The new intimacy had only lately been begotten out of a chance rencounter, and perhaps it would never have been born if Roland, her eldest brother, had not condemned Lily from the altitude of his twenty-year-old priggishness and found in Dorothy a supporter of his point of view. That the brother and sister on either side of her should be hostile to a friend of hers was enough to make Norah fond of Lily, who belonged to a type of ethereal blonde that she hoped did not compete too successfully with herself. Occasionally, at the beginning of the new friendship, Norah was assailed by doubts about this, which intensified her prejudice against blue eyes, not to mention excessive slimness and immoderate length of neck. However, though Lily was not really at all interesting, it was impossible to deny that she was something more than pretty, and when, after a few carefully observed walks, Norah discovered that the percentage of people who looked twice at herself exceeded the percentage of those who looked twice at Lily, she was almost inclined to admit that Lily was beautiful. Quite sincerely, therefore, she was able to call down that she was awfully glad to see her friend; quite honestly, too, she was able to admire her standing there on the sunny pavement below.

The fine autumn weather had allowed the young women of West Kensington to prolong their summery charms with brightly tinted dresses, and in all the dull decades of their existence the houses of Lonsdale Road, even in their first lilac-scented May, had perhaps never beheld a truer picture of spring than this autumnal picture now before them of that tall, slim girl in her linen dress of powder-blue swaying gently as a fountain is swayed by the wind, and above her, framed by dingy bricks that intensified the brilliance of the subject, that other girl in a kimono tea-rose hued from many washings, herself like a tea-rose of exquisite color and form. Yet Mrs. Caffyn, when she hurried into Norah's room, could deduce no more from this rebirth of spring in autumn than a cause for the critical stares of neighbors, and begged her either to invite her friend indoors or to come away from the window.

"I wanted to ask Lily to lunch," said Norah, fretfully.

Mrs. Caffyn was in despair at the notion.

"You have plenty of time to talk to her. It's not yet twelve o'clock," she urged, "and with the children coming home from school and having to be got off again it *is* so difficult to manage with extra people at meals."

"Everything seems difficult to manage in this house."

"I'm sorry to disappoint you, but you must try to think of other people a little."

"It would be difficult to think of anything else in Lonsdale Road, mother dear. Lily," she called out from the window, "come up and talk to me before the animals come roaring home to be fed."

"Norah dear, I'd rather you didn't refer to your brothers and sisters like that," Mrs. Caffyn rebuked, with an attempt at authority that only made her daughter laugh. It may not have been a pleasant laugh to hear, and Mrs. Caffyn may have been right to leave the room with a shake of the head; but Norah's teeth were so white and regular that it was a delightful laugh to look at, and Norah was so intent on watching its effect in the glass that she did not notice her mother had gone away in vexation. Presently she and Lily were deep in the discussion of pompadour pads, so enthralling a subject that when Norah wanted to talk about her engagement it was nearly dinner-time, and she felt more than ever the injustice of not being able to invite her friend to the family meal.

"I must talk to you about Wilfred," she said. "We must have a long talk, because I'm determined to have it settled."

At that moment, with swinging of satchels and banging of doors and much noisy laughter, Agnes and Edna, getting on, respectively, for thirteen and fourteen, arrived back from the school that not so long ago Norah and Lily had themselves attended.

"But it's impossible to talk now," grumbled Norah; and as if to accentuate the truth of this remark her brother Vincent, aged ten, came tearing down the road, dribbling a tin can before him and intoxicated with the news of having been chosen to play half-back for his class. In another two years, he boasted, he would be in the Eleven.

"Why don't you come round to Shelley Mansions this evening?" Lily suggested. "We've invited some friends in."

One of the stipulations made about Norah's friendship with Lily had been that she should never visit the home of her friend, about whose mother all sorts of queer stories were current in West Kensington. To challenge family opinion on this point seemed to her an excellent preliminary to challenging it more severely by insisting on being openly engaged to Wilfred Curlew. She hesitated for a moment, and then announced that she would come.

"To supper?" Lily asked.

After another moment's hesitation Norah promised firmly that she would, and her friend hurried away just as Cecil, a loutish boy with sleeves and trousers much too short for him, slouched back from St. James's. The house which a little while ago had been gently murmurous with that absorbing conversation about pompadour pads now reverberated with the discordant cries of a large family; an overpowering smell of boiled mutton and caper sauce ousted the perfumes from Norah's room; her eyes flashed with resentment, and she went down-stairs to take her place at table.

II

If Norah had been a journalist like her suitor, Wilfred Curlew, she would have described the resolution she made on that September morning as an epoch-making resolution, for since the effect of it was rapidly and firmly to set her on the path of independence it certainly deserved one of the great antediluvian epithets.

Some months ago the Hadens had moved from their house in Trelawney Road because the landlord was so disobliging—as a matter of fact, he was unwilling to wait any longer for the arrears of rent—and they were now inhabiting Shelley Mansions, a gaunt block of flats built on the frontier of West Kensington to withstand the vulgar hordes of Fulham, and as such considered the ultimate outpost of gentility. Most of the tenants, indeed, like the Foreign Legion, were recruited from people who found that their native land was barred to them for various reasons; but if Shelley Mansions lacked the conveniences of civilized flat-life, such as lifts and hall-porters, they possessed one great convenience that was peculiar in West Kensington—nobody bothered about his neighbor's business. Mrs. Haden's elder daughter, Doris, was no longer at home, having recently gone on the stage and almost immediately afterward married; and the small flat, with two empty spare rooms so useful for boxes, was comparatively much larger than the Caffyns' house in Lonsdale Road, the respectability and solid charms of which were spoiled by overcrowding.

Mr. Haden was supposed to be in Burma; but people in the secure heart of West Kensington used to say that Mr. Haden had never existed, a topic that Norah remembered being debated at school, to the great perplexity of the younger girls, who could not imagine how, if there was no Mr. Haden, there could possibly be a Doris and Lily Haden. Nowadays, with years of added knowledge, Norah would have liked to ask her friend more particularly about her absent father; but she was of a cautious temperament, and decided it was easier to accept the Oriental interior of the Shelley Mansions drawing-room as evidence of the truth of the Burmese legend. Her instinct was always against too much intimacy with anybody, and she rather dreaded the responsibility of a secret that might interfere with the freedom of her relations with Lily. Whatever the origins of the household, she decided it was a much more amusing household than the one in Lonsdale Road, and if No. 17 could have achieved the same atmosphere by banishing Mr. Caffyn to Burma, Norah would willingly have packed him off by the next boat.

Mrs. Haden had a loud voice, an effusive manner, and a complexion like a field of clover seen from the window of a passing train. Her coiffure resembled in shape and texture a tinned pineapple; it was, too, almost the same color, probably on account of experimenting with henna on top of peroxide. Norah's inclination to be shocked at her hostess's appearance was mitigated by the pleasure it gave her in demonstrating that Lily's really golden hair was not more likely to prove permanent. Mrs. Haden earned her living by teaching elocution and by reciting. These recitations were mostly interruptions to the conversation of afternoon parties in private houses; but once a year at the Bijou Theater, Notting Hill, she gave a grand performance advertised in the press, when her own recitations were supplemented by a couple of one-act plays never acted before or since, for the production of which some moderately well-known professional friends used to give their services free in order to help Mrs. Haden and the authors. Notwithstanding her energy, she found it very hard to make both ends meet. Norah distinctly remembered that Doris and Lily Haden had left school on account of unpaid fees, and some of the objections raised now to her friendship with Lily were due to Mrs. Caffyn's knowledge that the tradesmen of West Kensington would not allow even a week's credit to the residents of Shelley Mansions. If Mrs. Haden could have overcome their prejudice, her hospitality would doubtless have been illimitable; with all the difficulties they made, it was extensive enough, and she need not have bothered to consecrate a special day to it. But perhaps it pleased her to think that she owned one of the days of the week, for she used to refer to the fame of her Thursdays with as much pride as if they were family jewels.

It was to one of these enslaved Thursdays that Lily had invited Norah, who at first sat shyly back in a wicker chair within the shade of a palm, afraid, so fiercely did Mrs. Haden fix her during a recitation of "Jack Barrett Went to Quetta," that the creakings of her chair were irritating the reciter. Gradually the general atmosphere of freedom and jollity communicated itself to the strange guest, and when the room was so full of tobacco smoke that it was impossible for anybody to recite or to sing or to dance without being almost asphyxiated, she had no qualms about obeying Mrs. Haden's deafening proclamation that everybody must stay to supper. A young man with a long nose, a long neck, an extravagantly V-shaped waistcoat like a medieval doublet, and a skin like a Blue Dorset cheese attached himself to Norah and advised her to sit close to him because he knew his way about the flat. Presumably the advantage of knowing your way about the flat was that you sat still while other people waited on you, and that you obtained second helpings from dishes that did not go round once. Norah seldom resisted an invitation that enabled her to keep quiet while others worked, not because she was lazy, but because rushing about was inclined to heighten her complexion unbecomingly; moreover, since the young man in the V-shaped waistcoat was enough like her notion of a distinguished actor to rouse a mild interest in him, and not sufficiently unlike a gentleman to destroy that interest, she was ready to listen to the advice he was anxious to give her about all sorts of things, but chiefly about the stage.

"Are you studying with Mrs. Haden?" he asked; and when Norah shook her head he turned to her gravely and said: "Oh, but you ought, you know. They may tell you she's a bit old-fashioned, but don't you believe them. Pearl Haden knows her job in and out, and if you've got any talent she'll produce it. Look at me. I was going out with Ma Huntley this autumn as her second walking gentleman, but she wouldn't offer more than two ten, and, as I told her, I really didn't feel called upon to accept less than three. After all, I can always get seven by waiting, and I didn't see why Ma should have me for two ten, especially as she expected me to find my own wigs and ruffles. No, you take my advice and study with Pearl Haden."

"You really recommend her, do you?" asked Norah, condescendingly.

She had never until that moment thought of going on the stage or of taking lessons in elocution from anybody, but the idea of being able to patronize the mother of a friend appealed to her, and, though she was a little doubtful of the way her brothers and sisters would accept her rendering of "Jack Barrett Went to Quetta," she supposed that Wilfred would admire it. One of the charms of being engaged was the security of admiration it provided.

"Though, of course," continued the gentleman in the V-shaped waistcoat, "with your appearance you oughtn't to have to bother much about anything else."

This was very gratifying to Norah; even if there should be trouble when she got home, the evening would have been worth while for this assurance that her looks were capable of making an impression upon artistic society.

"You really think I ought to go on the stage?" she asked, assuming the manner of a person who for a long while has been trying to make up her mind on this very point.

"Everybody ought to go on the stage," the gentleman in the V-shaped waistcoat enthusiastically announced; "at least, of course, not everybody, but certainly everybody who is obviously cut out for the profession like you. But don't be in a hurry to make up your mind," he added. "You're very young." He must have been nearly twenty-five himself. "There's no need to hurry. I was driven to it."

Norah appeared interested and sympathetic. She really was rather interested, because the idea had passed through her mind that Wilfred might go on the stage. If this young man could earn seven pounds a week, surely Wilfred, who was much better looking, could earn ten pounds a week, in which case they might be married at once.

"What drove you to it?" she asked, and then blushed in confusion; being driven to anything was associated in Norah's mind with drink, and she thought the young man might be embarrassed by her question.

"Oh, a woman!" he replied, in a lofty tone. "But don't let's talk about things that are past and over. Let's eat and drink to-day, for to-morrow—Did you ever read Omar Khayyam? A man in our crowd introduced me to him last year. I tell you, after Omar Khayyam Kipling isn't in it. I suppose you read a good deal of poetry?"

"A good deal," Norah admitted. "At least, I used to read a good deal."

This was true; she had read several volumes at school under the menaces of the literature mistress.

"Well, if I may offer you some advice," said the young man, "go on reading poetry. I may as well confess right out that poetry has been my salvation. Have some more of this shape? It's a little soft, but the flavor's excellent." After supper Norah took Lily aside and told her she must go home at once.

"But, Norah," protested the daughter of the flat, without being able to conceal a slight inflection of scorn, "the evening's only just beginning. Lots of people come in after supper always."

Norah resented Lily's tone of superiority; but inasmuch as this was her first experiment in open defiance, she decided not to go too far this time, especially as she was not quite sure how far her father's unreasonableness might not extend.

"Cyril Vavasour will see you home," said Lily. "He's awfully gone on you. He told me you were one of the most beautiful girls he'd ever met."

Norah could not help feeling flattered by such a testimonial from one whose experience among women had evidently been immense, and though she might have expected a superlative without qualification from somebody who met her in a West Kensington drawing-room, she realized that she must expect a slight qualification from a world-wanderer like Mr. Vavasour. A few minutes later Norah and her appreciative new acquaintance descended the echoing steps of Shelley Mansions and were soon safe from any suggestion of Fulham in the landscape and walking slowly through the familiar streets of West Kensington, which in the autumnal mistiness looked grave and imposing. The sky was clear above them, and a fat, yellow moon was rolling along behind a battlement of chimney-tops.

"O moon of my delight who know'st no wane!" quoted Mr. Vavasour, in a devout apostrophe.

Perhaps it was because he imagined himself in a Persian garden much farther away from West Kensington than even Fulham was that he allowed himself to take Norah's arm; nor did she make any objection. After all, he considered her one of the most beautiful girls he had ever met, and, being engaged to be married, she could allow her arm to be taken without danger or loss of dignity.

"And so you really advise me to go on the stage?" she asked, as if she would insinuate that the taking of her arm was only a gesture of interrogation.

"Absolutely," Mr. Vavasour replied.

"Yes, but of course my father's awfully old-fashioned, and he may think I oughtn't to go on the stage."

"Too much exposed to temptation and all that, I suppose?" suggested Mr. Vavasour.

"Oh no," said Norah, irritably, withdrawing her arm. "I didn't mean that. I meant he might think the family wouldn't like it."

She had intended to give the impression of belonging to a poor but noble family without giving the impression of being snobbish, and she was rather annoyed with Mr. Vavasour for not understanding at once what she meant.

"Oh, but people from the best families go on the stage nowadays," he assured her.

"Yes, I suppose they do," Norah agreed.

"And of course you could always change your name," he added.

"Yes, of course I could do that," she admitted.

"I changed mine, for instance," he told her.

"I like the name Vavasour."

"Yes, I rather liked it myself," he said; but he did not volunteer his own name, and she did not ask him to reveal what Howards or Montagus had plucked him forever from their family tree. In any case this was not the moment to embark on fresh confidences, for they were approaching the main street and Norah was almost sure that the figure standing at the corner of Lonsdale Road on the other side was her eldest brother, Roland.

"Don't come any farther," she said. "Perhaps we'll meet again at Lily's some day."

"We shall," Mr. Vavasour announced, with conviction. "Good night." He swept his hat from his head with a flourish and Norah shook hands with him. She had been rather afraid all the way back that he would try to kiss her good night, but gentle blood and the bright arc-lamp under which they were standing combined to deter him, and they parted as ceremoniously as if his V-shaped waistcoat was really a medieval doublet.

"Oh, it *was* you," said Roland.

"How do you mean it *was* me? Who did you think it was?"

"Do you know what the time is? Half past ten!"

"Thanks very much," said Norah, sarcastically. "The wrist-watch you gave me at Christmas is not yet broken."

"Don't be silly, Norah," he protested. "Father's in an awful wax. I've been hanging about here for the last half-hour, because I couldn't stand it."

They were walking quickly down Lonsdale Road, and Norah was thinking how clumsily he walked compared with Mr. Vavasour and yet how much better looking he was.

"Did Wilfred come?" she asked.

Her brother nodded. "Yes, but I told him you weren't in, and he went off in a bit of a gloom."

They had reached the gate of No. 17 by now, and the house seemed to Norah unreasonably hushed for this hour of the evening. Beyond the railway line the sky was lit up with the glare of the Exhibition, and the music that the military band was playing—it was a selection from "The Earl and the Girl"—was distinctly audible.

"Why should father object to my going out in the evening?" she asked, turning to her brother sharply. "He used to object to your smoking."

Roland removed from his mouth the large pipe and thought ponderously for a minute. It was quite true that only two years ago his father had objected to his smoking, and that with great difficulty he had been able to persuade him that bank clerks always smoked. Since that struggle his father had yielded him a grudging admission that he was grown up. The long years before he should be a bank manager rose like a huge array of black clouds before his vision, and though he disapproved of sisters acting on their own initiative, something in this autumnal night—perhaps it was only the sound of the distant band—created in him a sudden sympathy with any aspirations to freedom. Perhaps, if Norah had encouraged him at that moment, he would have stood up for her independence; but he felt that his company only irritated her and without a word he led the way up the steps, dimly aware that he and she had already set foot upon the diverging paths of their lives.

The dining-room had been cleared for action. Ordinarily at this hour the room was full of young people playing billiards on the convertible dining-table; but to-night the table had not been uncovered, the children had all gone to bed, and Mr. Caffyn was reading the *Daily Telegraph*, not as one might have supposed with enjoyment of the unusual peace, but, on the contrary, in a vague annoyance that his perusal of the leading article was not being interrupted by the butt-end of a cue or the chronicle of London Day by Day being punctuated by billiard-balls leaping into his lap. His patriarchal feelings had, in fact, been deeply wounded by his daughter's behavior, and though for the first time in months he had been able to put on his slippers without having to hold up a noisy game while they were being looked for, he was not at all grateful.

"I've had my supper," Norah informed him, brightly.

This really annoyed Mr. Caffyn extremely, for he had been looking forward to telling his daughter that her supper had been kept waiting until ten o'clock, when it had finally been removed in order to allow the servants to go to bed. At this moment Mrs. Caffyn, who had hurried down-stairs to the kitchen as soon as she heard Norah coming, arrived in the dining-room with a tray.

"She's had her supper," said Mr. Caffyn, indignantly.

"Oh, I was afraid—" his wife began.

"Oh no, she's had her supper," said Mr. Caffyn. "Good Heavens! I don't know what the world's coming to!"

Since her father was making a cosmic affair of her behavior in going out to supper without leave, Norah decided to give him something to worry about in earnest, and, seating herself in the arm-chair on the other side of the fireplace, she prepared to argue with him. Mrs. Caffyn began to murmur about going to bed and talking things over when father came back from the office to-morrow, but Norah waved aside all procrastination.

"I want to talk about my engagement," she began.

Roland, who had just reached the door, stopped. Wilfred Curlew was a friend of his; in fact, it was he who had first brought him to the house, and though he knew that anything in the nature of an engagement between him and one of his sisters was ridiculous, he hoped that a soothing testimony from him would prevent Wilfred's final exclusion from the family circle.

"Norah, dear child, it isn't nice to begin playing jokes upon your father at this hour, especially when he isn't very pleased with you," Mrs. Caffyn said, waving her eyes in the direction of the door.

"I'm not at all sleepy," said Norah, coldly. "And I'm not joking. I want to know if father is going to let Wilfred and me be openly engaged?" she persisted, holding up her left hand so that the gaslight illuminated the ring upon the third finger.

"And who may Wilfred be?" demanded Mr. Caffyn.

This seemed to Roland a suitable moment for his intervention, and, though he had for some time been aware that his father was growing impatient of their habitual visitor, he pretended to accept this attitude of Olympian ignorance and reminded him that Wilfred was a friend who sometimes came in during the evening.

"You said once, if you remember, that he was rather a clever fellow. As a matter of fact he's doing well, you know, considering that he's not long gone in for journalism. He's just been taken on the staff of the *Evening Herald*. He's been doing that murder in Kentish Town."

Mr. Caffyn rose from his chair and with an elaborate assumption of irony inquired if his daughter proposed to engage herself on the strength of a murder in Kentish Town. Norah had got up when her father did and was listening with a contemptuous expression while he dilated on the folly of long engagements.

"Yes, but I don't intend it to be a long engagement," Norah proclaimed, when he paused for a moment to chew his heavy mustache. "I intend to get married."

Mr. Caffyn swung round upon his heels and faced his daughter.

"This, I suppose, is the result of the education I've given you. Insolence and defiance! Don't say another word or you'll make me lose my temper. Not another word. Norah, I insist on silence. Do you hear me? You have grievously disappointed my fondest hopes. I have not been a strict father. Indeed, I have been too indulgent. But I never imagined *my* daughter capable of a folly like this. If I'd thought, twenty-one years ago, when I bought this house with the idea of creating a happy home for you all, that I should be repaid like this I would have.... I would have...."

But Mr. Caffyn's apodosis was never divulged, because, seized with an access of rage, he turned out the gas and hurried from the room. In the hall he shouted back to know if his wife was going to sit up all night. Mrs. Caffyn hurried after her husband as fast as she was able across the darkened room.

"I'm coming, dear, now. Yes, dear, I'm coming now. Ouch! My knee!... I'm sure Norah will be more sensible in the morning," she was heard murmuring on her way up-stairs.

"I suppose he thinks I shall go on living with him forever," exclaimed Norah, savagely throwing herself down into her father's arm-chair. "In my opinion most parents are fit to be only children. Light the gas again, Roland; I want to write a note to Wilfred."

III

By the time morning was come Norah had decided that she would rather go on the stage than be engaged to Wilfred Curlew. The extraordinary thing was that she should never have realized, before her conversation with Mr. Vavasour, how obviously the stage was indicated as the right career for her. It was true that she had never until now seriously contemplated a career, and the mild way she had accepted herself merely as the most important member of a large family was sufficient answer to the silly accusations made by her father last night. Perhaps he would begin to appreciate her now when he was on the point of losing her; perhaps he would regret that he had ever suggested she was indifferent to the claims of family life; in future she should take care to be indifferent to everybody's feelings except her own; she would teach her father a lesson. It never entered Norah's head that there would be any difficulty about going on the stage apart from paternal opposition, and she wondered how many famous people had owed their careers to a fortuitous event like her meeting with Mr. Vavasour. At any rate, it would not be more difficult to obtain her father's permission to embark on this suddenly conceived adventure than it would be to obtain his permission to wear on the third finger of her left hand the rather cheap ring that was the outward sign of her intention to marry Wilfred. Confronted by the two alternatives— success in the theater and matrimony with Wilfred—she felt that success was much the less remote of the two; in fact, the more she thought about it the farther away receded matrimony and the more clearly defined became success. "I don't want to be a great actress," she explained to herself; "I want to be a successful actress." She half made up her mind to go out and talk to Lily about the new project, but on second thoughts she decided not to alarm her parents by any prospect so definite as would be implied in availing herself of the practical assistance that Lily and her mother could afford her in carrying out her plan. It would be more tactful to present as alternatives the definite fact of being engaged to Wilfred or the indefinite idea of being able some time or other in the future to adopt the stage as a profession. The more Norah thought about Wilfred the less in love with him she felt, and the less in love with him she felt the easier would be her task to-night. In her note she had told him to come in after supper, as usual, but she had not said a word about her intention to precipitate their affair. Would it impress her father if she and Wilfred were to meet him at the station and approach the subject before supper? No, on the whole, she decided, it would be more prudent to provoke the final scene otherwise, and her heart quickened slightly at the thought of the surprise she was going to spring upon the family that evening.

Norah was unusually pleasant to everybody all day: she gave Vincent some sweets that she did not like herself; she offered to take Gladys and Marjorie for a walk in Kensington Gardens, because a rumor had reached her of a wonderful display of hats in one of the big shops in Kensington High Street. She noticed that when her father came back from the office he seemed to have forgotten about the scene of last night, and she saw her mother's spirits rising at the prospect of an undisturbed evening. After supper Mr. Caffyn sat down as usual in his arm-chair; Gladys and Marjorie, tired after their long walk and exhausted with the contemplation of shop-windows in which they had perceived nothing to interest themselves, went off to bed without trying for a moment's grace. The upper leaves of the dining-table were removed, and a party of billiards was made up with Norah and Cecil matched against

Roland and Dorothy; Vincent was allowed to chalk the tips of the cues, Agnes and Edna to quarrel over the marking. Mrs. Caffyn, with a sigh of relief for the comfortable wheels on which the evening was running, took the arm-chair opposite her husband and read with unusual concentration what she imagined was yesterday's morning paper, but which, as a matter of fact, was the morning paper of a month ago. Soon the front-door bell rang, and a friend of Roland's, called Arthur Drake, with whom Norah had been in love for a week about a year ago and of whom Dorothy was slightly enamoured at the present, came in full of a new round game for the billiard-table that he had just learned in another house. Cecil went off to his home-work and left Arthur to explain the new game—a complicated invention in which five small skittles, a cork, and a bell suspended from the gas-bracket each played a part. Mr. Caffyn fended off the butt-ends of the cues that were continually bumping into him amid a great deal of shouting and laughter; Agnes trod on her mother's corn; Vincent grazed his knuckles in fielding a billiard-ball that was bound for his father's head.

"And where's old Wilfred?" Arthur Drake suddenly inquired.

Another ring at the front door answered his question and Norah's suitor came in. He was a loose-jointed young man of about twenty-two, with tumbled wavy hair, bright gray eyes, and a trick, when he was feeling shy, of supporting with one arm the small of his back. His long, dogmatic chin was balanced by an irregular and humorous mouth; his personality was attractive, and if he had earned five times as much as he earned as reporter on the staff of the *Evening Herald*, or even if he had been paid for the fierce and satirical articles he wrote on the condition of modern society for a socialist weekly called *The Red Lamp*, he might not have been considered an unsuitable mate for Norah. As it was, Mr. Caffyn looked up at him with as much abhorrence as he would have betrayed at the entrance into his dining-room of the dog that his children were always threatening to procure and the purchase of which he was constantly forbidding. Wilfred tried hard to lose himself in the round game, and whenever he was called upon to make a shot from the corner where Mr. Caffyn was sitting he did so with such unwillingness to disturb Mr. Caffyn that he always missed it. Every time he found an opportunity to pass Norah in the narrow gangway between the wall and the table he tried to squeeze her hand; and he did his best by bribing Vincent with some horse-chestnuts he had collected that morning at Kew, where his work had taken him to investigate an alleged outrage in the Temperate House, to inspire Vincent with an unquenchable desire to play Up Jenkins. Norah, however, had a plan of her own that made the notion of occasionally clasping Wilfred's hand under the table during Up Jenkins seem colorless, and Wilfred, who in his most optimistic prevision of the evening had not counted upon more than two or three kisses snatched by ruse, suddenly found himself invited by her to abandon the game and come into the drawing-room next door.

The drawing-room of No. 17 was invested every Wednesday afternoon by a quantity of punctilious ladies who came to call on Mrs. Caffyn. Owing to the number of its ornaments and the flimsiness of its furniture, it was not considered a suitable room for general use; moreover, as secretary of the Church of England Purity Society, it occasionally fell to Mr. Caffyn's lot to interview various clergymen there on confidential matters, and in a house like 17 Lonsdale Road, worn and torn by children, it was essential to preserve one room in a condition of gelid perfection. So rarely was the room used that the over-worked servants had not bothered to draw the curtains at dusk, and when Wilfred and Norah retired into its seclusion the chilly gloom was accentuated by the street-lamps gleaming through the bare lime-trees at the end of the garden. Norah told her lover to light the gas, and not even the sickly green incandescence availed to make her appear less beautiful to him in this desert of ugly knickknacks.

"No, don't pull the curtains," she said, quickly, "and don't kiss me here, because people might see you from the street. I didn't ask you to come in here to make love."

Perhaps a sense of the theater had always been dormant in Norah, for she went on as if she were making a set speech; but Wilfred was much too deep in love to let the cynicism upon which he plumed himself apply to her, and he listened humbly.

"We can't go on like this forever," she wound up. "We must be engaged openly. I told father that last night, but he won't hear of it, so what are we to do?"

"Darling, I'm ready to do anything."

"Oh, anything!" she repeated, petulantly. "What is anything? He'll be here in a minute, and you've got to tell him that unless he consents to our being engaged you'll persuade me to elope."

"Do you think he'd give way then?" Wilfred asked, doubtfully. He was very much in love with Norah, but he could not help remembering that he, too, had a father who, after an argument every Sunday evening, still allowed him ten shillings a week for pocket-money. If he were to elope, he should not only be certain to lose that supplement to his own earnings, but he should also involve in deeper discredit the profession he had adopted instead of the law, which Mr. Curlew, senior, had designed him to enter by way of the office of an old friend who was a solicitor.

Norah wished that her father would come in and interrupt what should have been a passionate scene, but which was in reality as cold as the room where it was being played. She watched herself and Wilfred, whom the incandescent gas did not set off to advantage, in the large mirror that formed the over-mantel of the fireplace, and she realized now, as she had never realized before in her life, how amazingly she stood out from her surroundings.

"You haven't kissed me once this evening," Wilfred began; but she shook herself free from his tentative embrace, and with one eye on the door for her father's entrance and the other on the mirror, or rather with both eyes at one moment on the door and immediately afterward on the mirror—a movement which displayed their brilliancy and depth—she went on enumerating to her suitor the material difficulties that made their engagement so hopeless.

"But I'm getting on," he insisted. "The editor was very pleased with the way I handled that Kentish Town murder. They don't consider me at all a dud in Fleet Street. I'm sure I give everybody in this house quite a wrong impression of myself because I feel nervous and awkward when I'm here; but I don't think there's really much doubt that in another couple of years I shall be in quite a different position financially. Besides, I hope to do original work, and if a friend of mine can raise the money to start this new weekly—"

"Oh, if, if, if!" interrupted Norah, impatiently.

"Norah, don't you love me any more?"

"Of course I love you," she said. "Don't be so stupid."

"You seem different to-night."

"You wouldn't like me to be always the same, would you?"

"No, but—" He broke off, and turned away with a sigh to regard the melancholy street-lamps twinkling through the lime-trees at the end of the garden.

"I think it's I who ought to be angry, not you," said Norah. "I offered to marry you at once, and you instantly began to make excuses."

"Norah!" protested the young man.

"Oh, how I hate everything!" she burst out, looking round her with a sharper consciousness than she had ever experienced before of the drawing-room's ugliness and life's banality. At this moment Mrs. Caffyn put her head timidly round the door.

"You'd better come back to the dining-room, dear," she advised. "I think father's just noticed you're not there."

"That's exactly what I meant him to do."

"Norah!" exclaimed her mother, in a shocked voice. "What has come over you these last two days?"

Wilfred was supporting the small of his back in an unsuccessful effort to look at ease, and Norah was wondering more than ever how she could ever have fancied herself in love with him. How awkward he appeared standing there, almost—she hesitated a moment before she allowed herself to think the worst it was possible to think of anybody—almost common! She looked half apprehensively at Wilfred to see if he had divined her unspoken thought. She would not like him to know that she was thinking him—almost common; he might never get over it. She was sure he was particularly sensitive on that point because in *The Red Lamp* he was always declaiming against snobbery.

Suddenly they heard the dining-room door open, and Mrs. Caffyn had barely time to breathe an agonized, "Oh, dear, what did I tell you would happen?" before the head of the house came in. Upon the dining-room an appalled silence must have fallen when Mr. Caffyn rose from his chair, and one could fancy the frightened players, cues in hands, huddled against the wall in dread of the imminent catastrophe. The whole house was electric as before an impending storm, and above the stillness the mutter of a passing omnibus sounded like remote thunder. With so much atmospheric help Mr. Caffyn ought to have been able to achieve something more impressive than his, "Oh, you're in here, are you? I wish you wouldn't light the gas in the drawing-room when there's no need for it."

"I thought you wouldn't like us to sit in the dark," Norah murmured, primly.

"Don't deliberately misunderstand me. You know perfectly well what I mean. Moreover, I don't think it's nice for the children; it may put all sorts of ideas into their young heads."

Inasmuch as Mr. Caffyn was secretary of the Church of England Purity Society with private means of his own, while his daughter's suitor was an agnostic journalist who had never yet earned more than thirty-five shillings in one week, it is perhaps not astonishing that the young man should have begun to apologize for lighting the gas needlessly. To Norah, however, these apologies sounded infinitely pusillanimous; from having been very much in love yesterday morning she had already reached indifference, and this final exhibition of cowardice brought her to the point of positively disliking Wilfred. Nevertheless, she managed somehow to impress her father with her intention to die rather than give him up, and after an argument of about ten minutes, in the course of which Norah did all the talking, her father all the shouting, and her mother and suitor all the fidgeting, Mr. Caffyn was at last sufficiently exasperated and ordered Wilfred Curlew to leave the house immediately. In spite of Mrs. Caffyn's entreaties the pitch of her husband's voice had been so piercing that he had probably managed not merely to put ideas into the heads of the children still in the dining-room, but even to corrupt the dreams of the sleeping innocents up-stairs.

"Gilbert dear," his wife besought. "The servants!"

"I pay my servants to attend to me, not to my affairs," said Mr. Caffyn, majestically. His wife might have replied that under the terms of their marriage contract it was she who paid the servants out of her own money; but having been married twenty-one years she had long ceased to derive any satisfaction from putting herself in the right. Poor Wilfred, finding that he must either say something to break the silence which had succeeded Mr. Caffyn's denunciation of his behavior or retire, preferred to retire, and with one arm firmly wedged into the small of his back he stumbled awkwardly down the hall to the front door. Norah made no attempt to alleviate the discomfiture of his exit; but Arthur Drake, with a chivalry, or, to put it at its lowest valuation, with a social tact that amazed her, covered Wilfred's retreat by such a display of farewell courtesies as made even the practical Dorothy pause and consider if there might not be something in love, after all.

"Bolt the door," Mr. Caffyn commanded. "And be sure that the chain is properly fastened."

Then rather at a loss how to maintain the level of his majesty and wrath, he luckily discovered that Vincent had not yet gone to bed, and exhorted the assembled family to tell him if he paid £8 a term to Mr. Randell for Vincent to grow up into a pot-boy or a billiard-marker. Cecil, the recent winner of a senior scholarship at St. James's, had been grinding at his home-work in the bedroom, and he came out into the hall at this moment to plead pathetically for a few doors to be shut. His father improved the occasion by holding up Cecil as a moral example to the rest of the family, who were made to feel that if Gilbert Caffyn had not produced Cecil Caffyn, Gilbert Caffyn's life would have been wasted. The more he descanted upon Cecil's diligence and dutifulness the more sheepish Cecil himself became, so that with every fresh encomium his sleeves revealed another inch of ink-stained cuff. The only way to stop Mr. Caffyn and restore Cecil to the algebraical problem from which he had been raped by the noise outside his room seemed to be for everybody to go to bed. Agnes and Edna, their heads stuffed full of new ideas, went giggling up-stairs, whither Dorothy, yawning very elaborately, followed them. Roland decided that Cecil groaning over an algebra problem would be more endurable than having to listen to a renewal of the argument between Norah and his father, and he, too, retired. The gradual melting away of the audience quieted Mr. Caffyn, who, when he had lowered or extinguished all the gas-jets except those in the dining-room, felt that he had shown himself master of his own house, and returned to his arm-chair with the intention of nodding over the minor news in the paper until he was ready for bed himself. Norah, however, in spite of her mother's prods and whispered protests, brought him sharply back to the matter in dispute.

"Suppose I insist on being engaged to Wilfred?" she began.

"Good Heavens!" cried Mr. Caffyn. "Am I never to be allowed a little bit of peace? Here am I working all day to keep you clothed and fed, and every night of my life is made a burden to me. You don't appreciate what it is to have a father like me." His wife patted him soothingly and flatteringly upon the shoulder as if she would assure him that they all really appreciated the quality of his fatherhood very much. "Why, I know fathers," went on Mr. Caffyn, indignantly, "who spend every evening at their clubs, and upon my soul, I don't blame them. I was talking to the Bishop of Chelsea to-day. He came into the office to consult me about the scandalous language used at the whelk-stalls in Walham Road on Saturday nights—we're taking up the question with the municipal authorities. He told me I looked tired out. 'You look tired out, Mr. Caffyn,' he said. 'I am tired out, my lord,' I answered. And *he* was very sympathetic."

"You hear that, Norah dear?" said Mrs. Caffyn, twitching her fingers with nervousness. "Now don't worry your father any more."

"As soon as he answers my question I sha'n't worry him any more. Suppose I insist on being engaged to Wilfred Curlew? Suppose I run away and get married to him?"

"Have you any conception what marriage means?" demanded Mr. Caffyn. "Do you realize that I waited two years to marry your mother, and that I didn't propose to her until it was quite evident that my poor father must soon die? I suppose you don't want me to die, do you? Don't imagine that my death will make any difference, please."

"Gilbert, Gilbert!" begged his wife.

"Well, really, nowadays children behave in such an extraordinary fashion that it wouldn't surprise me at all to hear Norah was counting on my death."

"Gilbert, Gilbert!" she repeated, and looked in agony at the gas, as if she expected it to turn blue at such a horrible suggestion.

"If I don't marry Wilfred," Norah went on, "I must earn my own living."

"How?" inquired her father, with an assumption of blustering incredulity.

"By going on the stage."

"On the stage?" he repeated. "Do you realize that only yesterday I had to deal with the question of our attitude toward the posters of several theaters?"

"That wouldn't have anything to do with me," said Norah.

"But how are you going on the stage?" her father continued.

"I should try to get an engagement."

"Oh, would you, indeed? Ha-ha! Your mind seems to be running on engagements, my child. However, this engagement is even more visionary and improbable than the other one," said Mr. Caffyn, with a laugh. "I'm afraid you think it's easier than it is, my dear girl. I have a little experience of the stage—I regret to say chiefly of its worst side—and I can assure you that it's not at all easy, really."

"But if I can get an engagement?" persisted Norah.

"Why, in that case we'll talk about it," said her father. "Yes, yes, there'll be plenty of time to talk about that later on. And now if you have no objection I should like to read what Mr. Balfour is saying about Protection. It's a pity you don't try to take some interest in the affairs of your country instead of— However, I suppose that's *too* much to expect from the younger generation."

"I must have your promise," Norah insisted. "If I write to Wilfred to-night and tell him he mustn't come to the house any more, will you let me go on the stage?"

"We'll see about it," parried Mr. Caffyn.

"No, I must have a definite promise."

"Must, Norah? Do, dear child, remember that you're speaking to your father," murmured her mother.

"Oh, that's the modern way we bring up our children," said Mr. Caffyn. "Before I know where I am I shall have Vincent ordering me up to bed."

His wife laughed with such conjugal enthusiasm at his joke that the last vestige of Mr. Caffyn's ill humor disappeared, and, being suddenly struck with the extreme beauty of his eldest daughter as she waited there bright-eyed in expectation of his answer, he promised her that if she would break off all communication with that confounded young Curlew and could obtain an engagement for herself, he would probably not create any difficulties. Her face lit up with satisfaction and, bending over, she kissed her father on the forehead with as much good will as a young woman kisses an elderly lover who has promised her some diamonds she has long desired.

IV

Norah kept her word and wrote a letter to Wilfred Curlew in which she pointed out the impossibility of embarking on a prolonged and quite indefinite engagement, wished him good luck for the future, and made it clear that she did not intend to have anything more to do with him. The portion of the letter on which she most prided herself was the postscript: "*Don't think that I bear you any ill will. I don't.*" The peace that had lately fallen over South Africa left Wilfred no opportunity of putting his despair at the service of his country; but Norah's behavior benefited the young journalist in the long run by teaching him to mistrust human nature as much as God, a useful lesson for a democrat. Norah, having disembarrassed herself of her suitor, set out in earnest to get on the stage and confided her ambition to Lily. Mrs. Haden's advice was asked, and Norah as a friend of her daughter was given lessons in elocution and deportment without being charged a penny. Mrs. Haden demonstrated to her that she stood very little chance of getting on the stage until she could recite "Jack Barrett Went to Quetta" or "Soldier, Soldier, Come from the Wars" with what she called as much intention as herself; in other words, until the story of Jack Barrett was awarded as much pomp of utterance as the Messenger's speech in Hippolytus and the demobilized soldier greeted with Ophelia's driveling whine. Mrs. Haden would not allow that her pupil's looks were nearly as important as her ability to mouth Rudyard Kipling—perhaps, the pupil thought, because her mistress had a pretty daughter of her own. September deepened to October, October dimmed to November while Norah was wrestling with her dread of seeming ridiculous and was acquiring the unnatural diction that was to be of such value to her first appearance. The lessons came to an abrupt end soon after Mrs. Haden had begun upon her deportment, which to Norah seemed to consist of holding her hands as if she were waiting to rinse them after eating bread and treacle, and of sitting down on a chair as if she had burst one suspender and expected the other to go every minute. One morning when she arrived at Shelley Mansions for her lesson Lily came to the door of the flat and with fearful backward glances cried out that her mother was lying dead in bed.

"Dead?" echoed Norah, irritably. She was always irritated by a sudden alarm. "I wish you wouldn't—" She was going to say "play jokes," but she saw that Lily was speaking the truth, and, having been taught by Mrs. Haden how to suit the action to the word, the expression to the emotion, she contrived to look sympathetic.

"She must have died of heart, the doctor says. I went to see why she didn't ring for her tea and she didn't answer, and when I thought she was asleep she was really dead."

Norah shuddered.

"I'm awfully sorry I've disturbed you in the middle of all this," she murmured.

"But I'm glad you've come," said Lily.

"It's awfully sweet of you, my dear, to be glad; but I wouldn't dream of worrying you at such a moment. And don't stand there shivering in your nightgown. Take my advice and dress yourself. It will distract your mind from other things. You must come round and see me this afternoon, and I'll try to cheer you up. I shall stay in for you. Don't forget."

Norah hurried away from Shelley Mansions, thinking while she walked home how easily this untoward event in the Haden household might hasten the achievement of her own ambition. Lily would obviously have to do something at once, and it would be nice for her to have a companion with whom she could start her career upon the stage. Norah had not intended to take any definite steps until her nineteenth birthday in March, but she was anxious to show her sympathy with Lily, and it was much kinder, really, to make useful plans for the future than to hang about the stricken flat, getting in everybody's light. If Lily came this afternoon they would be able to discuss ways and means; it would be splendid for Lily to be taken right out of herself; it would be nice to invite her after the funeral to come and stay in Lonsdale Road, so that they could talk over things comfortably without always having to go out in this wet weather; yet such an excellent suggestion would be opposed by the family on the ground that there was no room for a stranger. How intolerable that the existence of so many brothers and sisters should interfere with the claims of friendship! Perhaps she could persuade Dorothy to sleep with Gladys and Marjorie for a week or two. She and Lily should have so much to talk over, and if Dorothy were in the room with them it would be an awful bore. Full of schemes for Lily's benefit, she approached her sister on the subject of giving up her bed.

"Anything more you'd like?" asked Dorothy, indignantly.

"I think," said Norah, "that you are without exception the most selfish girl I ever met in all my life."

Dorothy grunted at this accusation, but she refused to surrender her bed, and Norah soon gave up talking in general terms about people who were afraid to expose themselves to a little inconvenience for the sake of doing a kind action, because Lily arrived next day with the news that her sister had obtained leave to be "off" for a week and was advising her to do everything she could to get an engagement as soon as possible. There were problems of arrears of rent and unpaid bills from the solution of which it would be advantageous for Lily to escape by going on tour. The few personal possessions of their mother the sisters would divide between them, and the undertaker was to be satisfied at the expense of a fishmonger who, being new to West Kensington, had let Mrs. Haden run an account.

"And your father?" Norah could not help asking; but Lily avoided a reply, and Norah, who had been too well brought up to ask twice, formed her own conclusions.

"Anyway, my dear," she assured her friend, "you can count on me. I hadn't intended to do anything definite until I was nineteen, but of course I'm not going to desert you. So we'll go and interview managers together."

"Doris advises me to try Walter Keal," said Lily. "Dick—her husband—has given me a letter for him which may be useful, he says."

"Who's Walter Keal?"

"Don't you know?" exclaimed Lily. "He sends out all the Vanity shows."

Norah bit her lips in mortification. She hated not to know things and decided to avoid meeting Doris, who as a professional actress of at least a year's standing would be likely to patronize her.

"You see," Lily went on, "he'll be sending out 'Miss Elsie of Chelsea' at the end of December, and if we could get in the chorus we should be all right till June."

"The chorus?" echoed Norah, disdainfully. "I never thought of joining the chorus of a musical comedy."

"It might only be for a few months, and when you're with Walter Keal there's always the chance of getting to the Vanity."

"A Vanity girl!" repeated Norah, scornfully. "For everybody to look at!"

Lily told her friend that it was better to be looked at as a Vanity girl than to spend her life looking at other people from a window in West Kensington.

"But I can't sing," Norah objected.

"Sing! Who ever heard of a chorus-girl that could sing?"

The lowly position of a Vanity girl was not proof against the alchemy of Norah's self-esteem; she made up her mind to renounce Pinero and all his works and go into musical comedy.

When the two friends reached the small street off Leicester Square and saw extending up the steps of the building in which the offices of Mr. Walter Keal were situated an endless queue of girls waiting to interview the manager, Norah was discouraged.

"Oh, he has lots of companies," Lily explained. Then she addressed herself to a dirty-faced man with a collar much too large for him who was in charge of the entrance.

"You give me your letter, and it'll be all right."

"But it's for Mr. Keal himself," Lily protested.

"That's all right, my dear; your turn'll come."

The women immediately in front looked round indignantly at Lily, and Norah, who was beginning to feel self-conscious, begged her not to make a fuss. This was advice Lily always found easy to take, and, the introduction from her brother-in-law stowed away in the dirty-faced man's pocket, she and Norah took their places in the queue. Every ten minutes or so a good-looking girl, obviously well pleased with herself, would descend briskly from the glooms above; but mostly at intervals of about thirty seconds depressed women, powdering their noses as nonchalantly as possible, came down more slowly. Foot by foot Norah and Lily, who by now had a trail of women behind them, struggled higher up the steps. There was a continuous murmur of sibilant talk punctuated by shrill laughter, and the atmosphere, thickly flavored with cheap scent, perspiration, damp, clothes, and cigarette smoke, grew more oppressive with each step of the ascent. At last they turned the corner of the first landing and saw ahead of them a shorter flight; half-way up this, another landing crowded with girls came into view, the three doors opening on which were inscribed "Walter Keal's Touring Companies" in white paint; a muffled sound of typewriting seemed auspiciously business-like amid this babbling, bedraggled, powdered mass of anxious women. By the central door another dirty-faced man was ushering in the aspirants one at a time.

"We ought to have given my letter to him," said Lily.

"Well, don't go back for it now," Norah begged, looking in dismay at the throng behind.

They must have been waiting over two hours when at last they found themselves face to face with the janitor. A bell tinkled as a bright figure emerged from the door on the left and hurried away down the steps without regarding the envious glances of the unadmitted; immediately afterward the door in front of them opened, and they passed through to the office.

"One at a time," the janitor called; but Norah quickly shut the door behind them, and she and Lily were simultaneously presented for the inspection of Mr. Walter Keal.

The office was furnished with a large roll-top desk, three chairs, and a table littered with papers which a dowdy woman in pince-nez was trying to put in some kind of order. The walls were hung with playbills; the room was heavy with cigar smoke. Mr. Walter Keal, a florid, clean-shaven man with a diamond pin in his cravat, a Malmaison carnation in his buttonhole, and a silk hat on the back of his head, was bending over the desk without paying the least attention to the new-comers. Standing behind him in an attitude that combined deference toward Mr. Keal with insolence toward the rest of the world was a young man of Jewish appearance who stared critically at the two girls.

"You don't remember me, Mr. Keal," began Lily, timidly. "I was introduced to you once in the Strand by my brother-in-law, Richard Granville."

"I'm sure you were," interrupted Mr. Keal, curtly; but when he looked up and saw that Lily was pretty he changed his tone. "That's all right; don't be frightened. I've met so many girls in my time. Well, what can I do for you?"

"I had a letter of introduction from my brother-in-law, Mr. Granville," Lily began again.

"Never heard of the gentleman," said Mr. Keal.

Norah, feeling that she and Lily stood once more on an equality, came forward with assurance.

"We thought you were choosing girls for the chorus in 'Miss Elsie of Chelsea.'"

"Full up," the manager snapped.

The Jewish young man bent over and whispered something to his master, who took a long look at the girls.

"However, I might find you two extra places. What experience have you had? None, eh? Can you sing? You think so. Um—yes—all girls think they can sing. Well, I'll give you a chance, but I can't offer more than a guinea a week of seven performances. If you don't like to take that, there are plenty who will and be grateful. It's my Number One company."

Norah did not wait for Lily, but accepted for both of them.

"Are they going to let us have the club in Lisle Street, Fitzmaurice?" the manager turned to inquire of his assistant.

"Yes, Mr. Keal. The club has arranged to lend their concert-room every morning and afternoon this week, but if you want any evening calls we shall have to make other arrangements."

"But —— it all," Mr. Keal exclaimed, "when are we going to get the stage?"

"They won't be able to let us have it till the week before Christmas."

"That's a nice ruddy job," grumbled Mr. Keal. "All right, dears," he said, "go in there and get your contracts." He pointed to the room adjoining, where, amid an infernal rattle of typewriters, Lily and Norah sold their untried talents to Mr. Keal for a guinea a week of seven performances, extra matinées to be paid for at half rate, and a fortnight's salary in lieu of notice to be considered just. When she took up the pen to sign the contract Norah paused.

"You've put your own name, Lily," she said, doubtfully.

"Oh, I can't be bothered to think of a new name. Besides, my own is quite a good one for the stage."

"Yes, but I ought to change mine. I think I shall call myself Dorothy Lonsdale. Do you like that?"

"You've got a sister called Dorothy. Won't she be rather annoyed?"

Norah tried to think of another name, but she was confused by the noise of the typewriters, and at last she ejaculated, impatiently:

"Oh, bother, I must be Dorothy! I've always known it would suit me much better than her. I shouldn't mind if she called herself Norah. Besides, I sha'n't be Dorothy Caffyn, so what does it matter?"

They were told that their contracts would be handed to them at the rehearsal called for to-morrow morning at the Hungarian Artistes' Club, Lisle Street, Leicester Square.

"How easy it is, really," said Norah, when she and Lily were going down-stairs again, past the line of tired women still waiting to be admitted. "Though I thought his language was rather disgusting. Didn't you?"

"I didn't notice it," said Lily. "But you'll have to get used to bad language on the stage."

"I shall never get used to it," Norah vowed, with a disdainful glance at a particularly common-looking girl who, tossing the feathers in her hat like a defiant savage, called out:

"God! Flo, look at Mrs. Walter Keal coming down-stairs."

The girls round her laughed, and Norah hurried past angrily. She had been intending to patronize Lily; after that remark it was not so easy.

Just as they reached the foot of the first flight of steps the dirty-faced janitor bawled over the balustrade, "Mr. Keal can't see any more ladies to-day."

Sighs of disappointment and murmurs of indignation rose from the actresses; then they turned wearily round and prepared to encounter the December rain.

"You'd better come and call for me to-morrow," said Norah, "so that we can go to the rehearsal together. Think of me to-night when I'm trying to explain to father what I've done."

"Will he be very angry?"

"Yes, I expect he will, and though I know how to manage him it's always a nuisance having to argue," said Norah. "You're lucky not to have a father."

Lily looked at her friend quickly and suspiciously.

"I mean you're lucky to be quite on your own," she explained.

The moment Mr. Caffyn came home from the city that evening Norah revealed to him that she had got an engagement in a touring company and reminded him of his promise. As she had expected, he tried to go back on his word, and even brought up the old objection to a daughter of his going on the stage.

"Nobody will know that I'm your daughter," she said. "I shall change my name, of course."

"But people are sure to hear about it," Mr. Caffyn argued.

Norah pulled him up suddenly.

"It's no good going on about it, father. I've got an engagement and I'm going to accept it. If you try to prevent me I shall do something much worse."

Mr. Caffyn's dislike of the stage may not have been as deep as he pretended, or he may have thought that his daughter really intended to do something desperate and that he might be called upon to support her in married life, which would be more expensive than supporting her on the stage. Moreover, she seemed so confident that perhaps he might never have to support her on the stage, and what a delightful solution of her future that would be! After all, she was the eldest of six girls, and six girls rapidly growing up might become too much even for the secretary of the Church of England Purity Society to control successfully.

Mrs. Caffyn melted into tears at the idea of her eldest daughter's earning her own living, and Norah decided to profit by maternal weakness.

"The only thing, mother dear, is that I shall be very poor."

"Darling child!"

"You see, I don't like to ask father to make me a larger allowance than he makes at present."

"Oh no," agreed Mrs. Caffyn, apprehensively. "I beg you won't ask him to do that."

"So my idea was—" Norah began. She paused for a moment to think how she could express herself most tactfully. "Mother, you have a certain amount of money of your own, haven't you?"

"Yes, dear."

"And I suppose it's really you who makes me my allowance of twenty-five pounds a year? What I thought was that perhaps you'd rather give me a lump sum now when it would be more useful than go on paying me an allowance. Another thing is that I should hate to feel I was coming into money when you died, and, of course, if you gave me my money now I shouldn't feel that."

"My dear child, how am I to find any large sum of money now? It's very sweet of you to put it in that way, but you don't understand how difficult these matters are."

"How much money have you got of your own?" asked Norah.

Mrs. Caffyn thought this was rather an improper question; but Norah was looking so very grown up that she did not like to elude the answer as she had been wont to elude many answers of many childish questions through all these years of married life.

"Well, dear," she said, with the air of one who was revealing a dangerous family secret, "I suppose you're old enough to hear these things now. I have three hundred pounds a year of my own—at least, when I say of my own, you mustn't think that means three hundred a year to spend on myself. Your father is very just, and though he helps me as much as he is able, all the money is taken up in household expenses."

"Well, twenty-five pounds a year," said Norah, "at five per cent. is the interest on five hundred pounds."

"Is it, dear?" asked her mother, in a frightened voice.

"If you give me five hundred pounds now you wouldn't have to pay me twenty-five pounds a year. And if you lived for another twenty-five years you'd save one hundred and twenty-five pounds that way."

Mrs. Caffyn looked as if she would soon faint at these rapid calculations.

"How am I to get five hundred pounds?" she asked, hopelessly.

"You must go and see the manager of your bank."

"But Roland is a clerk in my bank," Mrs. Caffyn objected. "And what would *he* say?"

"Roland!" repeated Norah, with scorn. "You don't suppose Roland knows everything that goes on in the bank?"

"No, I suppose he doesn't," agreed Mrs. Caffyn, wonderingly.

"If you like *I'll* go and see the bank manager," Norah offered. "He took rather a fancy to me, I remember, when he came to supper with us once."

"Norah, how recklessly you talk!" protested Mrs. Caffyn. But Norah was firm and she did not rest until she had persuaded her mother to ask for an interview with the manager, to whom she made herself so charming and with whom she argued so convincingly that in the end she succeeded in obtaining the £500.

"Though what your father will say I don't like to think, dear," said Mrs. Caffyn, as she tremblingly mounted an omnibus to go home.

"I don't see why father should know anything about it, and if he does he can't say anything. It's your money."

"Let's hope he'll never find out," Mrs. Caffyn sighed, though she had little hope really of escaping from detection in what she felt was something perilously like a clever bank robbery—the sort of thing one read about in illustrated magazines.

Norah determined to be very cautious at rehearsals and she advised Lily to be the same.

"Of course, we shall gradually make friends with the other girls, but don't let's be in too much of a hurry, especially as we've got each other. And if you take my advice you'll be very reserved with the men."

Since Norah had found how easy it was to get on the stage her opinion of Mr. Vavasour had sunk, and since she had found how easy it was to get out of love her opinion of men in general had sunk. On the other hand, her opinion of herself as an actress and as a woman had risen proportionately. Meanwhile the rehearsals proceeded as rehearsals do, and the No. I company of "Miss Elsie of Chelsea" was harried from club-room to club-room, from suburban theater to metropolitan theater, until it was ready to charm the city of Manchester on Boxing Night.

On Christmas Eve, the last evening that Norah would spend at home for some time, she decided in an access of honesty to tell Dorothy that she had taken her name for purposes of the stage. Most unreasonably, Dorothy protested loudly against this, and it transpired in the course of the dispute that she had all her life resented being the only one of the family who had not been given two names. Norah's own second name, Charlotte, which was also her mother's, had never struck her before as anything in the nature of an asset, but now with much generosity she offered to lend it to Dorothy, who refused it as scornfully as she could without hurting her mother's feelings.

"Why couldn't you have taken Lina or Florence or Amy or Maud?" Dorothy demanded. These were the second names of the other sisters. "And, anyway, what's the matter with your own name?"

"I don't know," said Norah. "Dorothy Lonsdale struck me as a good combination, and the more I think of it the better I like it."

"Lonsdale," everybody repeated. "Are you going to call yourself Lonsdale?"

"It's the family name," Norah reminded them.

This was quite true; Lonsdale had been the maiden name of Mrs. Caffyn's mother, who, according to a family legend, had been a distant kinswoman of Lord Cleveden. Indeed, before Mr. Caffyn was married he had often used this connection to overcome his father's opposition to a long engagement. When he had bought the house in Lonsdale Road he had liked to think for a while that in a way he was doing something to restore the prestige of a distant collateral branch; the transaction had possessed a flavor of winning back an old estate. Naturally, as he grew older, he ceased to attach the same importance to mere birth, especially when he found that he did not require any self-assertion to get on perfectly well with the bishops who came to consult him about diocesan scandals. Therefore he was inclined to take his eldest daughter's part and applaud her choice of a stage name.

"But suppose I wanted to go on the stage myself?" Dorothy insisted. "I might want to use my own name."

"Well, so you could," Norah urged. "You could be Miss Dorothy Caffyn. But you won't go on the stage, so what's the good of arguing like that? Anyway, I've signed the contract as Dorothy Lonsdale, so there's nothing to be done. *I* can't change."

"I do think it's mean of you," expostulated the real Dorothy, bursting into tears.

Norah would not allow anybody to come and see her off at Euston on Christmas morning, and Mr. Caffyn, who did not at all like the idea of a four-wheeler's waiting outside his house on such a day, helped his daughter's plans by marshaling the whole family for church half an hour earlier than usual, so that the farewells were said indoors. Lily had left the flat a fortnight ago and, having been staying in some Bloomsbury lodgings recommended by her sister, was to meet her friend at the station. At a quarter to eleven, amid the clangor of church bells, the cab of Norah Caffyn turned out of Lonsdale Road into the main street of West Kensington, and at noon on the platform at Euston Miss Lily Haden wished a Merry Christmas to Miss Dorothy Lonsdale.

CHAPTER II

I

THE ostriches of northern Patagonia are said to indulge in co-operative nesting: half a dozen hens one after another proceed to lay in a shallow cavity numerous eggs, the incubation of which is left to a male bird. Similarly, for the consummation of a musical comedy half a dozen lyrists, librettists, and composers lay their heads together in a shallow cavity and leave the result of their labor to be given life by a producer. "Miss Elsie of Chelsea," not being an exceptional musical comedy, will not repay a more thorough analysis. The first act developed in a painter's studio; in the second act everybody from the models in the chorus to the millionaire and his daughter whom the painter wanted to marry were transported to Honolulu. It was produced at the Vanity Theater under Mr. John Richards's management in the early autumn of the year 1902, and for many seasons it attracted large audiences all over the civilized world.

During the first fortnight of the tour, a fortnight of unending rain in Manchester, Dorothy, as she must be called henceforth, was inclined to think that life on the stage was not much more exciting than life in West Kensington, and certainly twice as tiring. It was holiday time, with two performances a day for eight days, and only in the second week—or more strictly in the third week, for Boxing Day fell upon a Friday that year—was she able to look about her in the small world where she must spend the next six months of her existence. She soon came to the conclusion that such an environment would not be tolerable for longer, and she made up her mind to escape from touring as soon as possible into a London engagement.

While she was still rehearsing in town she had paid one or two visits to the Vanity Theater, partly because it pleased her to hand in a card inscribed, "Miss Dorothy Lonsdale. Mr. Walter Keal's Miss Elsie of Chelsea Co.," but chiefly with the object of studying the demeanor, dress, appearance, and talents of the various members of the Vanity chorus, especially of the show-girls. The result of her observations was a strong belief that she was as graceful, as well able to set off clothes, as beautiful, and as good an actress as any of them. At the same time, she had begun to hear girls in the company talk about "getting across the footlights" and had realized that her own personality's powers of projection were still untested. If at the end of the tour it was brought home to her that with all her qualities "off" she lacked the most important one of all "on," she should immediately retire from the stage forever. The life itself did not attract her, and to spend years growing older and older in the environment of a provincial company seemed to Dorothy wilful self-deception; liberty at such a price would be worse than a comfortable servitude to suburban convention.

When on that wet Christmas morning at Euston she had seen the companions to close contact with whom she was bound for six months—a polychromatic group of crude pink complexions, mauve veils, electric seal, and exaggerated boots, looking in the mass like a shop-window in a second-rate thoroughfare, the sort of shop-window that has bundles of overcoats hanging outside the doorway, which indeed the men resembled—she had felt a sudden revulsion from them all, which those days in Manchester had done nothing to cure.

The first fortnight's bills for board and lodging had already shown Dorothy that existence on a guinea a week was not going to be easy; if she were ever engaged for London, she should require money to dress herself well at the beginning of her career, and it was imperative to save every penny she possibly could now in order to preserve intact the £500 she had obtained from her mother. An immediate economy would be effected in their weekly expenses if she and Lily could persuade another girl to share lodgings with them, and Dorothy began to study the ranks of the chorus for a suitable partner. Of course, from a social point of view she would have preferred to live with one of the principals, but the principals had not yet paid any attention to her, and she would not risk making advances first; besides, their standard of living might be too high for one who did not intend to waste money on the provinces. But when she considered her companions of the chorus, the dreadful language many of them used, the outrageous stories they told at the top of their voices, and, worst of all, their cockney accents, Dorothy shrank from extending the enforced intimacy of the dressing-room to her weekly home. This problem had not been solved when on the third Sunday after Christmas the company left Manchester for Birmingham, and by the newly arranged order of traveling Miss Dorothy Lonsdale found herself allotted to share a compartment with Miss Lily Haden, Miss Fay Onslow, and Miss Sylvia Scarlett.

Miss Onslow was unmistakably the senior member of the chorus and had reached the happy period of an actress's life when she has no more need to bother about keeping her reminiscences too nicely in focus. She was, in fact, as even she herself admitted, not far off forty; in a railway train on a wet January afternoon the kindest observer would have assumed that her next landmark was fifty. A month ago Dorothy would have shuddered to find herself on an equality with such a person; but asperous is the astral road, and she had to make the best of Miss Onslow by treating her with at least as much cordiality as she would have shown to a small dressmaker from whom she wanted a dress by the end of the week. Gradually, as her new surroundings became familiar, Dorothy had brought herself to call Miss Onslow "Onzie," and though the abbreviation made her gorge rebel as from cod-liver oil, she bravely persevered. Instinctively she knew that this was the only woman in the chorus whose counsel she could trust, the only one who would honestly tell her if she looked better with or without an artificial teardrop. The sum of Onzie's experience was hers for the asking; the middle-aged actress was an academician of grease-paint, serving alike as a warning and an example to the student; while her knowledge of the various towns in which the company had dates was evidently profound. Already she had provided Dorothy with an address for Birmingham; but these rooms to be enjoyed without the prickings of extravagance required a third partner. Dorothy, anxious to profit still further by Onzie's experience, suggested that she should join Lily and herself; but that very experience for which the novice was greedy made the old professional shake her head:

"No, thank you, ducky," she said. "I always live alone nowadays. You see, I've got my own little peculiarities. Besides, when my best boy comes down to see me he likes to see me alone. When I was with the 'Geisha' crowd last year I obliged one of the girls by sharing rooms with her in Middlesbrough, and as luck would have it George selected Middlesbrough to pay me a little visit. He was really very aggravated indeed, and he said to me, 'Fay,' he said, 'whatever's the use of me coming all the way up to Middlesbrough if I can't ever see you?' So I had to tell the other girl—Lexie Sharp her name was— that the arrangement didn't work, and what do you think she did? Well, if you'll believe me, she went about telling everybody that I was jealous of her over George! Luckily for me she was a girl who was very well known for her tongue and nobody paid any attention to her; still, it was uncomfortable for me, though I deserved it for breaking one of my rules. Who knows? George may come up to Birmingham. It's just the sort of place he would select for a visit, because, being a London fellow, he feels out of it in too small a town. Of course, he has nothing to do with the stage himself. Oh dear me, no, nothing whatever! He lives at Tulse Hill with two aunts, one of which has a growth in the throat and may go off at any moment, which prevents George working, as she's so particular about having him always close at hand. Well, any one ought to understand an aunt's feelings—I'm sure I can—but some of the girls last year used to criticize him something dreadful behind my back, until really I was glad to say good-by to them all. But this seems a much nicer crowd we're in now."

"We've only been in it a fortnight," said Miss Scarlett from the other corner of the carriage.

Dorothy looked at the speaker curiously. She was a girl who had joined the company for the last three rehearsals and during this first fortnight in Manchester had kept herself apart. Lily had spoken to her once or twice, but Dorothy, who was afraid there might be an unpleasant reason for such deliberate seclusion, had begged Lily not to be in too great a hurry to make friends with her. During Onzie's monologue Miss Scarlett had apparently been unconscious of what was happening in the compartment, and from the corner opposite Lily she had been staring out at the landscape, that was scarred and grimed and misshapen by industry like the hands of the toilers who lived in it. She was different from all the other girls, Dorothy was thinking—rather foreign-looking with her deep, brown, slanted eyes and mass of untidy brown hair, her wide nose, high cheek-bones, and distinctly ugly mouth, the underlip of which only just escaped protruding. She was dressed, too, in a style that was quite unlike that of anybody else and without any regard for the prevailing fashion. Dorothy remembered with a flickering smile that when she had first seen her at rehearsals she had thought she was one of the Hungarian artistes who had come to see why her club-room was being used by a theatrical company. Now when in a deep voice she suddenly turned round and commented on Fay Onslow's last remark Dorothy was astonished to hear that she spoke the same kind of English as herself; she indeed, in her surprise, almost gave utterance aloud to her thought that this gipsy creature was a lady.

"Hell! I've left my cigarettes behind," the lady ejaculated.

"There now, what a nuisance for you!" said the good-natured Onzie. "Have one of mine, dear."

"Which are they? Turks or Virgins?" asked Miss Scarlett, leaning over and screwing up her eyes to see what Onzie was offering.

Dorothy corrected her opinion and decided that Miss Scarlett had been a lady once upon a time; yet even while she was condemning her vulgarity she was thinking that her ladyhood was not so far away in the past. Her speech and manner had the assurance of age, but she could not be much more than twenty-two or twenty-three, perhaps not even so much as that.

Presently the train stopped for a dreary Sunday wait, and while some of the gentlemen of the company, with a view to future favors, were scuttling about the platform in search of tea for the ladies from whom they would demand them, Dorothy took this opportunity of asking Lily what she thought about inviting Sylvia Scarlett to share their rooms at Birmingham.

"She seems quite different from the other girls," Dorothy explained. "I mean, she talked as if she was a lady. Don't you think so? And really, you know, we can't afford these rooms unless we do get a third person."

Lily was quite ready to accept Miss Scarlett's company, though, as Dorothy thought impatiently, she would have been equally willing to accept the dresser's, if Dorothy had thought of inviting the dresser to share rooms with them.

"Do you want a cup of tea, Lil?" a young man came along and asked at this moment. When Lily declared that she should love a cup of tea, he hurried off toward the buffet.

"Do you know him?" asked Dorothy, in surprise.

"Only since we joined the company."

"But he's one of the chorus-boys, isn't he?"

"Yes."

"And you let him call you Lily already?" Dorothy hoped it was no worse than Lily; it had sounded dreadfully like Lil.

"Why shouldn't I?"

"Of course, it's your own business," said Dorothy, turning coldly away to eye Sylvia Scarlett, who was striding up and down the platform with both hands in the pockets of a frieze overcoat and looking so independent of everybody in the world that she felt shy of interrupting her. At that moment Lily was carried off by the chorus-boy for a cup of tea, which, had it been arsenic, Dorothy could not have declined more indignantly, and she found herself alone upon the platform and exposed to the glances of the comedian, a debased sport from the famous Vanity comedian whose mannerisms he had reproduced in the provinces as well as he was able for fifteen years, and would probably continue to reproduce for as many more. A small and ugly man, Joe Wiltshire had become so hardened to women's snubs that by sheer recklessness and indiscrimination he managed to fill his bag. If he was weak with rocketing pheasants he never hesitated to pot a sitting rabbit; in other words, he made love to every woman he met and found 5 per cent. of them amenable. Now with a view to impressing the prettiest girl in the chorus he was being funny with two bottles of stout and a corkscrew; but though he managed to cheer up the porter on duty, he failed to amuse Dorothy, who seized an opportunity of escaping from the performance by attaching herself to Sylvia Scarlett on her return promenade.

"I say," she began, in her best West Kensington manner. "I hope you won't think it awful cheek on my part, but my friend and I—you know, that pretty, fair girl who was in our carriage—would be awfully glad if you'd join us this week in our digs. Awfully nice rooms, but rather expensive for two, though we ought to be able to manage quite reasonably with three. Of course, if you're already fixed—"

"I've never been fixed in my life," said Miss Scarlett, sharply, "and I certainly don't intend to be fixed in Birmingham."

"No, I say, shut up; don't laugh. Have you been on the stage long?"

"Two weeks and two days."

"Oh, I say, really, then this is your first shop?"

Dorothy felt more at ease now that she knew she had not got to deal with a veteran of the profession; this new girl was obviously not one to be patronized, but there was now no reason to anticipate patronage on her side. With the removal of this danger Dorothy became more natural in her manner, and by the time the line was cleared for the theatrical special to proceed the bargain had been struck by which Sylvia Scarlett would share rooms with herself and Lily.

"I say, I hope you don't mind my making personal remarks," said Dorothy, "but you're looking most awfully tired."

She had intended this remark to effect a breach in the other girl's reserve, but it apparently had the contrary effect of raising the barrier still higher. She drew back slightly huffed, and Sylvia, leaning over, with a quick expansive gesture put a hand on her arm and told her not to be offended if she was not being confidential, but that she was enjoying the luxury of complete privacy after a period of disagreeable publicity. Dorothy would have preferred more exact information; even in childhood she had always felt inclined to cry when people had asked her riddles, and Roland's favorite way of teasing her had been to invent riddles without answers; however, she comforted herself with the reflection that Sylvia really was a lady, which at any rate ought to be a guaranty that the answer to that conundrum was not vulgar like the dreadful answers to dressing-room conundrums.

The train dragged on through the wet January dusk and into the dripping night of blurred lamps and distant furnaces, of ghostly Sunday travelers and long platforms like stagnant streams. Conversation in the compartment hung heavily upon the air like the moist breath of the tired women in the four corners of it. Dorothy, whose touchstone of behavior was self-respect, asked herself why Fay Onslow should mind living with other girls, such intimate revelations of her private habits was she making in the course of this journey. If a woman as fat as she was did not feel the loss of her dignity in searching for a flea like that, why should she want to live alone? And that was by no means the least dignified thing she had done. This ostentatious disregard of life's little decencies was certainly a regrettable side of theatrical life. However, the fact that she herself had gone on the stage prevented Dorothy from betraying her disapproval of such behavior. It would have been contrary to her method of dealing with life to admit that she could even expose herself to anything unseemly, still less that she might succumb to it. From the moment that Dorothy went on the stage the profession became above criticism, and the sense of collective propriety that she inherited as her father's daughter was no longer capable of being shocked. She crucified her fastidiousness; she was persecutor and martyr at the same time and derived an equal consciousness of superiority from either aspect of herself; in fact, the only thing in life that seriously troubled Dorothy was a minute bleb of skin on her left eyelid, and even that could be removed by a beauty doctor.

It was raining harder than ever when the train reached Birmingham, and the girls decided to indulge in the luxury of a cab. The rooms looked as if they really would be very comfortable, and the landlady insisted proudly that managers had been known to stay in them, not mere business managers whose only aim in life seemed to be making fusses about the starching of their white shirts, but acting managers, one of whom had even brought his children, which, as she pointed out, proved that the lodgings were homely.

Sylvia was some time getting ready for supper, and Dorothy, thinking it would not be nice to begin without her, made Lily wait quite half an hour. When Sylvia did come down at last, Dorothy was nearly sure that she had been crying, and the mystery of her origin once more obtruded itself. Dorothy wished now that she had arranged for Sylvia and herself to share the second room instead of Lily and herself. This strange new girl perplexed her self-assurance, and she proposed that if the new association prospered— they drank to its success in the pale India ale which the landlady provided— they should take it week about to sleep in the single room. Dorothy tried to extract confidences from Sylvia by confiding in her the history of Lily as far as she knew it; when that did not elicit anything she offered a gilded version of her own prior circumstances. The following week at Derby she shared the bedroom with Sylvia and went so far as to give her an almost truthful account of the Wilfred Curlew business, but nothing could she get from Sylvia in return. Moreover, there was nothing in her belongings that afforded a clue to her history; there was not a single photograph or initialed ornament; all her possessions were left lying about the room, and her trunk was never locked; and when every morning the girls called at the stage door for their correspondence she only in the company never received a letter, nor even bothered to look if there was one waiting for her in the rack. But if Sylvia was mute about the past she was not at all reserved about the present. There was nobody like her for seizing upon the eccentricities of the various members of the company to make merry with, and if sometimes Dorothy felt that she went too far in laughing at herself, she could not be angry because she used to laugh as much, indeed more, at Lily. She was a match, too, for any landlady; and gradually, as the association begun at Birmingham hardened into permanency, Dorothy and Lily left the entire management of their weekly home to Sylvia: who had a delightful capacity for keeping the weekly bills reasonable without ever seeming to be economical.

Dorothy was too firmly convinced of the reality of her own beauty to be an idealist, but if in after life any portion of her early experience on the stage seemed to her worthy of idealization these first weeks with Sylvia and Lily seemed so. Partly this was due to her discovery that touring was not so unpleasant when she did not have to bother about anything except her own appearance; but chiefly it was due to her growing conviction of ultimate success. There was beginning to be no doubt that even from the chorus of a musical comedy company on tour her personality was getting across the footlights. Even Sylvia, the mercilessly critical Sylvia, had prophesied success for her, and Dorothy's dreams went past to the music of approaching triumphs. Her mind was all a pageant, and the commonplace of touring existence—the aroma of the theater, the flight from the great manufacturing towns on still Sabbath mornings of black frost, the kaleidoscopic mustering of the company at railway stations, the emptiness of new rooms untouched as yet by the transience of the three girls, the garish mirrors hung with velvet that held her beauty, the undulating horsehair sofas, the sea-shells on the mantelpiece, the fire glowing in the grate, the dim gas when they came home from the performance, the smell of Cheddar cheese in the little room, the bright gas shining on the three places laid for supper, the petticoats hanging over the bed up-stairs, the oil-cloth in the passages, the noise of the landlady's family in the stuffy kitchen—all these and a hundred more externals of touring existence were in the years to come regarded affectionately as winter is beheld from the radiance of a summer afternoon.

So from Derby "Miss Elsie of Chelsea" went to Leeds, from Leeds to Bradford, from Bradford to Liverpool, from Liverpool to Newcastle. Then from Newcastle the company ascended into Scotland, where genial landladies and cakes and enthusiastic audiences compensated for east winds.

II

Gradually, under the pressure of Sylvia's teasing, Dorothy allowed herself to make friends with the other girls and to be superficially polite with the men. She was never popular in the company in the way that for different reasons Sylvia and Lily were popular; but perhaps her disdain and conceit were pardoned as tokens of future success, because she was not ostracized as she certainly would have been ostracized without the fascination that favorites of fortune always exert upon the rest of mankind. Besides, people said such spiteful things behind her back that they had to be fairly pleasant to her face. The men in the chorus one after another tried in vain to attract her attention whenever the requirements of the scene gave them an excuse for talking to her. But Dorothy used to respond as if the dialogue could really be heard by the audience, which may have been artistic, but did not allow her admirers much opportunity of cultivating a friendship. Off the stage she would have nothing to do with any of them. The comedian made one or two more attempts to charm her with buffoonery, but she told him that he was even less funny off the stage than on, upon which he lost his temper and swore she was a stuck-up cow; an alleged lack of humor in Scotland had recently deprived Mr. Wiltshire of some of his best laughs, and he was in no mood to be criticized by a chorus-girl.

"If you speak to me again like that," said Dorothy, primly, "I shall complain to Mr. Warren."

"Wow-wow-wow!" the comedian mimicked.

"Never mind, Joe," said Sylvia, who was standing close by in the wings. "If you manage to break your leg with your next entrance you'll get a laugh, all right."

"You think yourself very funny, don't you?" growled Mr. Wiltshire.

"Yes, but I haven't got to convince a Scotch audience that I am," said Sylvia.

The comedian's cue came before he could retort, and, falling over his feet in a way that would have made a more southerly audience rock with mirth, he took the stage.

"Vulgar little beast!" said Dorothy.

Mr. Wiltshire never relaxed his efforts to charm the people of Edinburgh, Glasgow, Dundee, and Aberdeen to laughter, but he gave up trying to amuse Dorothy, and thenceforth devoted himself to girls with a keener sense of humor.

Once when Dorothy had refused to go for a long walk in the country round Aberdeen, the glittering of the granite buildings on a fine March morning tempted her out too late, and she wandered by herself along the sea-shore toward the mouth of the Don until she was able, so windless was the day, so warm the sun against the low sandy cliffs, to sit down on the beach. It happened that Mr. David Bligh, the tenor in "Miss Elsie of Chelsea," passed that way, and, seeing Dorothy, took a seat beside her. She had never intended her reserve with the other men in the company to include David Bligh, and from having felt rather sad at being left behind by Sylvia and Lily she now congratulated herself on her good fortune.

"All alone?" asked the tenor, fluting with his voice, as he always did when he was speaking to a woman.

"All alone," said Dorothy. "Isn't it too bad?"

They discussed loneliness with poetic similes harvested from the sea, upon the horizon of which nothing but a solitary tramp, hull down, was visible. So long as Mr. David Bligh's attention had been devoted to Miss May Seymour, the leading lady, Dorothy had been inclined to think that he was not very good-looking, that he did not possess a very good voice, and that probably he was not quite a gentleman. Now that he was beside her on this lonely beach she was inclined to modify all these judgments in his favor, and when suddenly he burst forth into "*Che gelido manino*," suiting the action to the word by simultaneously taking hold of her hand, she decided that not merely was his voice rather good, but that it was lovely.

"You really have a lovely voice," she told him.

He shrugged his shoulders, sighed, and with his stick drew some notes of music in the sand.

"I wonder why you never took up opera," she inquired, in tender astonishment.

"What's the good? The British public doesn't want British singers. Oh no," he said, with a glance full of reproach for the indifference of the sky, "I'm not fat enough for opera."

He went up the tonic scale to "la," frightening away some small sea-birds that had just alighted on the gleaming sand by the tide's edge.

"Let me hear your voice," he asked, abruptly.

Dorothy was gratified by this request. She had taken for granted the tenor's interest in her appearance, but that this should extend to her voice seemed to indicate something more profound than a casual attraction. She assured him that she was too shy, but he continued to persuade her, and at last she sang a part of one of the leading lady's songs.

"Yes, it would be worth while taking some trouble with it," he judged. "If you like I'll give you lessons. Have you got a piano in your rooms?"

"We have got a piano this week, as it happens," said Dorothy, "though I should doubt if it had ever been played on. Come to tea this afternoon, and we'll try it."

"You live with that Haden girl, don't you?"

"Do you think she's pretty?" Dorothy asked.

The tenor shrugged his shoulders.

"Oh yes, so-so. I really haven't noticed her much. She dyes her hair, I suppose."

"No, it's natural," said Dorothy, resisting the temptation to insert a qualifying, "I believe."

They discussed the varieties of feminine beauty; when the tenor had managed to convey without direct compliments that Dorothy had every feature a woman ought to have, she was convinced by his good taste that her voice must be out of the ordinary.

"Good gracious! It's past two o'clock," she exclaimed, at last, when her appetite began to assert itself in spite of ozone and flattery. "How time flies!"

"*I* dine at half past two. We'd better be strolling back."

It was after that hour when they reached Aberdeen, because David Bligh was continually stopping on the desolate roads that led across the low-lying lands between the city and the sea to illustrate with snatches of song many episodes of his adventurous life as an actor in musical comedy. Dorothy might have been bored by all this talk about himself if he had not made it so clear that he really did admire her; as it was, she assented warmly when he murmured, outside her lodgings:

"How quickly one can make friends sometimes!"

How quickly, indeed, when a man will show his admiration with his eyes and a woman with her ears.

The others had not returned from their expedition along Deeside when tea was finished, so Dorothy and the tenor took down the photographs and china ornaments from the top of the piano, and presently an unfamiliar sound brought in Mrs. Maclachlan, the landlady, to say that the piano had not been used since her eldest daughter died ten years ago, and that she would prefer that it was not used now. This was the kind of occasion on which Dorothy missed Sylvia, who would have known how to deal with the old woman; but David Bligh, without heeding her protests, continued to strum. Mrs. Maclachlan at once put the bass clef out of action by sitting down upon the notes, where, with arms akimbo, she maintained her position and poured forth a torrent of unintelligible Scots labials. Dorothy, horrified at the idea of a brawl with a woman who, even if she did let rooms, obviously belonged to the servant class, begged the actor not to play any more. In the end he agreed to resign from the contest with Mrs. Maclachlan on condition that Dorothy would try her voice on the piano in his rooms, where he was so encouraging about its quality that she gave herself up to serious study, one result of which was that henceforth she always had the second bedroom to herself, because her voice seemed to require most exercise when Sylvia and Lily required most sleep. The other girls in the company showed no inclination to believe that Dorothy's friendship with David Bligh was founded upon his skill in voice-production and they used to declare with conscious virtue that such singing-lessons were merely an excuse for making love.

"Be careful, dear, with Bligh," Fay Onslow warned Dorothy. "He's known all over the road for the way he treats girls. Look at May Seymour! Really, I'm quite sorry for the poor thing. I'm sure she's beginning to look her age."

This was good news about May Seymour, who had ignored her when she joined the company; but though in other respects the leading lady's fate might serve as a warning, Dorothy was much too secure of herself to need any advice about David Bligh. To be sure, he had several times seized the opportunity of examining his pupil's throat to kiss her, but she had accepted the kisses with no more sense of their reality than if they had been a doctor's bill, which in a way they were. However, Dorothy was not accustomed to let herself be over-charged, and these kisses were the only honorarium Mr. Bligh ever got. He was so much piqued by her indifference that he mistook for a grand passion the mortification set up by his failure to get her hopelessly in love with him, and he made such a complete fool of himself over Dorothy that the girls of the company were more annoyed than ever, and from having at first been charitably anxious about her virtue they now became equally severe upon her cruelty.

"The poor boy's getting quite thin," Fay Onslow declared. "You really oughtn't to treat him like that. It's beginning to show in his acting."

Dorothy consulted Sylvia about David Bligh's decline, not because she cared whether he was declining or not, but because it was an excuse to talk about herself.

"Serve him right," said Sylvia.

"But I shouldn't like to think that he was really suffering on my account."

"Lily and I are the only people who really suffer," said Sylvia.

"What do you mean?"

"My dear Dorothy, *we* have to listen to the practising."

"You don't really mind my practising, do you?"

"I get rather bored with it sometimes."

"Yes, I suppose it is rather boring sometimes."

Dorothy decided that it was also rather boring of Sylvia to switch the topic from her effect on David Bligh to the slight annoyance her practising might sometimes cause her friends. However, she forgave her by remembering that Sylvia had not the same inducement as herself to study singing.

Meanwhile, Dorothy's occupation of the leading man left Lily free to develop her deplorable taste for chorus-boys, and Dorothy found that her own habit of practising scales in the morning and going out for walks with David Bligh in the afternoon had resulted in continuous tea-parties at their rooms, to which, whenever she wanted to stay at home in the afternoon, she was most unfairly exposed. She might have put up with Lily's behavior for the rest of the tour if at last a moment had not come when it inconvenienced her personally. At Nottingham, which the company reached in mid-April, the weather was so fine that Dorothy accepted an invitation from an admirer in the front of the house to go for a picnic on the river Trent. Until now she had discouraged all introductions effected by the footlights, and she often marveled to Sylvia at the way other girls accepted invitations to private houses without knowing anything about their hosts. Perhaps she was already beginning to feel that David Bligh had taught her all he knew about voice-production, or perhaps the exceptionally smart automobile grumbling outside the stage-door struck her as a proper credential, or perhaps these April airs were irresistible.

"Really, you know, Sylvia," she said, "I think it would be rather fun to go. But I'm shocked at myself for suddenly breaking my rules like this. I wonder why I am breaking them. It must be the spring."

"The what?" repeated Sylvia.

"The spring," said Dorothy, hoping she did not look as affected as she felt.

"If you had said the springs," said Sylvia, "I would have agreed with you."

The owner of the car was the spoiled son of a rich lace manufacturer, and, according to the stage-door keeper, famous in Nottingham for his entertainment of actresses. What seemed more important to Dorothy was that he had just arrived from Cambridge for the Easter vacation, which decided her to accept his hospitality.

"You'll bring two friends?" suggested the young man.

"I'll bring the two girls with whom I share rooms."

"Topping!" he ejaculated, and with a sympathetic tootle of satisfaction the champing car leaped forward into the night.

"You can't come to-morrow?" gasped Dorothy, when with much graciousness she had advised Lily of the treat in store for her.

"No; I've promised to go with Tom to Sherwood Forest."

"Never mind, Maid Marian," said Sylvia. "We shall get along without you. If you see the ghost of my namesake Will in the greenwood, give him my love."

Dorothy was too angry to speak, and her resentment against Lily was increased next morning when the big car arrived with three young men, one of whom would have to spend an acrobatic day balancing himself on tête-à-têtes. Nor was the picnic a great success; early in the afternoon it came on to rain, and anything more dreary than the appearance of the river Trent was unimaginable.

"Never mind," said the host, "you'll have to come up to Cambridge; we'll entertain you properly there."

Apart from the rain which spoiled her hat, and the absence of Lily which ruined any intimate conversation about herself, Dorothy was chiefly upset by the contemptuous way in which these young Cambridge men referred to the leading man.

"Why on earth do managers dress actors up in yachting costume?" asked one of them. "I never saw such an ass as that man looked—David Blighter or whatever he calls himself."

Dorothy could see Sylvia checking an impulse not to accentuate her discomfiture by announcing her friendship with the despised tenor; but she felt sufficiently humiliated without that, and when they got back to their rooms she implored Sylvia to speak to Lily on the subject of being too friendly with the men in the company.

"It makes us all so cheap," Dorothy pointed out. "Of course, we're on tour and not likely to meet many friends who know us in London. Still, it is unpleasant. You heard the way those boys talked about David? What would they have said to Tom Hewitt? Besides, I get worried about Lily. She *is* very weak and she has been badly brought up. I'm awfully fond of her, as you know, and I'd do anything for her; but really I cannot stand that Hewitt creature, and I don't see why Lily should force him upon us."

"I think it's rather foolish of her myself," agreed Sylvia. "At the same time, I'm afraid that with Lily it's inevitable."

"Yes, but she lets him make love to her," protested Dorothy. "She doesn't care a bit about him, really, but she's too lazy to say 'no'. I came down the other day to find her sitting on his lap! Well, I think that's disgusting. *You* don't sit on people's laps; *I* don't sit on people's laps. Why should she? I know perfectly well what it is to be in love; I've been in love lots of times. I don't want you to think I'm setting out to make myself seem better than I am. As I told you, the only reason I went on the stage was because I couldn't marry the man I loved. So who more likely to have sympathy with people in love than myself? What I object to is playing about with boys of the company. Look at them! The most awful set of bounders imaginable. It's so bad for you and me to have them coming in and out of our rooms at all hours. That Hewitt creature actually proposed to come back to supper the other night. However, I told Lily that if he did I should go to a hotel. After all, we are a little different from the other girls of the company."

"I wonder if we are?" Sylvia queried.

"Of course we are," said Dorothy. "You surely don't consider yourself on a level with Fay Onslow? Or with Sadie Moore and Clarice Beauchamp? Those awful girls!"

"I think we're all about the same," said Sylvia. "Some of us drop our aitches, some of us our p's and q's, some of us sing flat and the others sing sharp; but alas! my dear Dorothy, we all look very much alike when we're waiting for the train on Sunday morning."

"I sing perfectly in tune," said Dorothy, coldly.

"Please don't snub, me, Dorothy," Sylvia begged. "I can hardly bear it."

"There's no need for you to be sarcastic; you must admit I'm right about Lily."

Sylvia suddenly produced an eye-glass and, fixing it in her eye, stared mockingly at Dorothy.

"What about David?" she asked.

"You can't compare me with Lily."

"No, but I might compare David with Tom," she said, letting the eye-glass drop in a way that Dorothy found extremely irritating.

After their host's remarks about the tenor Dorothy felt she could not argue the point farther, and now in addition to her anger against Lily she began to hate her singing-master. However, Sylvia must have felt that she was right and have spoken to Lily, because the following week at Leicester Lily, with most unwonted energy, attacked her on the subject:

"I don't know why you should grumble to Sylvia about me. I don't grumble to her about you. When have I ever grumbled about your practising? You say the only reason you let yourself get talked about with David Bligh is because he's useful to you. You say he's helping you with your voice. Well, Tom helps me with my bag. What's the difference? It's only since you were asked out by those men who had a car that you suddenly discovered how impossible Tom was and began laughing at his waistcoats. I didn't laugh at Cyril Vavasour's waistcoat, which was more extraordinary than Tom's."

"I've never grumbled about Tom's carrying your bag," Dorothy explained, patiently. "What I said to Sylvia was that I didn't think you ought to let him kiss you. I don't think it's dignified."

"Well, as long as he doesn't want to kiss you, I don't see what you've got to complain about."

The bare notion of Tom's wanting to kiss her was so unpleasant to Dorothy that she had to withdraw from the conversation. Thenceforth the breach between her and Lily began to widen; in fact, if it had not been for Sylvia she would have told Lily that she could not share rooms with her any longer. She was afraid, however, that Sylvia might be so sorry for Lily that she would find herself left alone, which would put her in an undignified position, because the other girls might say that it was because she wanted to carry on, as they would vulgarly express it, with Bligh; besides, living alone was too expensive.

Since Nottingham, Dorothy had been criticizing the tenor almost as sharply as she criticized Tom Hewitt, and she was in no mood to encourage the idea that there was anything between him and her; all her lessons now were merely repetitions of what he had taught her already, and it became obvious to Dorothy that he was what he was in the profession simply because he was not good enough to be anything better. He had so often bragged to her about his success with other girls that he deserved to suffer on her account, and she felt quite like Nemesis when soon after this, while they were walking in the town of Leicester, she told him that this was to be their last walk together.

"Don't stand still in that theatrical way," she commanded. "Everybody's looking at you."

The kidney-stones of the Leicester streets had been hurting her feet, and she was in no mood for mercy.

"So this is the end," fluted David Bligh, with such emotion that the top note narrowly escaped being falsetto. "After all these weeks you're going to throw me away like an old chocolate-box."

He swished his cane with such demonstrative violence that, without seeing what he was doing, he cut a passer-by hard on the knuckle and thereby provoked a scene of humble apologies that made Dorothy more furious than ever.

"At least you might not make me look a fool in a public thoroughfare," she told him.

"I'm awfully sorry, Dolly. I didn't know what I was doing for the moment."

"Don't call me Dolly," she said. "You know how I hate abbreviations."

"I don't seem to be able to do anything right this morning."

"Look at the ridiculous walk you've brought me! Nothing but cobble-stones, and passers-by bumping into one, and now we're getting down among the factories. You know how I hate being stared at."

"You didn't mind being stared at in Nottingham the week before last."

"Oh God! aren't you impossible!" cried Dorothy, herself now dramatically turning right round and leaving him undecided whether to follow her or retire in the opposite direction.

Half a dozen factory-girls, arm in arm, who, with the horrible quickness of their class for anything that causes discomfort to other people, had noticed the quarrel, began to shout after Dorothy that her little boy was crying for his mother; while she, in torments of rage and humiliation, and of hatred for the man who was the cause of them, hurried uphill toward a more civilized quarter of the town. Five minutes later the tenor overtook Dorothy and begged pardon for losing her like that; he explained that, having got involved in a crowd of factory-girls, he could not hurry without making himself more ridiculous.

"You don't mind making me ridiculous," she said, bitterly.

"My dear girl, it was you that turned away, not me."

"Oh, go to the devil!" she burst out. "I'll have nothing more to do with you. You can console yourself with May Seymour."

The people who turned to stare after the lovely girl that seemed an incarnation of this blue-and-white April day might have been as shocked as Dorothy was at herself to think that she had just descended to the level of an actor by telling him to go to the devil.

III

The month of May found the "Miss Elsie of Chelsea" company billed to appear in the suburban theaters, and Dorothy was called upon to make up her mind whether she should take rooms with Sylvia and Lily in the center of London or economize for a few weeks by staying at home. Four months of separation from her family had not made her particularly anxious to return to them. At the same time, since she was not yet a London actress, it might be more prudent to wait a little while before she cut herself off too completely from Lonsdale Road. The only thing that worried her about staying at home was the thought that all the members of her family would inevitably insist on going to see her act during the week that they were to play at the Grand Theater, Fulham. Even if her father should be shy of patronizing a musical comedy so near the Bishop of London's palace, she saw no way of preventing at any rate Roland and her sister Dolly from going; since she had stolen her sister's name, Dorothy, notwithstanding her dislike of abbreviations, had always managed to think of her as Dolly. Yes; it was obvious that whether she stayed up in town or stayed in West Kensington, she should be unable to prevent some of the family from going to see her, and, as they would not appreciate the fact that not even the greatest actresses begin by playing Lady Macbeth, she must make the best of their inspection.

So, one Sunday afternoon when the laburnum buds were yellowing in Lonsdale Road, Dorothy drove back to No. 17. Everything was much the same except that Dolly—Dorothy was firm from the moment she entered the house about refusing to answer any more to Norah—had, presumably in revenge for the loss of her name, taken her sister's bed. Mr. Caffyn was glad to hear that the difficulties and dangers of stage life had been exaggerated, and promised that he would warn the Bishop of Hampstead, who was billed to preside at a forthcoming meeting of the Church and Stage Society, not to make too much of them in his anxiety about theatrical souls. Dorothy succeeded in deterring her relations from going to the theater the first week at Camberwell; but the following week, when the playbills of "Miss Elsie of Chelsea" flaunted themselves in every shop-window of West Kensington, a large party, not merely of the immediate family, but of uncles and aunts and cousins raked together from every obscure suburb in London, swarmed for the Thursday matinée, and, what was worse, insisted on buzzing round Dorothy outside the stage-door in order to take her out to tea between the performances. They alluded with some disappointment to the inconspicuousness of the part she played, and they all agreed that the outstanding feature of the performance was the comedian. They thought it must be very nice for Dorothy to have such a splendid humorist perpetually at hand.

"But he's not funny off the stage," explained Dorothy, crossly.

This seemed greatly to surprise the aunts and uncles, who evidently did not believe her. In the middle of tea the party was joined by Roland, Cecil, and Vincent; not having been able to get away for the matinée, they had arrived to swell the family reunion before going to the evening performance, for which they had booked stalls in the very front row, where, later on, to Dorothy's intense disgust, she saw Wilfred Curlew sitting with them'. However, he did have the decency not to wait after the play to accompany herself and her brothers back to West Kensington.

The next morning, before she was dressed, Dorothy was informed that a young gentleman was waiting to see her in the drawing-room, and discovered, when she got down, that a representative of a monthly magazine called *The Boudoir* had come to ask for an interview. The young man, talking rather as if the magazine was a draper's shop, told her that his paper was making a special feature of beautiful actresses. He cannonaded Dorothy with all sorts of questions, and forced her to surrender the information that her favorite parts were Lady Teazle, Viola, Portia, and Beatrice.

"Comedy, in fact?" said the young man.

"Oh yes, comedy," Dorothy agreed, after a moment's hesitation to decide whether Portia, whose speech about the quality of mercy she had once declaimed at a school breaking-up, ought to be considered a comic figure.

"You have no ambitions for tragedy?"

"No," she told him. "I think there's enough tragedy in ordinary life."

"Would you recommend the stage as a profession?" he inquired.

"Rather a difficult question. It depends so much on the girl."

"Quite," agreed the young man, wisely. "But have you any advice for beginners?"

"My advice is to be natural," said Dorothy.

"Quite," agreed the young man again.

"Natural both on the stage and off," she added.

The young man, with an air of devout concentration, wrote down this valuable maxim, while Dorothy, looking at herself in the mirror, allowed various expressions of delicious naturalness to stand the test of her own critical observation.

"With whom did you study?" the interviewer inquired next.

"Principally with the late Mrs. Haden," said Dorothy, feeling very generous in mentioning Lily's mother after the way the daughter had behaved with Tom Hewitt. "A delightful teacher of the old school, now, alas! no longer with us."

The young man shook his head sadly.

"But my real lessons," Dorothy added, brightly, lest the loss of Mrs. Haden to art might be too much for the interviewer's emotions—"my real lessons were derived from watching famous actresses. No famous actress, continental or English, ever came to London whom I did not go to see. I often went without"—she paused to think what she could have gone without, for it might sound absurd to say that she went without clothes—"I often walked," she corrected herself, "in order to have the necessary money to buy a seat."

"That'll interest our readers very much," said the young man. "Yes, that's the personal note which always appeals to our readers." He sucked his pencil with relish. "And who is your favorite actress?"

"In England or abroad?"

"Oh, in England," the young man hurriedly explained; probably he was jibbing at the prospect of having to write a foreign name.

"In England, Ellen Terry, decidedly," Dorothy replied.

"Quite"; the young man sighed with relief. "Perhaps you would care to give me a photograph of yourself," he suggested.

"With pleasure," she said, taking from the mantelpiece one that she had sent her mother about a month ago.

"Of course," the interviewer hemmed, nervously, "that will be twelve and sixpence for the cost of reproduction."

"Twelve and six?" repeated Dorothy.

"The block will cost twelve and sixpence, that is to say."

"Twelve and six?" she repeated once more.

But she gave him the money; controlling her annoyance at the idea that this young man might be making a profit out of her innocence, she conducted him cheerfully to the door and presented him with a tulip from one of Dolly's flower-pots.

"You're fond of gardening?" he asked, with half-open note-book.

"I adore flowers," said Dorothy. "Good-by."

To her mother she explained the sad necessity she had been under of having to give away her favorite photograph.

"But, mother, I'll write for another one," she promised.

"Oh, Norah dear, I hope you will," said Mrs. Caffyn, much distressed.

"Only, as they're rather expensive, you won't mind giving me a guinea, will you?" Dorothy murmured, with a frown for the old "Norah."

"No, darling Norah—darling child, I mean, of course not. I'd no idea you were spending your salary like that," said Mrs. Caffyn, searching in her purse for the money.

That evening, during the first act a note was sent round to Dorothy from Wilfred Curlew to say that he had been to see her every night this week, and that he had persuaded a friend of his to give her some publicity in a magazine with which he was connected.

"At a cost of twelve and six," Dorothy scoffed to herself.

She did not send a word of thanks to Wilfred, and being unable from the stage to perceive his presence anywhere in the theater, she supposed that, having been there every night this week, he must by now have reached the gallery.

When the interview appeared the other girls were very jealous, and all of them vowed that they had never heard of *The Boudoir*.

"With a blush Miss Lonsdale handed our interviewer an exquisite bunch of flowers culled by the beautiful young actress from her garden, a 'thing of beauty' in the dreary desert of London streets," read out one of the girls.

"Good God, have mercy on us!" exclaimed Clarice Beauchamp, holding a hairpin dipped in eye-black over the gas. "It's a wonder the editor hasn't written before now to ask if he can't keep you."

The irritation in the dressing-room caused by the interview was allayed by a rumor that John Richards would visit the Alexandra Theater, Stoke Newington, where they were playing their last week in the suburbs, with a view to choosing girls for the Vanity production in the autumn. No confirmation could be obtained of this; but the chorus put on extra make-up and acted with all its eyes and all its legs for a shadowy figure at the back of one of the private boxes. After the first act the business manager, who had come behind for some purpose, was surrounded by all the girls, each of whom in turn begged him to tell her confidentially what Mr. Richards had said about the show and if he had had any criticisms to make about herself.

"Mr. Richards?" repeated the manager.

"Now, don't pretend you know nothing about it," they expostulated. "*We* know he's in front."

"Well, you know more than I do," said the manager.

"Then who is it at the back of the box on the prompt side?"

"You silly girls! That's the late mayor of Hackney."

"Then why do they make such a fuss of him?" persisted the girl who had started the rumor. "There was a carriage outside the box-office half an hour before the overture, and people were all round it, staring as if it was the king."

"It's a very sad story," the manager explained. "He's blind, poor fellow, and now, whenever he goes to the theater, they watch him being helped out of his brougham."

During the second act not an eye nor a leg was thrown in the direction of the mysterious stranger, whose identity was a great disappointment to the girls; they had counted on Mr. Richards visiting them in the course of the tour, and here it was coming to an end without a sign of him.

However, they were consoled by being told at the last minute that they were going to play three nights at Oxford before the tour came to a definite conclusion. Everybody agreed that it would be a delightful way to wind up, and when the company assembled at Paddington on a brilliant morning in earliest June, they seemed, in the new clothes they had been able to buy during the last month in London, more like a large picnic-party going up to Maidenhead than a touring company.

Dorothy had decided that the visit to Oxford was an occasion to justify breaking into the £500 she had got out of her mother, which was still practically intact, owing to the economy exerted all these weeks. Her new dresses and new hats, combined with that interview in *The Boudoir*, gave the rest of the chorus an impression that there was somebody behind Dorothy, and they regarded her with a jealous curiosity that was most encouraging.

IV

The three girls had only just finished dinner at their lodgings in Eden Square when Sylvia proposed a walk round Oxford. Dorothy agreed to go out if she were allowed time to change her things; but Lily declared that she was tired after the journey, and preferred to look at illustrated papers in deshabille. Many undergraduates turned their heads to stare at Dorothy's beauty or Sylvia's eye-glass when the two girls were walking down the High toward St. Mary's College, through the gates of which Sylvia calmly suggested that they should pass in order to explore the gardens.

"But suppose they tell us that girls aren't allowed to go in," Dorothy demanded, in a panic.

"We'll go out again."

"But we should look so foolish."

"We always look foolish," said Sylvia. "Anything more foolish than you look at the present moment I can't imagine, except myself."

Before Dorothy could prevent her, Sylvia had asked a tall and haughty undergraduate if there was any reason why they should not take a walk in the college grounds. The young man blushed painfully, and Dorothy, who could see that his embarrassment at being spoken to by an actress was causing intense delight to a group of idlers in the college lodge, was angry with Sylvia for exposing the two of them to a share in the ridicule.

"All right, Dorothy," said Sylvia, cheerfully. "He says we can."

The tall and haughty undergraduate strode away up the High to escape from his friends' chaff, and the two girls wandered about the college until they found themselves in the famous St. Mary's Walks, where upon a seat embowered in foliage they listened to the bells that were ringing down the golden day and ringing in the unhastening Sabbath eve. Close at hand, but hidden from view by leafy banks, the pleasurable traffic of the Cherwell sounded continuously in a low murmur of talk that, blending with the swish of paddles and comfortable sound of jostling punts, seemed the very voice of indolent June. Dorothy supposed that she, like nature, must be looking most beautiful in this bewitching light, and regretted that the only passers-by should be ecclesiastical figures bent in grave intercourse, or a few young men arguing in throaty voices about topics she did not recognize.

"I don't think we've chosen a very good place," she complained, with a discontented pout.

"We've chosen the place," said Sylvia, "where nearly four years ago, on a Sunday afternoon in August, I agreed to get married."

"Married?" repeated Dorothy, in amazement. "Are you married?"

"Yes, I believe I'm married for the present; but I sha'n't be soon."

"Oh, Sylvia, do tell me about it! I won't say a word to anybody else."

But Sylvia, having said so much, would say no more; jumping up and insisting that she was thirsty, she reminded Dorothy that they had promised to help Charlie Clinton entertain his brother and some undergraduate friends. Charlie Clinton was an obscure member of the company who had suddenly sprung into considerable prominence by revealing that he had a brother at Oxford and was himself the black sheep of a respectable family. Dorothy, realizing that the blackest sheep is better form than the whitest goat, had accepted the invitation, but she was not much impressed by the collection of undergraduates gathered in his rooms, and was vexed that she had wasted her most becoming hat on young men who wanted to talk about nothing but music. She was vexed, too, at finding that David Bligh had been invited, and that he was talking affectedly about good music and sounding with his fluty voice rather like an undergraduate himself. Lily came and danced a classical dance which seemed to please everybody else, though Dorothy could not see anything in it. Bligh sang German songs, and was so much applauded that he condescendingly proposed that his pupil should sing, who refused so angrily that none of the undergraduates dared approach her. It was indeed a thoroughly boring evening, and she wondered if Oxford was going to produce nothing better than this.

The theater on Monday night, notwithstanding the fine weather, was packed; but the audience was noisy, and the men in the chorus who had not been invited to Charlie Clinton's party severely condemned the bad manners of undergraduates.

"They're a rowdy lot of bounders, that's what they are," Tom Hewitt proclaimed, loosening the collar around his aggressive neck.

Dorothy, who had been looking forward to astonishing some of the girls in the dressing-room with her news about Sylvia, forgot everything in a delightful triumph she was able to enjoy at the expense of Clarice Beauchamp. A note was brought round after the first act addressed:

To the fair artist's model in pink.   Front row.   O. P. side.

Clarice Beauchamp had the impudence to contest Dorothy's right to open this note, and while some of the artist's models were rapidly transforming themselves into Polynesian beauties and others as rapidly assuming the aristocratic costumes of a millionaire's yachting-party, Clarice and Dorothy, who belonged to the latter division, argued heatedly. At last Fay Onslow, to whom the note could not possibly refer, was allowed to open it and give her verdict:

Fair lady, my name is Lonsdale. On the Grampian hills my father feeds his flock! In other words, will you and the lady with the monocle who yesterday afternoon picked out quite the most unattractive man in St. Mary's as your guide come and picnic with me on the upper river to-morrow? A friend of mine at the House is dying to meet you, but he is much too shy to write himself. If you can come, just send back your address by bearer and I'll send my tame cab to fetch you to-morrow at twelve o'clock.

Yours sincerely,
ARTHUR LONSDALE.

"I knew it was for me," said Dorothy. "Sylvia and I were in St. Mary's College yesterday afternoon."

Clarice Beauchamp, much mortified, had to surrender her claim to the note.

"But what a strange coincidence that he should be called Lonsdale!" Onzie exclaimed. "Most extraordinary, I call it. Who knows? He might be a relation."

"He might be," said Dorothy, calmly.

Lily looked up from her place as if she were going to speak, but, though she said nothing, Dorothy was glad that the terms of the note gave her no excuse for asking her to-morrow, even if Sylvia did maliciously propose that Lily should go instead of herself.

"Oh, but they particularly want you," Dorothy protested.

"Anyway, I can't go," Lily said; "I've promised to go round some of the colleges with Tom."

Dorothy winced at the threatened sacrilege.

Next morning a cab jingled up to the girls' lodgings, and they were driven to the nearest point of embarkation for a picnic on the upper river. Their host, a short young man with very fair hair and a round pink face, introduced himself and led the way to the Rollers, over which punts and canoes were dragged from the lower level of the Cherwell to the wider sweeps of the Isis. A tall young man who was standing by a couple of canoes moored to the bank came forward to greet them. His most immediately conspicuous feature was a pair of white flannel trousers down the seams of which ran stripes of vivid blue ribbon; but when he was introduced to Dorothy as Lord Clarehaven she forgot about his trousers in the more vivid blue of his name. All sorts of ideas rushed through her mind—a sudden dread that he might think Sylvia more attractive than herself, a sudden contempt for the party of the evening before, a sudden rapture in which blue sky, blue blood, and the blue stripes of the trousers merged exquisitely, and a sudden apprehension created by her pleated reflection in the water that she was not looking her best. After Lord Clarehaven she should not have been surprised if the first young man had also had a title; but he was apparently only Mr. Lonsdale, and, though entitled to respect as a friend of Lord Clarehaven, would probably interest Sylvia more than herself.

Dorothy's dread that she and Lord Clarehaven might not find themselves in the same canoe was soon dispelled, because Lord Clarehaven was evidently as eager for her company as she was for his, and they were soon leaving the others behind. There is no form of conveyance which makes for so much intimacy of regard as a canoe, and Dorothy, when she had once been able to reassure herself by means of a pocket-mirror that she had not been ruffled by the cab-drive or by the nervous business of getting gracefully into a wabbling canoe, settled herself down to be admired at a distance of about four feet. Moreover, she indulged for the first time in her life in the pleasure of admiring somebody else, a state of mind which doubled her charm by taking away much of her self-consciousness. If Lord Clarehaven was below the standard of aristocracy set by our full-blooded lady novelists, he was equally far removed from the chinless convention of banal caricature. He had the long legs, the narrow hips and head, and the big teeth of the Norman; but his fair hair was already thinning upon a high, retreating forehead, his nose was small, and if the protuberant eyes that one sees in Pekinese spaniels and other well-bred mammals were a faint intimation of approaching degeneracy in the stock, Dorothy was not sufficiently versed in physiognomy to recognize such symptoms; already fascinated by his title and his trousers, she was quite ready to be fascinated by his eyes.

"I was lunching in St. Mary's yesterday with Arthur Lonsdale," he was explaining, "and I noticed you from the lodge. I should have come up and spoken to you myself, but I was rather frightened by your friend's eye-glass. In fact, I'm still not at all at ease with her. She looks deuced clever, I mean, don't you think?"

"She is awfully clever."

"Poor girl, but I suppose it's not such a bore for a girl as it would be for a man. I'm an awful ass myself, you know. I mean, I'm absolutely incapable of doing anything."

"How did you know we belonged to the company?" asked Dorothy, implying that with all his modesty he must possess acute powers of judgment hidden away somewhere.

"Well, to tell you the truth, we didn't know. Somebody said your friend was a medical student, only I wasn't going to have that, and some man said he'd noticed you at the station, so Lonnie and I went to the theater on the off-chance and tried to spot you."

"Which you did?"

"Oh, rather. Only, then we couldn't spot your name. I was all for Clarice Beauchamp."

"She's an awfully horrid girl," said Dorothy, quickly.

"Is she? I'm sorry to hear that. And Lonnie betted you were Fay Onslow. So we were quits. Funny thing you should have the same name as Lonnie. No relation, I suppose?"

He was evidently so sure of this that Dorothy was rather piqued and asked, loftily, which Lonsdale he was.

"Cleveden's son."

"Oh, then I am a relation," said Dorothy. "Though of course a very, very distant one."

"By Jove! that's great!" said Clarehaven.

He seemed enthusiastic, but Dorothy could not make out whether he believed her or not, and she rather wished she had kept the relationship for the dressing-room. She hoped that Sylvia would not give Lonsdale an impression that she claimed to be his first cousin; this abrupt plunge into the whirlpool of society might make her act extravagantly. What a pity that she had not known who he was before they met, and "Oh!" she cried, aloud.

"What's the matter?" Clarehaven asked.

"Nothing. At least I think I touched a fish," said Dorothy.

But her exclamation was caused by dismay at recalling that she had addressed him as "Arthur Lonsdale, Esquire," when for the first time in her life she might have written "The Honorable Arthur Lonsdale," for everybody to see. What must he have thought of her ignorance? And now here in a canoe with her was Lord Clarehaven, but, owing to the foolish modesty that English titles affect, she did not know if he was a marquis, an earl, a viscount, or a mere baron. The prospect of the green river was leaden with the thought of her stupidity.

"You're looking very sad," said Clarehaven. "What's the matter?"

"I was thinking how beautiful it was here," she sighed.

"Topping, isn't it?"

"Topping," she echoed, awarding to the utterance of the epithet as much emotion as if it were robbed from Shakespeare's magic store. Amid a sweet smell of grass and to the accompaniment of lapping water and a small sibilant wind they lunched on the salmon and mayonnaise, the prawns in aspic, the galantine and cold chicken, the meringues and strawberries of how many Oxford picnics. Above them dreamed a huge sky; elm-trees guarded the near horizon; wasps had not begun, nor did Sylvia tease Dorothy about being related to Lonsdale when Clarehaven presented them as long-lost cousins.

By the end of the afternoon Dorothy had sufficiently confirmed her admirer's first impression to be invited to lunch with him at Christ Church the following day, in which invitation Sylvia was of course included. Then slowly they drifted back down the river, on the dimples and eddies of which the overhanging trees cast a patina as upon the muscles of an ancient bronze.

"How unreal the theater seems!" sighed Dorothy when they drove up to the stage-door.

"Does it?" Sylvia laughed. "It seems to me much more real than our pretty behavior this afternoon."

V

Dorothy slept badly that night. Her regret for the mistake she had made in addressing Arthur Lonsdale as esquire magnified itself horribly in the mean little bedroom of the lodgings in Eden Square. All night long she was waking up to reproach herself for her stupidity in not taking the trouble to make sure who he was before she sent back the note. Her blunder was all the more unpardonable because she should have been sufficiently interested in receiving a letter from a namesake to take this trouble. And now suppose Lord Clarehaven were to put her under the necessity of addressing him on the outside of an envelope? How was she to know what to write? "Lord Clarehaven, Christ Church College"? It sounded rather empty. In any case, she should have to ask for him at the lodge to-morrow, and how the porter would sneer behind her back if she should make a mistake! In despair Dorothy wandered into the next room where Sylvia and Lily were sleeping tranquilly.

"Oh dear!" she lamented.

"What's the matter?" asked Sylvia, jumping up in bed.

"Sylvia, I can't sleep. I think there's a rat in my room. I suppose Arthur Lonsdale didn't say if Lord Clarehaven was a marquis, did he?"

"Damn your eyes, Dorothy, did you wake me up to ask that? Go and get hold of Debrett, if you want to know so badly."

Dorothy went back to her bedroom in peace of mind. Of course! How easy it was, really, and she fell into a delicious sleep, from which, notwithstanding her disturbed night, she was early awake to dress and be out of the house by ten o'clock in order to search the Oxford bookshops for a *Peerage*.

"We have a *Baronetage*" said one bookseller.

Dorothy shrugged her shoulders compassionately, and went from shop to shop until she found the big red volume of her desire. She paid without a moment's hesitation the price of it, called a cab, and drove back to Eden Square, that she might have plenty of time to devour the contents before going to Christ Church. Her breath came fast when she actually read Clarehaven and began to absorb the wonderful information below:

CLAREHAVEN, EARL OF. (Clare) [Earl U.K. 1816. Bt. E. 1660.]

ANTHONY GILBERT CLARE, 5th Earl, and 10th Baronet; *b.* Oct. 15, 1882; *s.* 1896; ed. at Eton and Christ Church; is 2d Lieut, in North Devon Dragoons, and patron of one living.

Arms—Purpure, two flanches ermine, on a chief sable a moon in her complement argent. *Crest*—A moon in her complement argent, arising from a cloud proper. *Supporters*—Two angels vested purpure, winged and crined or, each holding in the exterior hand a key or. *Motto*—*Claro non clango*.

Seat—Clare Court, Devonshire. *Town residence*—129 Curzon Street, W. *Club*—Bachelors'.

SISTERS LIVING

Lady Arabella. b. 1885.

Lady Constantia. b. 1887.

Augusta (Countess of Clarehaven) 2d dau. of 9th Earl of Chatfield: *m.* 1880 the 4th Earl who *d.* 1896. *Residence*—Clare Court, Devonshire.

PREDECESSORS—[1] Anthony Clare, *M.P.* for Devon (a descendant of Richard Fitzgilbert, Baron of Clare, a companion of the Conqueror, son of Gilbert Crispin, Earl of Brione in Normandy, who was son of Geoffrey, a natural son of Richard I. Duke of Normandy), was cr. a Bt. 1660; *d.* 1674; *s.* by his son [2] *Sir* Gilbert, 2d Bt.; *d.* 1710; *s.* by his son [3] *Sir* Anthony, 3d Bt.; *d.* 1747; *s.* by his nephew [4] *Sir* William, 4th Bt.; *d.* 1764; *s.* by his cousin [5] *Sir* Anthony, 5th Bt.; cr. *Baron Clarehaven* (peerage of Great Britain) 1796; *d.* 1802; *s.* by his son [6] Gilbert, 2d Baron; cr. *Viscount Clare* and *Earl of Clarehaven* (peerage of United Kingdom) 1816; *d.* 1826; *s.* by his son [7] Richard Crispin, 2d Earl. *b.* 1788. *m.* 1818 Lady Caroline Lacey who *d.* 1859, 2d dau. of 3d Marquess of Longlan; *d.* 1864; s. by his son [8] Geoffrey William, *P.C.*, 3d Earl. *b.* 1820; sometime Lord Lieut. of Devon; M.P. for S. Devon (C); Vice-Chamberlain of H. M. Queen Victoria's Household. *m.* 1845 the Hon. Louisa Travers, who *d.* 1890, dau. of the 26th Baron Travers; *d.* 1867; *s.* by his son [9] Gilbert Crispin, 4th Earl, *b.* 1845; Lieut. Royal Horse Guards, 1866-67: *m.* 1880 Lady Augusta Fanhope, 2d dau. of 9th Earl of Chatfield; *d.* 1896; *s.* by his son [10] Anthony Gilbert, 5th Earl and present peer; also Viscount Clare and Baron Clarehaven.

Half a dozen times word for word she read through these magic pages, until she felt that she simply could not make a mistake at lunch. Then a page or two farther on, past Clarendon and Clarina, she came to:

CLEVEDEN, BARON. (Lonsdale) [Baron G.B. 1762.]

CHARLES ARTHUR BRABAZON LONSDALE. *G.C.M.G., G.C.I.E.* 5th Baron; *b.* Oct. 10, 1858; *s.* 1888; ed. at Eton and at Ch. Ch. Oxford. (B.A. 1880); is a J.P. and D.L. for Warwickshire and Verderer of the Forest of Arden; Hon. Col. of Yeo.; sat as M.P. for West Warwick—(C) 1880-1884; was Assist. Private Sec. to the Premier—(M. Salisbury) 1885-6; Gov. and Com. in Ch. of E. Australia. 1893-99; and Gov. of Central India. 1899-1901; *K.C.M.G.* 1893; *G.C.M.G.* 1898; *G.C.I.E.* 1899: *m.* 1882 Lady Helen Druce (an Extra Woman of the Bed-chamber to H.M. Queen Victoria), dau. of 10th Earl of Monteith and has issue.

Arms—Argent, an oak tree englanté vert. *Crest*—A bugle horn or, enguiché and stringed vert. *Supporters*—On either side a forester sounding a horn proper. *Motto*—J'y serai.

Seat—Cressingham Hall, Warwick. *Clubs*—Carlton. Travellers'.

SON LIVING

Hon. ARTHUR GEORGE MORNINGTON. *b.* Feb. 24, 1883.

DAUGHTER LIVING

Hon. Sylvia May. *b.* 1885.

"Sylvia?" Dorothy said to herself. But she decided to stick to the name Dorothy, and went on reading about her family.

BROTHER LIVING

Rev. the Hon. George, *b.* 1860; ed. at Eton, and at St. Mary's Coll. Oxford. (B.A. 1883. M.A. 1886); is R. of Bingham-cum-Bingham Monachorum; *m.* 1894 Mary Alice, dau. of the late Rev. Francis Greville, V. of St. Wilfred's, Tilchester, and Hon. Canon of Tilchester, and has issue living, Arthur Brabazon—*b.* 1896. Mary—*b.* 1898. Georgina Maud—*b.* 1900. *Residence*— Bingham Rectory, Hants.

SISTERS LIVING

Hon. Frances Louisa, *b.* 1863. *m.* 1885 Sir William Honeywood-Greene, 6th Bt. *Residence*—Arden Towers, Warwick.

Hon. Caroline, *b.* 1865. *m.* 1886 Sir Stanley Pinkerton, K.C.V.O. Master of the King's Spaniels. *Residence*—210 Eaton Square, S.W.

Hon. Horatia. *b.* 1867.

There followed a couple of pages devoted to collateral branches of the Lonsdales. These were something new: the Clares apparently lacked collaterals. Presently it dawned on Dorothy that these collaterals treated of the more distant relations of the family, and in a fever she began to search for confirmation of the legend in Lonsdale Road that through their grandmother, Mrs. Doyle, the Caffyns were connected with Lord Cleveden. On and on she read through colonels and rectors with their numerous offspring, through consuls and captains and judges and doctors even; but there was no mention of Doyles, still less of Caffyns. The connection must indeed be very remote: perhaps it was hidden among the predecessors.

PREDECESSORS.—[1] George Lonsdale, Verderer of the Forest of Arden; M.P. for Warwickshire 1740-62; cr. *Baron Cleveden*, of Cressingham, co. Warwick (peerage of Great Britain) 1762; *d.* 1764; *s.* by his son [2] Arthur, 2d Baron; *d.* 1822; *s.* by his son [3] Charles, 3d Baron; *b.* 1790: *m.* 1830 the Hon. Horatia Brabazon, who *d.* 1851, dau. of 3d Viscount Brabazon; *d.* 1840; *s.* by his son [4] George Brabazon, 4th Baron; *b*. 1832; a Lord-in-Waiting to H. M. Queen Victoria 1858-64: *m*. 1856 Lady May Mornington, who *d*. 1895, 3d dau. of 11th Earl of Belgrove; *d*. 1888; *s*. by his son [5] Charles Arthur Brabazon, 5th Baron and present peer.

Dorothy sighed her disappointment, but resolved that she would adopt the family crest and motto as her own. *J'y serai* underneath a bugle-horn: how well it would look on her note-paper. Fired by its inspiration, she began to dress herself for lunch with the Earl of Clarehaven, and when, an hour later, she ushered Sylvia into the Christ Church lodge with a hardihood that contrasted strongly with the reluctance she had shown when Sylvia had dragged her into St. Mary's on Sunday, there was no need to inquire for Lord Clarehaven by his correct title, because the host was there himself to meet his guests and escort them across the spaciousness of Tom Quad to his rooms in Peckwater. It appeared that at the last minute an urgent summons to play cricket for the Eton Ramblers had prevented Lonsdale from coming. Dorothy, notwithstanding her knowledge of the Lonsdale collaterals, was not sorry, for she did not wish to discuss the relationship with one of the family, especially before Sylvia, to whom she now turned with a hint of patronage.

"My dear, you will be disappointed. Mr. Lonsdale is not coming to lunch."

Sylvia said she would try to put up with the disappointment and hoped that an equally entertaining substitute had been provided.

"I've asked a fellow called Tufton," said Clarehaven. "His father's a sleeping partner or something of jolly old John Richards at the Vanity, and I thought he might be useful. Besides, he's not at all a bad egg. We elected him to the Bullingdon this term."

Dorothy looked at her host gratefully and admiringly.

"How awfully sweet of you!" she murmured, with the lightest, briefest touch of her fingers on his wrist, and thinking how well the people who mattered knew how to do things.

They had reached Peckwater by now, the architecture of which, brightened by many window-boxes in full bloom, reminded Dorothy of streets in Mayfair. Her morning with Debrett had in fact turned her head so completely that she sought everywhere for illustrations of grandeur in the life around her; in this regard Clarehaven's rooms, by conforming perfectly to her notions of what they should be, made her want to kiss herself with satisfaction. To begin with, the door of his bedroom, slightly ajar, allowed a glimpse of numerous pairs of boots running up the scale from brogues to waders, which somehow spoke more eloquently of riches and leisure than if the luncheon-table had been laid with gold. Dorothy was contemplating the tints of these boots like a poet in an autumnal glade when Clarehaven presented Mr. Tufton, who, to do him justice, looked as well turned out as one of his host's hunting-tops and in a chestnut-colored suit with extravagantly rolled collar maintained his personality against the boots and the cigars and the brown sherry and the old paneling and the studies of grouse by Thorburn that gave this room its air of mellow opulence.

Dorothy told Mr. Tufton brightly that he had missed a wonderful afternoon yesterday.

"I was playing polo," he explained.

Dorothy, having an idea that polo was nearly as dangerous as bull-fighting, shuddered.

"I say, do you feel a draught?" inquired the host, anxiously.

"Oh no, it's delicious here."

A voice from the quad was shouting "Tony," and Dorothy, remembering Anthony from Debrett, could not resist telling Clarehaven that he was being called. Clarehaven was moving over to the window to discourage whoever was demanding his presence, when another voice came clearly up through the June air.

"Shut up, Ridgway! Tony's lunching some does, you silly ass!"

Dorothy could not help thinking that Sylvia ought to have pretended not to hear this allusion instead of bursting out into what was really a vulgar peal of laughter.

"I think there *is* a draught," said Mr. Tufton, closing the windows so gravely that one felt much of his inmost meditation was devoted to the tactful handling of moments like this.

"Are these your sisters?" Dorothy asked, picking up a photograph of two girls, each holding a foxhound.

"Yes, those are my sisters Bella and Connie," Clarehaven replied. "They're awful keen on puppy-walking."

Perhaps, after all, abbreviations were sometimes tolerable, and names like Arabella and Constantia were rather long.

"Isn't your second name Gilbert?" she asked.

"Yes. Dreadful infliction, isn't it?"

Dorothy decided not to say that her father's name was Gilbert, to which she had been leading up, and took her seat at table, noticing with pleasure that the full moon of the house of Clare adorned the silver. After lunch they looked at albums of snapshots, during the examination of which Mr. Tufton was most useful, because he was continually saying: "By Jove! Isn't that Lady Connie?" or: "By Gad! Isn't that the covert where Lady Bella got her left and right last October?" or: "Hello! I see Lady Clarehaven has followed my advice about the pergola." If Mr. Tufton could advise countesses as stately as the Countess of Clarehaven and refer to the daughters of an earl as Lady Bella and Lady Connie, what might not Dorothy do with patience and discretion? Meanwhile she took no risks, and if she had to mention the members of her host's family she alluded to them as "your mother" or "your elder sister" or "your younger sister."

"But what a glorious place Clare Court must be!" she exclaimed.

"Oh, I don't know," said the owner of it. "The train service is absolutely rotten."

"You'll have your new car this vac.," Mr. Tufton reminded him. "I wrote the firm a very strong letter yesterday." Then seeing that his friend was growing gloomy at the prospect of Devonshire even with a new car, he suggested a stroll round Meadows, and cleverly arranged to lag behind with Sylvia.

Clarehaven when he was alone with Dorothy did not find much more to say, but he was able to look at her with a more open admiration than when his glances had been disconcerted by Sylvia's monocle.

"You know I'm tremendously quelled by your friend," he avowed. "By Jove! you know, I feel she's always criticizing a fellow. Now with you I feel absolutely at my ease."

"I'm glad," Dorothy murmured. Then for two full moments she let her deep eyes flash into his.

"I say, when you look at me like that," said Clarehaven, solemnly, "you absolutely bring my heart into my mouth. By Gad! I feel it being hooked up like a trout."

"I'm afraid it's a very easy heart to hook," she laughed.

"Oh no, it's not! Oh no, really it's not! I can assure you that I'm not in the least susceptible."

"Ah, you'll forget all about me to-morrow."

"My dear Dorothy! You don't object to my calling you Dorothy? My dear Dorothy, if you knew how unlikely I am to forget all about you to-morrow...."

"Well?"

"Well, I'm not going to forget about you, that's all."

"We shall see."

"Yes, we shall," said Clarehaven, fiercely.

Dorothy was anxious to add still a small touch to his obvious appreciation, and she conceived the daring idea of inviting him back to tea in the lodgings. She felt that there in the dingy little room her grace and beauty would appear more desirable than ever, and if he should fancy from her invitation that she intended to make herself cheap he would soon perceive from her behavior how far removed she was from the average chorus-girl. Clarehaven applauded the suggestion, and though Sylvia looked rather bored by it, Tufton was enthusiastic; so they visited a pastry-cook's and bought lots of expensive cakes and chocolates, for which the guest of honor paid.

"How the poor live!" exclaimed Dorothy, pointing with a dramatic gesture at the drab little houses of Eden Square as if she would comment upon an aspect of Oxford that was hardly credible after Christ Church.

"Yes, this is our quad," chuckled Sylvia. "Old Tom!"

"I've never been here before," said Clarehaven, anxious to convince Dorothy that really he was not susceptible. "I've heard of Eden Square, of course, but this is my first visit. It's where all the theatrical people stay, isn't it, Tuffers?"

"It may be," replied Mr. Tufton, who, having paid for everything he possessed with money his father was making out of the theater, naturally did not wish to show himself too familiar with its domestic life.

"Number ten," said Dorothy, gaily. "Here we are!"

She opened the front door and led the way along a narrow passage to the sitting-room, and, flinging wide open the door, drew back for Clarehaven to enter first.

"You'll have to excuse the general untidiness," she warned him.

The sentence was out before she had time to realize that the general untidiness included a searing vision of Lily in an arm-chair, imparadised upon the lap of the impossible Tom Hewitt. Sylvia dashed forward to the rescue of Dorothy, who was standing speechless with mortification, and began introducing everybody to one another as fast as she could. Clarehaven's devotion to the stage did not seem impaired by this abrupt manifestation of low life behind the scenes, and Tufton, who in other company would probably have been as much outraged as Dorothy herself by such a reflection upon the source of his wealth, copied his friend's lead. Tom Hewitt with a mumbled excuse about having to see the manager retired as soon as possible. Lily, notwithstanding that her left cheek was flushed and that the hair on the left side of her head was more conspicuously a part of the general untidiness than the hair on the right, seemed utterly unconscious of having as good as torn up the Debrett in which Dorothy had invested this morning, and actually talked away in her languorous style to Clarehaven and Tufton as if Tom Hewitt's lap was the natural place on which to pass a lovely summer afternoon.

For Dorothy that tea-party was a martyrdom from which she began to think that she should never recover. Wherever she looked she saw that horrible picture of Lily and Tom. Once Clarehaven asked for another lump of sugar, and, tormented by the vision, she put two chocolates in his cup. Tufton passed his cup for a little more milk, and she emptied it away into the slop-bowl. Finally in an effort to restore her equanimity she took a chocolate that concealed a sticky caramel within, and when her mouth was all twisted and her teeth felt as if they were being pulled out by the roots Clarehaven asked if she could not spare him a photograph. He was being kind, thought Dorothy, miserably; the Fitzgilberts and Crispins and Clares of all those generations were gathering to help him hide the contempt he must feel for this tea-party; Lacy and Travers and Fanhope were behind him, pleading the obligations of nobility. And if he were not being kind she must suppose that he rather liked Lily, which would be worst of all. But what a lesson she had been given, what a lesson, indeed! If but once it might be granted to her that a folly should be expiated in the pain of the moment, she would never play tricks with fortune again.

When Clarehaven rose to make his farewells Dorothy did not attempt to detain him, but with a sorrowful grace shook his hand and would not even give him the photograph.

"No, no, I'd rather send you one from London."

"But you'll forget," he protested.

"No, I sha'n't. One hundred and twenty-nine Curzon Street. Or will you be at Clare Court?"

"I'll write to you."

"No, no," said Dorothy. It would never do for him to write to Lonsdale Road; besides, he might take it into his head to visit her there, which might be more disastrous than this tea-party. What would he think, for instance, of the misshapen boots that were usually waiting outside Roland's room like two large black-beetles? No, when she had thought out her campaign she would send him a photograph, and if, looking back on this afternoon, he decided that she was not worth while—well, she must put up with it. Dorothy was so sorry for herself that Clarehaven was flattered by her melancholy countenance into supposing that he had made a deep impression. In the narrow passage Tufton slipped behind and whispered to her that she must look her best to-night.

"Why?"

"Stable information," he said, and hurried after his friend, Lord Clarehaven.

When the three girls were alone together in the fatal sitting-room Dorothy's repressed rage with Lily broke out uncontrollably.

"I hope you don't think I'll ever live with you again after that disgusting exhibition. I suppose you think just because you went with me to Walter Keal that you can do as you like. I don't know what Sylvia thinks of you, but I can tell you what I think. You make me feel absolutely sick. That beastly chorus-boy! The idea of letting anybody like that even look at you! Thank Heaven, the tour's over. I'm going down to the theater. I can't stay in this room. It makes me blush to think of it. I'll take jolly good care who I live with in future."

Something in Lily's fragility, something in her still untidy hair and uncomprehending muteness, inflamed Dorothy beyond the bounds of toleration, and in despair of just words to humiliate her sufficiently she slapped her face.

"Hit her back, my lass," cried Sylvia, putting up her eye-glass to watch the fray; but Lily collapsed tearfully into the arm-chair, and Dorothy rushed out of the room.

The sight of Debrett's scarlet and gold upon her dressing-table was enough to reconjure all her mortification, and she was just going to weep her heart out upon the bed as, no doubt, below Lily was weeping hers out upon the shoulders of a ghostly Tom Hewitt, when Tufton's parting advice recurred to her. She had to look her best to-night. Why? He must have some reason to say that.

"*J'y serai?*" cried Dorothy, mustering all her family pride to keep back her tears.

VI

Although fortified by the motto, Dorothy was still suffering from the memory of that afternoon, and when she arrived at the theater to dress and saw Tom Hewitt standing by the stage-door she tried to pass him without acknowledging his salute.

"Mr. Richards will be in front to-night," he told her, portentously.

"Oh, we're always hearing that," said Dorothy. "I don't believe it."

"It's a fact. Warren told me so himself. And Mr. Keal's come down with him."

So this was why Tufton had advised her to look her best to-night; the visit could only mean that the great man wanted girls for the autumn production at the Vanity. Dorothy began to cheer up. Even if Lily's behavior had disgusted Lord Clarehaven irreparably, such behavior would not spoil her own chance of being engaged by John Richards, and at the Vanity there would be plenty of titled admirers. No doubt most of them would be younger sons or elder sons who had not yet succeeded, but ... "*j'y serai*," murmured Dorothy. "It's a good thing that I don't fall in love very easily. And it's lucky I didn't let myself cry," she added, congratulating her reflection in the dressing-room mirror.

Every girl was painting herself and powdering herself and pulling up her stockings and patting her hair and, regardless of the undergraduates she had met during the week, preparing to act as she had never acted before. Dorothy took neither more nor less trouble with her appearance than she took every night.

This time rumor was incarnate in fact, for the great Mr. Richards came and stood in the wings during a large portion of the play, and Dorothy, convinced that the one thing she ought not to do was to throw a single glance in his direction, devoted all her attention to the front of the house. There were lots of flowers; but nobody, neither principal nor chorus-girl, was handed such a magnificent basket of pink roses as herself, and nobody who had not suffered as she had suffered that afternoon in the depths could have been so gloriously thrilled on the heights as Dorothy was when the curtain fell at the close of the performance amid the shouts and cheers of youthful art-loving England, and she was stopped in the wings by Mr. Water Keal.

"Come here, dear," he said. "I want to introduce you to Mr. Richards."

The impresario was a large and melancholy man whose voice reverberated in the back of a cavernous throat with so high a palate that consonants were lost in its echoes and his speech seemed to consist entirely of vowels.

"Who sent you the prehy flowers, dear?" he asked, lugubriously.

"The Earl of Clarehaven," said Dorothy, with a brilliant smile.

"Ha—ha, vehy 'ice, vehy 'ice," he muttered, fondling the card attached. "Goo' gir'! Goo' gir'!"

The millionaire's yachting friends wore evening gowns for the latter part of the second act, and Dorothy in old rose, with her basket of flowers and exquisite neck and shoulders, was indeed looking her best.

"Goo' gir'!" Mr. Richards boomed once more; then as she passed from the royal presence he patted her shoulder in congratulation, dusted the powder from his fingers, lit an enormous cigar, and wandered away with Mr. Keal.

When Dorothy reached the dressing-room every girl was speculating on the depth of the impression she had made upon Mr. Richards, but not one of them could claim that the great man had patted her on the back or noticed her flowers. Presently the call-boy came with a message that Miss Lonsdale was to be at the theater to-morrow morning at eleven o'clock without fail, and it was obvious to the most jealous observer that Dorothy's chance had come. She was so much elated by her good fortune that she was reconciled to Lily, told everybody what a delightful lunch she had had with Lord Clarehaven and what a delightful picnic she had had with Lord Clarehaven and how she had met a cousin of hers, Arthur Lonsdale, who was the only son of Lord Cleveden.

"You know, he was governor of Central India," Dorothy reminded the dressing-room.

"India!" echoed Miss Onslow. "That sounds hot stuff, anyway."

Dorothy buried her face in the roses to get rid of the effluvium of such vulgarity. And then in the middle of her success, just when her true friends should have been most pleased, Sylvia, who had shared—well, not shared, but had been allowed to assist at her triumph—Sylvia it was who asked, in a voice audible to the whole dressing-room:

"On which side of the road are you related to young Lonsdale?"

Luckily the joke was too obscure to be generally understood; but Dorothy decided to banish Sylvia from the list of her friends that in Lily's company she might henceforth inhabit an outer darkness unlit by Debrett's scarlet and gold.

"I expect I shall soon forget what an awful life touring is," said Dorothy to herself that night, as she turned back the limp cotton sheets and looked distastefully at the hummocky mattress. There was a trenchant symbolism, too, in massacring a flea with Debrett; no other volume would have been heavy enough.

The next morning Mr. Richards seemed to be inviting her—so gentle were his accents, so soft his intonation—to join the Vanity company next September at three pounds a week. Mr. Keal and his Jewish assistant, Mr. Fitzmaurice, were present at her triumph; and when Dorothy was going down-stairs from the manager's office, Mr. Fitzmaurice hurried after her and begged her not to forget that it was he who had been the first to recognize her talents.

"Well, call me a cab, there's a good boy," said Dorothy, to reward him; and Mr. Fitzmaurice, who only six months ago had looked at her so critically on that wet December morning in Leicester Square, now ran hither and thither in the summer weather until he had found her a cab.

"What swank!" Dorothy heard Clarice Beauchamp say when, with a rattle and a dash, she drove up to the station, where the company were mustering for their last journey together. But she had only a gracious smile for poor Clarice; and at Paddington, although she parted with Sylvia and Lily cordially enough, she did not invite either of them to come and see her in Lonsdale Road.

CHAPTER III

I

NOT even the Irishman's passion for originality is strong enough to resist the common impulse of human nature to follow the course of the sun; he must migrate westward like the Saxon before him, and it is surely remarkable to find a theater holding out against a social tendency to which an Irishman succumbs. When a flood of new thoroughfares submerged old theatrical London in the last years of the nineteenth century and created a new theaterdom farther west; when the barbarous hoardings of the Strand Improvement obliterated so many resorts of leisure, and, like the people of Croton, the London County Council diverted a stream of traffic to flow where once was the Sybaris of Holywell Street and the Opéra Comique; when the Lyceum and the Adelphi changed the quality of their wares; when Terry's became a cinema palace and His Grace of Bedford sold Drury Lane overnight—the Vanity was almost the only theater that preserved its position and its character. The peak of Ararat was not more welcome to the water-weary eyes of Noah than to patrons a theater as old-fashioned as the Ark was the sight of that little island upon which the Vanity maintained itself amid the wrecks and ruins of the engulfed Strand. Close by, as if to commemorate the friendly rivalry of Church and Stage, upon another island St. Clement Dane's cleft the traffic of Fleet Street long after Temple Bar had been swept away; and it was agreeably appropriate that the church where Doctor Johnson, our greatest conservative, was wont to bow his head before the slow grinding of God's mills should have for company in a visible protest against the illusion of progress that monument of English conservatism, the Vanity Theater. More secure upon its island in the Strand than the Eddystone Lighthouse upon its rock in the Channel, the illuminated portico of the Vanity blazed away as brightly as it ever did before the destruction of the mean streets that used to obscure its glory. Not far off, the Savoy Hotel served as prologue and epilogue to its entertainments; and no alliance between one of the new theaters in Piccadilly and the Ritz or Carlton could yet claim to have superseded that time-honored alliance between the Vanity and the Savoy.

In the early 'seventies the sacred lamp of burlesque, as journalists moved to poesy by their theme have it, was lighted at the Vanity, and in the waning 'eighties the gas-lamp of burlesque, with nothing but an added brightness to mark the change, became the electric bulb of musical comedy. Time moved slowly at the Vanity; tenors grew hoarse and comedians grew stiff, but they were not easily superseded; many ladies grew stout, but the boards of the Vanity were strong, and even the places of those dearly loved by the gods who married young were only taken by others equally beloved and exactly like their predecessors; puns disappeared gradually from the librettos; the frocks of the chorus exaggerated the fashion of the hour; very seldom a melody was sufficiently novel to escape being whistled by the town; but in the opening years of the twentieth century the Vanity was intrinsically what the Vanity had been thirty years before and what no doubt it would be thirty years thence. The modish young men who applauded "Miss Elsie of Chelsea" sat in the stalls where their fathers and in some cases their grandfathers had applauded "Hamlet Up to Date." The fathers vowed that the Vanity had deteriorated since the days when mutton-chop whiskers were cultivated and the ladies of the chorus flirted bustles on the outside of a coach-and-four; but the sons were quite content with the present régime and considered jolly old John Richards as good as any impresario of the 'eighties. Unless the standard of beauty had universally declined at the dawn of the new century, that opinion of youth must be indorsed; it is doubtful if twenty more beautiful girls than the Vanity chorus contained in the autumn of 1903 could have been found in any other city or in any other country, and certainly not in any other theater. When a few years after this date John Richards was knighted for his services to human nature and applied to the College of Heralds for a grant of arms, a friend with a taste for Latin robbed Propertius for the motto and gave him *Tot milia formosarum*, which, though lending itself to a ribald translation of "The foremost harem of smiling Totties," was not less well deserved by John Richards than by Pluto, to whom the poet addressed the original observation.

Dorothy, by spending in complete seclusion the two months before rehearsals began, prepared herself to shimmer as clearly as she could in the shimmering galaxy that was to make "The River Girl" as big a hit as "Miss Elsie of Chelsea." She declined to accompany her family to the seaside in August, being sure that August at Eastbourne would be bad for her complexion; therefore she remained behind in Lonsdale Road with the cook, who by the time Dorothy had finished with her began to have ambitions to be a lady's maid. Nothing is more richly transfigured by unfamiliarity than the empty streets of a London suburb in mid-August, when their sun-dyed silence quivers upon the air like noon in Italy. At such a season the sorceress Calypso might not have disdained West Kensington for her spells; Dorothy, dream-haunted and with nothing more strenuous than singing-lessons and fashion papers to impinge upon the drowsy days, lived on self-enchantment. She never sent Lord Clarehaven the promised photograph, not did she even write him a letter; after deliberation she had decided that it would be more effective to appear upon his next horizon like a new planet rather than to wane slowly from his recollection like a summer moon. To write from an address at which it would be impossible to renew their acquaintance would be foolish. Besides, with such a future as hers at the Vanity was surely bound to be, did one Clarehaven more or less matter? He had served his purpose in demonstrating the ease with which she could reach beyond other girls; but, as Mary, the cook, had observed last night in recounting her rupture with the milkman, "plenty more mothers had sons," and if Clarehaven arrived impatiently at the same conclusion about the supply of daughters, that was better than exposing herself to the greater humiliation of being taken up in an idle moment and as readily dropped again. Dorothy's imagination had been touched by reading of three Vanity marriages that were now sharing the attention of the holiday press with giant gooseberries and vegetable marrows of mortal seeming. The younger son of a duke, the eldest son of a viscount, a Welsh baronet had, one after another, made those gaps in the Vanity chorus, to fill one of which Dorothy had been chosen by the provident Mr. Richards; she accepted the omen, and made up her mind that for her it should always be marriage or nothing.

It would be unfair at this stage in Dorothy's career to accuse her of formulating any definite plan to win a coronet, still less of casting her eye upon Lord Clarehaven's coronet in particular; but during these sun-drenched August days she did resolve to do nothing that might spoil the fulfilment of the augury. Left to herself, and free from the criticism of friends or relations, it would have been strange if Dorothy's estimate of her own powers had not been rather heightened by so much lazy self-contemplation. One day she had met an acquaintance marooned like herself upon this desert isle of holidays, and on being asked what she was doing in London at such a season, had replied truthfully enough that she was just looking round; but she did not add that she was looking round at herself in a mirror. This cloistral felicity lasted as long as the lime-trees in West Kensington kept their summer greenery; at the end of August the leaves began to wither, the rumble of returning cabs was heard more often every day, and the first rehearsal of "The River Girl" was called. Dorothy's seclusion was over; of the girls who passed through the Vanity stage-door that August morning there was none so fresh as she.

"How odd," she thought, "that only this time last year the notion of going on the stage had never even entered my head."

Dorothy had paused for a moment on the threshold of the theater, and was listening while the door swung to and fro behind her and syncopated the dull beat of the traffic in the Strand to a sort of ragtime tune. How different these rehearsals were going to be from those of last year in the Lisle Street club-room, and how right she had been to escape from the provinces so quickly.

From the first moment Dorothy felt more herself in the Vanity than she had felt all those six months of touring. She was, of course, stared at and criticized, but she was never acutely conscious of the jealousy that had glared from the eyes of her companions in the provinces. The beauty of her rivals in this metropolitan chorus only made her own beauty more remarkable; she, being the first to recognize this, accorded to her associates such a frank and such an obviously sincere admiration that she gained a reputation for simplicity, which the other girls ascribed to innocence. From innocence to mystery is but a short step in an ambient like the Vanity, and without a Lily or a Sylvia to tell the other girls too much about her, Dorothy developed the mysterious aspect of herself and left her innocence undefined. At the Vanity there was none of the destructive intimacy of touring life. Nobody ever saw the ladies of this chorus in polychrome on the wet platform of a Yorkshire railway station; nobody ever saw the ladies of this chorus tilting with a hatpin at pickled onions; nobody, in fact, had any excuse for being disillusioned by the ladies of the Vanity, because, being individually and collectively aware of their national importance, they were never really off the stage; indeed, except occasionally in their bedrooms, perhaps, they were never really behind the scenes. The fancy of a casual observer, who lingered for a moment at the stage-door to watch the ladies of the Vanity tripping out of their hansoms, was as much stimulated by the sight as the fancy of the regular patron who from the front of the house was privileged to observe them tripping on to the stage. They were brilliant butterflies by day and gorgeous moths by night; though nature forbids us to suppose that they never were caterpillars, their larval state is as unimaginable as the touch of time that worked the metamorphosis.

Dorothy did not allude to the chrysalis of West Kensington from which she had just emerged, nor did she mention more than she could help the caterpillar existence of touring. True to her native caution, she avoided committing herself to any sudden friendships that might afterward be regretted, but she fluttered round all the girls in turn, and with Miss Birdie Underhill and Miss Maisie Yorke, two members of the sextet sung from punts in the first act, she made a tolerably high excursion into the empyrean. Birdie and Maisie were tall blondes of the same type as herself, but, being some years older, they were beginning to think that, inasmuch as they had not been able to find even the younger son of a baron whose attentions conformed to his title, they ought to accept the hands of two devoted and moderately rich stock-brokers who had long and patiently admired them. Perhaps it was the first faint intimations of maternity demanding expression that led these two queens of the chorus to hint so graciously to Dorothy at the inheritance they designed for her. To pass from butterflies to bees for a metaphor, they fed her with queens' food (prepared by Romano's) and taught her that the drones must either be married or massacred—even both if necessary. Dorothy was too wise to think she knew everything, and, being acquisitive rather than mimetic, she gained from the two queens the cynicism of a wide experience without subjecting herself to the wear and tear of the process.

Lest a too exclusive attention to Miss Underhill and Miss Yorke should leave her stranded when they quitted the chorus, Dorothy frequented equally the company of a very lovely brunette called Olive Fanshawe, who was certainly the most popular girl in the dressing-room and of a sweet and gentle disposition, without either affectation or duplicity. Apart from the advantage of being friends with a girl so genuinely beloved, Dorothy was attracted to Olive Fanshawe's ivory skin and lustrous dark hair; that would set off her own roses and mignonette to perfection, and she was glad when Olive proposed that perhaps later on they might share a flat. She decided, however, to stay at home during the winter, or at any rate until she should have obtained a more prominent place in the chorus and be justified in launching out on her own with some prospect of practical homage in return.

Dorothy's early confidence in herself had been slightly shaken in the first six weeks of "The River Girl," because Clarehaven had not once been to see her, or, if he had, had never written to tell her how lovely she looked on the banks of a scene-painter's Thames. If he still took the least interest in her, he could easily have found out where she was, and it was significant that she had seen nothing of Tufton, either. Dorothy began to be afraid that those two days at Oxford had vanished from Clarehaven's memory; so, lacking as yet any great incentive to make the best of herself off the stage, she decided not to waste money either on a flat or on winter clothes. No address out of Mayfair would suit her, and no furs less expensive than sables would become her fair beauty. At nineteen she need not be in too much of a hurry, and she should certainly be wise to wait until the springtime would provide her with the prettiest frocks for much less outlay. As for taking a flat, why, anything might have happened by the spring.

Dorothy's plans, however, were precipitated by the behavior of her father. It appeared that a friendly archdeacon had warned Mr. Caffyn privately of the forthcoming sale of some church schools in the center of a large maritime town in the west of England in order that a cinema theater might be erected on their site to the glory of God, the profit of His Church, and the convenience of His little ones. The archdeacon drew Mr. Caffyn's attention to the clause in the contract by which the morality of every performance was secured, and strongly advised him to follow his own example and invest in the theater. Mr. Caffyn, who was not of a speculative temperament, felt that, though he should be unwise to risk brewery stock profitable enough at a date when the Liberal party had scarcely yet swelled the womb of politics, he was being offered an excellent opportunity to add to his wife's income, which was not yielding more than three and a half per cent. upon her capital. It was on top of this important decision that Dorothy came back from the theater one foggy November night to be met by her mother in the dim hall of No. 17.

"A most terrible thing has occurred," Mrs. Caffyn whispered. "Hush! Don't disturb Cecil. Tread quietly. The poor boy is tired out with working for his Christmas examinations, and father might hear us."

To Mrs. Caffyn the drawing-room seemed the only fit environment for an appalling problem the day had brought her, the only atmosphere that could brace her to confront its solution, but Dorothy, who was cold after her nerves by drinking the fresh tea brought in for a late arrival. Dorothy came downstairs, rather cross at having been disturbed from her afternoon nap, and Mr. Caffyn, a Cenci of suburban prose, confronted his wife and daughter.

"I have seldom felt such a fool," he began upon a note of pompous reminiscence that whistled in his mustache like a wind through withered sedge on the margin of a December stream. "I have *never* felt such a fool," he corrected himself, "as I was made to feel this afternoon by my own wife and my own daughter. I go to your bank," he proclaimed, fixing his wife's wavering eye—"I go to your bank, and there, in the presence of my eldest son, I ask to see Mr. Jones, the manager, with a view to improving your financial position."

"How kind of you, dear," she murmured, in an attempt to propitiate him before it was too late.

"Yes," Mr. Caffyn went on, apparently not in the least softened by the compliment. "In your interest I abandon for a whole hour my own work— the work of the society I represent, although, mark you, I knew full well that by so doing I should be kept in the office another whole hour after my usual time."

Dorothy looked sarcastically at her wrist-watch, and her father bellowed like a bull on the banks of that stream in midsummer.

"Silence, Norah!"

"Are you speaking to me?" she inquired. "Because if you are, I'd rather, firstly, that you spoke to me without shouting; secondly, that you didn't call me Norah; and thirdly, that you didn't say I was talking when I was only looking at my watch."

Mr. Caffyn, throwing up his head in a mute appeal for Heaven to note his daughter's unnatural behavior, swallowed a crumb the wrong way, the noisy attempts to rescue which allowed his wife a moment's grace to dab her forehead with a handkerchief; her tears, like the crumb, had chosen another route, and the fresh tea was excessively hot.

"Where was I?" Mr. Caffyn demanded, indignantly, when he had disposed of the crumb.

"I think you'd just got to my bank, dear," his wife suggested, timidly.

"Ah yes! Well, Jones and I were going into the details of your investments, and I was just calculating what would be the amount of your extra income should I consent to your investing your capital in accordance with the advice of the Archdeacon of Brismouth, when Jones, who I may remark *en passant* has been a friend of mine for twenty years and should know better, calmly informs me that without consulting your husband you have withdrawn five hundred pounds from your capital in order to fling it away upon your daughter. I thought he was perpetrating a stupid joke; but he actually showed me a record of this abominable transaction, and I had no alternative but to accept his word. I need hardly say that any chance I might have had of finishing off my work at the society vanished as far as this afternoon was concerned, and so"—here Mr. Caffyn became bitterly ironical—"I ventured to permit myself the luxury of a hansom-cab from the offices of your bank to the corner of Carlington Road, where the four-mile circle of fares terminates, and now, if you please, I should like an explanation of this outrage."

"The explanation is perfectly simple," Dorothy began.

"I was speaking to your mother, not to you. The money is hers."

"Precisely," said his daughter, "and that is the explanation."

"Dearest child," Mrs. Caffyn implored her, "don't aggravate dear father. We must admit that we were both very much in the wrong, particularly myself."

"Not at all," said Dorothy, quickly cutting short her father's sigh of satisfaction at the admission. "Not at all. We were both absolutely in the right. The transaction was a purely business one. Mother has allowed me twenty-five pounds a year since my seventeenth birthday."

"Mother has allowed you?" echoed Mr. Caffyn. "Even if we grant that this sum was technically paid out of your mother's income, you must understand that it should be considered as coming from me—from me, your father."

"You and mother can settle that afterward. It doesn't invalidate my argument, which is that such a lump sum is likely to be more useful to me at the beginning of my career on the stage than an annual pittance—"

"Pittance?" repeated Mr. Caffyn, aghast. "Do you call twenty-five pounds a pittance?"

"Please don't go on interrupting me," said Dorothy, coldly. "I'm now doing a calculation in my head. Twenty-five pounds a year is five per cent.—"

"Five per cent.!" shouted Mr. Caffyn. "Your mother was only getting three and a half per cent."

"Oh, please don't interrupt," Dorothy begged, "because this is getting very complicated. In that case mother owes me, roughly, about another two hundred and fifty pounds. However, we'll let that pass. You are both released from all responsibility for me, and if you both live more than twenty years longer you will actually be making twenty-five pounds a year out of this arrangement. In twenty years you'll be sixty-eight, won't you? Well, there's no reason why you shouldn't live to seventy-two, and if you do you'll make one hundred pounds out of me. So I don't think you can grumble."

"Dear child," sobbed Mrs. Caffyn, "I don't think it's very polite, and it certainly isn't kind, to talk about poor father's age like that. Let's admit we both did wrong and ask him to forgive us."

"I am not going into the question of right and wrong," replied Dorothy, loftily. "It's quite obvious to me that you have a perfect right to do what you like with your own money and that I have a perfect right to avail myself of your kindness. Father's extraordinary behavior has made it equally clear to me that I can't possibly stay on in this house; in any case, the noise the children make in the morning will end by driving me away, and the sooner I go the better."

"I forbid you to speak to your parents like that," said Mr. Caffyn.

Dorothy could not help laughing at his authority, and he played his last card:

"Do you realize that you are not yet of age and that if I choose I can compel you to remain at home?"

"I don't think it would be worth your while," she told him, "for the sake of five hundred pounds, which in that case you'd certainly never see again. I don't want to break with my family completely, but if I find that your prehistoric way of behaving is liable to spoil my career, I sha'n't hesitate to do so."

Dorothy guessed that she had defeated her father; Mrs. Caffyn, too, must have guessed it, for she suddenly gasped:

"I think I must be going to faint."

And by summoning the memories of a mid-Victorian childhood she actually succeeded. Luckily her husband had eaten most of the cakes; so that when she was rescued from the wreck of the tea-table and helped up to her room only one sandwich was adhering to her best gown.

II

It is hardly necessary to say that Dorothy did not confide in the girls at the theater what had happened at home, but she let it be generally understood that she was now looking out for rooms, and she talked a good deal of where one could and where one could not live in a flat. About a week later Olive Fanshawe took her aside and asked if she was serious about moving into a flat at last; and, upon Dorothy's assuring her that she was, Olive divulged under the seal of great secrecy that a friend of hers, a man of high rank with much power and influence in the country, was anxious to do something for her.

"He's a strange man," she told Dorothy, "and though I know you'll think it's impossible for anybody to want to look after a girl in a flat without other things in return, he really doesn't make love to me at all. He gets tired of society and political dinners and the Palace."

"The Palace?" Dorothy repeated.

"Buckingham Palace. You didn't think I meant the Crystal Palace?" said Olive, with a laugh.

Dorothy, with Debrett for a footstool, when she chose to treat the volume thus, was offended by this raillery, and explained that she had only wished to know whether she meant St. James's Palace or Buckingham Palace.

"Darling, I was only teasing you.... Well, my friend wants to have a place where he can lunch quietly sometimes or have tea and forget about the cares of grandeur. You won't mind if I don't tell you his name, will you?"

Dorothy did mind extremely, but inasmuch as she had affected an air of mystery about herself and her origin, she felt she could not reasonably object to Olive's secrecy.

"He told me to find another girl to live with me," Olive continued, "and he said he would pay the rent of the flat and find all that's necessary in the way of decorations and furniture. I've been waiting such a long time for the right girl; I thought you didn't want to live up in town or I should have suggested it sooner. He's seen you from the front, and he admired you very much and couldn't understand why I didn't ask you at once."

Dorothy was struck by Olive's frankness and still more was she struck by her incapacity for jealousy. She could not think of any other girl who would have been so obviously pleased as Olive was to hear a friend admired by their own man. Three months at the Vanity had made Dorothy chary of believing the assertion that there was nothing more between her and the mysterious great one than good-fellowship, because she was quite sure by now that all men expected more, and her judgment of Olive's character led her to suppose that Olive would be too kind to refuse him more. However, that was her business, and since there was evidently going to be a simulation of complete innocence about the transaction, no offer could have suited her better.

"My dear Olive," she said, "nothing could be nicer for me, and of course I happen to be one of the few girls who would or could understand that there is nothing in it. What a pity the weather's so wet for house-hunting."

"That's what the great man said, and he told me to hire an electric brougham until I've found the place I want."

"Of course," said Dorothy, as if the idea of searching for a flat outside an electric brougham, a rare luxury in those days, was inconceivable.

For a fortnight she and Olive glided here and there along the dim, wintry streets, until at last they noticed that the stiff Georgian houses at the far end of Halfmoon Street bulged out into an efflorescence of bright new flats, which on inspection seemed to provide exactly the address and the comfort they required.

"It's an awfully good address," said Dorothy. "Clarges Street would have been a little nearer to Berkeley Square, but...." She forgave the extra block or two with a gesture.

"It's so quiet," added Olive.

"And really not far from Devonshire House, though from Stratton Street we should have overlooked the garden."

"But we can take San Toy for her walks in Green Park." San Toy was Olive's Pekinese spaniel.

"I shall have my bedroom in apple green," Dorothy announced. "Apple green with rose-du-barri curtains; and you'd better have cream with café-au-lait in yours, unless you have eau-de-nil and sage.... I think the fourth-story flat was the nicest."

"Yes, it's more romantic to be high up," Olive agreed.

"And the light is better for one's dressing-table," Dorothy added.

In dread of a maternal attempt to bring about a reconciliation between herself and her father, Dorothy had hoped to avoid spending Christmas at home. But the flat could not be ready until February; so, partly to keep her mother quiet, partly because she was a little apprehensive of the paternal prerogative with which Mr. Caffyn had threatened her minority, she consented on Christmas morning to be kissed by his mustache. Perhaps he was more willing to forgive her owing to his wife's conduct of her financial affairs having provided an excuse to transfer them into his own hands.

Dorothy's absence from the last Christmas gathering at home had not sharpened her appetite for this kind of celebration, and she did not at all like the sensation of being in the bosom of her family; Gulliver was scarcely more disgusted by the Brobdingnagian maids of honor. Seizing the occasion to impress upon her younger brothers and sisters her disapproval of any inclination to boast about having a famously beautiful sister at the Vanity, she was mortified to learn that her career was regarded by the juniors as a slur upon their social standing. Cecil informed her bluntly that in his society—the society of industrious scholars at St. James's—actresses were regarded with horror, and that though an unpleasant rumor had pervaded the school of Caffyn's having a sister on the stage, he had managed to stifle such deleterious gossip. It seemed that the traditions of the preparatory school responsible for Vincent's budding social sense strictly forbade any allusion to family life in any form whatsoever; at Randell's *all* relatives were regarded as a disgrace, and only last term a boy had been called upon to apologize for the extraordinary appearance his mother had presented at the prize-giving. Another boy, whose father was reputed to belong to the Royal Academy, had been forced to allay with largess of tuck the hostile criticism leveled against a flowing cravat his parent had worn at the school sports. As for sisters, Vincent affirmed, their very existence was regarded as a shameful secret; but a sister on the stage ... he turned away in despair of words to express what a humiliation that would bring upon him were it known. Agnes and Edna assured Dorothy they had far too many enthralling topics of conversation already to bother about her; but when one or two of the mistresses had inquired how she was getting on and had regretted that she was not acting in Shakespeare, they had certainly not revealed that she was now called Dorothy Lonsdale, because the real Dorothy was also an old girl; so that even if one of the mistresses in an unbridled moment should visit the Vanity, she would search for Miss Norah Caffyn upon the program and come away no wiser than she went.

Meanwhile, the decoration and furnishing of the flat went on in strict accordance with Dorothy's ideas, since she had better taste than Olive, who, besides, was too much afraid of spending another person's money. Dorothy had not yet been introduced to the great man, but she was sure that he would like Olive to have all she wanted, or, in other words, all she herself wanted. They moved in during February, and it was arranged that the first Sunday evening should be dedicated to the entertainment of their benefactor, who had returned to town for the opening of Parliament. About six o'clock on the evening in question Dorothy rose from a deliciously deep and comfortable Chesterfield sofa, looked round her affectionately at her own drawing-room aglow with chintz and daffodils, and in her bedroom, when she sat down in front of a triple mirror to do her light-brown hair before dressing for dinner, apostrophized her good fortune aloud, and admired herself more than ever.

Dorothy acknowledged to herself that Olive's great man surpassed her preconception of him kindled by dressing-room legends; at first she had been inclined to criticize her friend's occasional ventures into political prophecy as self-importance or girlish credulity; but as soon as she saw the source of them she admitted that this time Olive's romanticism was justified. Their guest was a tall, grizzled man, more military to the outward eye than political, and he treated Olive with just the god-fatherly manner she had led Dorothy to expect. She made a good deal of fuss over him in the way of finding cushions for his head and mixing his cocktail with extra care; but nothing in her obviously sincere affection conveyed a hint of cloaking another kind of emotion. Although the great man preserved his own anonymity, he talked so freely about people of whom Dorothy had often read in the papers that his absorbing conversation soon made her forget the strain upon her curiosity to know who he was. He approved of the way the flat had been decorated and complimented the two girls on their good taste, all the credit of which Olive at once ascribed to her companion. About eleven o'clock the great man passed his hand over his eyes in a way that seemed to hint at a deep-seated, perhaps an incurable, fatigue, and announced that he must be going to bed.

"Though, unfortunately," he added, "I must write one or two letters first at my club. Happy children," he said, turning to them in the hall and holding a hand of each. "We must try to meet next Sunday evening; but I'm dreadfully busy, and I may not be able to get away."

Turning up the collar of his fur coat, he told Olive not to ring for the lift and walked very wearily, it seemed to Dorothy, down the stairs of the flats.

"I don't want to be inquisitive," she said, when they were back in the drawing-room still haunted by the ghost of an excellent cigar. "But I should like to know who he really is."

"Dorothy," her friend begged, "it's the only stipulation he's made, and I don't think it would be fair to break it."

"You don't trust me," Dorothy complained.

"My dear, it isn't that; but I certainly should have to tell him that I told you, and I'm sure he wouldn't like it. After all, we ought to be very grateful for this jolly flat where we're perfectly free and have nothing to bother about. Remember what happened to Psyche."

Dorothy was inclined to add "and also to Fatima"; but since she could not pretend that the great man did in any way remind her of Bluebeard and since the flat undoubtedly was delightful, she did her best to restrain her curiosity, even though sometimes it irritated her like prickly heat.

"It's a pity he had to go away to write his letters at a club," she said.

"But he couldn't write from this address."

"No, but we could keep some plain paper for him," said Dorothy. "And that reminds me, what is your crest?"

Olive looked alarmed.

"I don't think I've got a crest," she said. "My father's a solicitor in Warwickshire."

"Warwickshire?" repeated Dorothy. "That's an odd coincidence. I wonder if he knows Lord Cleveden."

Olive shook her head vaguely.

"He knows a good deal about Warwickshire; in fact, he's writing a book called *Warwickshire Worthies*. He's been writing it for years. Does Lord Cleveden come from Warwickshire?"

"Of course," said Dorothy, and then after a minute with a far-away look she added, "So do I."

"Oh, Dorothy, then there really is a mystery? I thought it was only dressing-room gossip."

"You have your secrets, Olive. Mayn't I be allowed mine? Though I suppose I haven't any legal right to it, I am going to put my crest on my note-paper, because I like the motto. It's a bugle-horn, and the motto is *J'y serai*. I needn't translate it for you, as you went to a convent in Belgium."

Olive laughed affectionately at her friend's little joke, and they decided to reap the full advantage of a quiet Sunday by going to bed early.

"He's a great dear, isn't he?" said Olive by the door of her room.

"Oh, a great dear. How horrid it is that a man like that would be so misjudged by the world that he has to keep his name a secret. But, of course, I understand his point of view. I've had some experience of family pride, and it's a tremendous thing to be up against. However, it will be all the same a hundred years hence. Good night, darling. Your great man is a great, great success."

"I'm so glad you like him, Dorothy dear."

"I like him immensely."

Just before Dorothy got into bed she called out to her friend, who in a dressing-gown of amber silk hurried to know what she wanted.

"I only wanted to tell you that you simply must get this new tooth-paste. I like it immensely."

"Oh, I'm glad it's a success," Olive exclaimed.

"It's a great, great success."

Dorothy wondered when she was fading into sleep how long it would be before she should be able to recommend a tooth-paste to the world at large, recommend it in glowing words with a photograph of herself smiling at the delicious tube.

III

Soon after Dorothy and Olive were established in Halfmoon Street Birdie Underhill and Maisie Yorke, by getting married on the same day at the same church to bridegrooms in the same profession, obtained as much publicity in the newspapers as was possible for two Vanity girls who had failed to acquire a title on abandoning the stage. The service in a double sense was fully choral, and the two queens had a train of bridesmaids from the Vanity, all looking as demure as Quakeresses in their dove-gray frocks, and certainly holding their own in the mere externals of maidenhood with the sisters of the bridegrooms, who were as fresh and rural as if Bayswater, their home, was in the Lake district and had been immortalized by Wordsworth in a sonnet. One reporter was so much impressed by the ceremony that his account of it was headed "Dignified Wedding of Two Vanity Girls."

"Yes," said Dorothy, when with Olive she was driving away from the reception, "it was charmingly done, of course; but, poor dears, it is rather a come-down."

"But I thought their men were awfully twee," said Olive.

"Twee" was society's attempt at this date to voice the ineffable, in which respect it was at least as successful as the terminology of most mystics and philosophers: yet although Plotinus might have been glad of it in the sunset-stained fog of neo-Platonism, the practical Dorothy considered that this was too transcendental for stock-brokers.

"After all," she said, poised serenely above the abyss of reality, "what is a stock-broker?"

"They'll be fairly well off, and they'll have nice houses, and children perhaps," Olive argued. "And I expect they're tired of the theater by now. I don't think either of them would ever have got anything better than the Punt Sextet; and Maisie told me when I was kissing her good-by and wishing her all happiness that she was twenty-seven. Isn't it terrible to think of?"

"Twenty-seven!" Dorothy echoed. She would have been less shocked if the sum had referred to Maisie's lovers rather than to her years. "Well, of course, she admitted once to me that she was twenty-four. I only hope that when I'm twenty-seven I sha'n't be singing with five other girls in punts."

"You won't be, darling. You'll either be a great star or you'll be brilliantly and happily married."

Olive was really a very easy girl to live with; and the former of these predictions seemed likely to come true when Dorothy was actually promoted to occupy one of the punts after the girl first selected had proved a failure in such a conspicuous position; the other vacant punt had been successfully filled by Queenie Molyneux. This girl, though she was not nearly so beautiful as Dorothy, had a good deal of talent, which gave even the two solo lines she was allowed in the sextet what any serious dramatic critic who had learned French at school would have called *espièglerie*. Miss Molyneux had reason to hope that such a phrase would one day be applied to her acting, because people whose judgment was to be trusted went about saying that she had a career before her, not merely in musical comedy, but perhaps even in real comedy, where she would be written about by critics who were not afraid to use foreign words at what they would call the "psychological moment." In view of the fact that Miss Molyneux might henceforth be considered a rival, Dorothy took care to be very friendly with her, and to be seen fairly often lunching with her at Romano's or supping at the Savoy, although she was a girl whose reputation even at the Vanity was whispered about, and whose private life far exceeded in *espièglerie* her two lines in the sextet. Notwithstanding this, it was Queenie Molyneux whom Dorothy chose to be her companion at a supper-party given by Lord Clarehaven soon after the beginning of the Easter holidays, seven months after the production of "The River Girl."

Clarehaven had reappeared without a word of warning, and in a note that he sent round to invite Dorothy and a friend to supper he seemed quite unconscious that there was anything in his behavior to be excused. He hoped that she had not forgotten him, as if his silence of nearly a year was perfectly natural; he mentioned that Lonsdale was with him, congratulated her upon her singing in the sextet, and begged for an answer to be sent down to the stage-door. Somehow it was not very difficult for Dorothy to forgive him, and she accepted the invitation. The obvious friend to have taken out with her would have been Olive Fanshawe, because Olive was a brunette and Queenie was not. However, if Clarehaven was capable of being even temporarily fascinated by another girl's outward charms, Dorothy felt that she might as well give him up at once; she did not intend her life to be spoiled by beauty competitions. Dorothy wanted to impress Clarehaven more deeply than with the skin-deep loveliness that belonged in her own style as much to Olive as to herself, and in order to impress him she felt that a moral contrast would be more effective than the hackneyed contrast between brunette and blonde. Of course, she did not mean the kind of moral contrast that Lily had provided on that dreadful afternoon in Oxford; that had been merely a painful exhibition of vulgarity. Olive was so sweet and good and well behaved that between them they might achieve the insipid, to obviate which Dorothy chose Queenie, who would set off, if not her complexion, at any rate her point of view.

At the end of the evening, when Clarehaven, hesitating for a barely perceptible moment, had said good-by to Dorothy outside Halfmoon Mansions and stepped reproachfully back into his hansom, she decided on her way up-stairs that the supper-party might be considered a success. To begin with, all the other people supping at the Savoy had stared at their table more than at any other. Then, Arthur Lonsdale had evidently taken a fancy to Queenie Molyneux, and if Dorothy was not mistaken Queenie had taken a fancy to him. His way of talking had been just the foil she required for her own, and when they drove away together to Ridgemount Mansions there was no doubt in Dorothy's mind that Lonsdale would tell the cab not to wait and end by missing that last train at Goodge Street. However, what happened to the cab or, for that matter, to Lonsdale and Queenie Molyneux was of slight importance beside the fact that Clarehaven had evidently lost nothing of his admiration for herself, or, if he had lost it, had regained it all and more this evening. When he and his friend compared notes to-morrow how sharply the difference between herself and some other Vanity girls would be brought home to him.

Yet, successful as the supper-party had been, it remained for the time another isolated event in the relations between herself and Clarehaven, from whom she had not heard another word during the vacation.

"He's frightened of you, that's what it is," said Miss Molyneux, whose friendship with Lonsdale, begun that night, was being hotly kept up, though she was running no risks by inviting Dorothy to be a spectator of it.

"Frightened of what?"

"Oh, he thinks you're too good to be amusing and not good enough for anything else. Arthur told me so. Not in so many words, but his lordship found the drive home rather lonely."

"Anything else?" repeated Dorothy. "What do you mean by anything else?"

"Why, to marry, of course," replied her friend.

It was strange that the first girl to express in words the thought that was haunting the undiscovered country at the back of Dorothy's mind should be the one girl at the Vanity to whom marriage probably meant less than to any other.

"But why not?" thought Dorothy, in bed that night. "He's independent. Nobody can stop him. Countess of Clarehaven," she murmured. The title took away her breath for a moment, and it seemed as if the very traffic of Piccadilly paused in the presence of a solemn mystery. "Countess of Clarehaven!"

The omnibuses rolled on their way again, and the idea took its place in the natural scheme of things. Queenie little thought that her scoffing allusion to the state of affairs between Clarehaven and herself would have such a contrary effect to what she intended. Queenie had meant to crow over her, but she had made a slip when she had let out that Clarehaven was frightened. It was not Clarehaven who was frightened; it was his friend Lonsdale. No doubt, Clarehaven had not yet whispered of marriage even to himself; no doubt he was merely thinking at present what a much luckier chap Lonsdale was than himself. But Lonsdale was frightened....

"And he has reason to be," said Dorothy, turning on the light and picking up Debrett.

It happened that the great man telephoned next morning to say that he was coming to lunch that day, and after lunch Dorothy alluded lightly to Lord Clarehaven.

"I believe I once met his mother," said the great man. "Wasn't she a daughter of Chatfield?"

Dorothy nodded.

"Yes, I remember the story now," he went on. "She had a good deal of trouble with her husband. But he's been dead some years, eh?"

"Eighteen ninety-six," said Dorothy.

"Yes, I thought so. I don't know anything about the son; he sounds, from your description, rather a young ass."

However deeply Dorothy would have resented such a comment from any one else, she accepted it from the great man as merited; she was even grateful to him for it; from the instant that Clarehaven presented himself to her vision as rather a young ass, it did not seem so impossible that she should one day marry him. These months at the Vanity had already considerably cheapened the peerage in Dorothy's estimation, and intercourse with the great man had imparted to her some of his own worldly contempt for inconspicuous young peers. Dorothy began to ponder the likelihood of being able to elevate Clarehaven from single "young assishness" to the dignity of the great man himself; a clever wife could do much, a beautiful wife more. She was so serenely confident of herself that when, a few days after this conversation, the subject of it telegraphed from Oxford to say he should call for her the following day to take her out to lunch, she was neither astonished nor at all unduly elated.

"You wouldn't mind his lunching here?" she asked Olive. "He's quite a nice boy. Rather young, of course, after the great man; but he'll improve."

Olive was delighted to welcome Clarehaven, and Dorothy was glad of an opportunity to display her independence and pleasant surroundings. She had warned Olive not to leave her alone with their guest after lunch, because she was anxious to avoid discouraging him too much by positively refusing to let him make love to her, although she wished him to go away with the impression that only luck had been against him.

"You seem very comfortable here," he commented, suspiciously, when, on his departure, Dorothy escorted him to the door of the flat.

"I am very comfortable," she admitted.

"Is it your flat or Miss Fanshawe's?"

"Both."

He looked round at the paneled hall and frowned.

"I can't make you out," he confessed.

"Isn't mystery woman's prerogative?" she asked, and then in case she had frightened him with such a long word she let him kiss her hand before he went away.

Certainly for a girl who was not much over twenty Dorothy could not be accused of clumsiness. Her admirer had gone away piqued by the richness of her surroundings, the correctness of her demeanor, most of all by the touch of her hand upon his lips. Yes, she might congratulate herself.

"Rather a dear!" said Olive.

"Yes," Dorothy agreed. "Rather—but dreadfully young. Though his title only dates back to the eighteenth century, the baronetcy is older, and his ancestors really did come over with the Conqueror."

And one felt that such antiquity compensated Dorothy for some of that youthfulness she deplored.

During the next fortnight Clarehaven paid several visits to town, but Dorothy was steadily unwilling to be much alone with him, and, finally, one hot afternoon in mid-May, exasperated by her indifference and caution, he went back to Oxford in a fit of petulance (temper would have been too strong a word to describe his behavior, which was like a spoiled child's) and relapsed into another spell of silence. A week or so after this Queenie Molyneux asked

Dorothy one day how long it was since she had heard from Clarehaven, and when Dorothy countered the awkward question by asking, rather bitterly, how long it was since she had heard from Lonsdale, Queenie admitted that he, too, had been silent for some time.

"I'm afraid I'm too expensive for Lonnie," she laughed, lightly. "He's a nice boy, but love in a cottage would never suit me, and love anywhere else wouldn't suit him. So that's that."

"You don't know what it is to be in love," said Dorothy.

"Cut it out!" said Miss Molyneux. "I'd rather not learn."

Dorothy would have liked to cut her own tongue out for playing her false by uttering such a sentiment to a girl like Queenie. However, she had no wish to seem a whit less hard than her rival—Dorothy was beginning to achieve such a projection of her personality across the footlights that Queenie really had become a rival, though Queenie might have put it the other way round— and she consoled herself for Clarehaven's absence by giving a great deal of attention to the new frocks that the fine weather demanded; also in consequence of a suggestion by the great man she began to take riding-lessons, with which she made as rapid progress as with her dancing, to which she had already been devoting herself for some time.

Toward the end of the month Dorothy and Olive were criticizing the fashions in the windows of Bond Street when somebody slapped her on the back and, turning round with half a thought that she was being called upon to reply to a novel method of attack by Clarehaven, she perceived Sylvia Scarlett. It was typical of Sylvia to greet her like this on meeting her again for the first time after a year, but the old awe of Sylvia prevented her from expressing her dislike of such horseplay in Bond Street, and a sudden shyness drove her into self-assertion. She began to talk about lunching at Romano's and supping at the Savoy and of the success she had made in "The River Girl" sextet, to all of which Sylvia listened with a smile until she broke abruptly into her discourse with:

"Look here! A little less of the Queen of Sheba, if you don't mind. Don't forget I'm one of the blokes as is glad to smell the gratings outside a baker's."

Dorothy did not think this remark particularly amusing; there was quite enough genuine cockney to be endured on the stage without having to listen to an exaggerated imitation of it in Bond Street. Olive, however, was laughing, and Dorothy decided to take Sylvia down a peg by asking what she was doing now.

"Resting, Dolly, but always open to a good offer. Same old firm. Lily and Skinner. The original firm makes boots; we mar them. The trouble is that I can't find anything to skin; I tried Rabbit's, the rival boot-shop, but even they wanted cash. However, Lily's quite content to go on resting, so that's all right."

"My dear," exclaimed Dorothy, in affected dismay, "you're not still living with that dreadful girl?"

"Oh, go to hell!" said Sylvia, sharply, and strode off down Bond Street.

"What an attractive girl!" Olive exclaimed.

Dorothy stared at her in bewilderment.

"What do *you* see attractive in *her*?"

"She's just the sort of person who would amuse the great man," Olive declared.

"I'm sorry that I bore him so much."

Olive seized her hand.

"Dorothy," she murmured, reproachfully, "you know you don't bore him. He was only saying yesterday that he wished he could ride with you in the Row."

"You'd better get Sylvia Scarlett to share the flat with you," went on Dorothy.

"How can you say things like that? You know I love you better than anybody in the world. You know how beautiful I think you, how clever, Dorothy; it's really unkind to suggest that any other girl could take your place."

"If you're so anxious to know her," Dorothy continued, "I'll write and ask her to come and see us."

"Dorothy, you quite misunderstand me."

"I shouldn't like you to think I would stand in the way of your meeting anybody you took a fancy to, man or woman."

Olive protested again and again that Dorothy had utterly misjudged her and that she never wished to see Sylvia Scarlett again. The argument lasted so long and the whole question of whether or not Sylvia should be invited to Halfmoon Mansions assumed such importance that after lunch Dorothy wrote and invited Sylvia, and not merely Sylvia, but Lily as well, to come and have tea with them the next day. She told herself when she had posted the letter that she was probably committing a great folly by introducing to her friends two people who knew so much about her, and she asked herself in amazement what mad obstinacy had led her into such a course of action.

"Most girls would avoid her," she thought. "But if I avoid her, she'll despise me; and I *do* hate the way she can make people look idiotic."

Dorothy was not accustomed to analyze her emotions much; she was usually too fully occupied with the analysis of her features; but before she went to sleep that night she had admitted to herself that she was thoroughly frightened of Sylvia.

In the morning a messenger-boy brought the answer.

MULBERRY COTTAGE,
TINDERBOX LANE, W.

DEAR DOROTHY,—Rudeness evidently pays, and as Lily is bursting with curiosity to see you, we'll come to tea to-morrow. I'm tremendously impressed by your note-paper. Is the trumpet hanging in the corner a crest or a trade-mark? I thought when I first opened your letter that you had gone into the motor business. "*J'y serai*" is good, but I suggest "I blow my own trumpet" would be better, or, if you must have a French motto, you could change your crest to a whip and put underneath "*Je fais claquer mon fouet.*" But perhaps this would suit me better than you. Lily has buried at least half a dozen Tom Hewitts since last June, so we'll come unaccompanied by any skeletons to your feast. Don't mind my teasing you. I believe you wish me well. I much look forward to hearing your Abyssinian friend singing of Mount Abora. Forgive my allusions to literature and display of idiomatic French. They're the only things I can set off against Romano's and the Savoy.

Yours ever,
SYLVIA.

P.S.—It was decent of you to apologize for what you said about Lily, and perhaps you were right to be a little haughty with me after that remark of mine in the dressing-room at Oxford. I'll try to keep a check on myself in future if you'll be as charming as you know how to be when you choose.

"I'm afraid," said Dorothy, when she read this letter, "that Sylvia has grown rather affected. Poor girl, it will be good for her to meet some nice people again."

She did not read the postscript to Olive, but she was much relieved by it, and she showed her relief by praising Lily's beauty and telling Olive that in taking a fancy to Sylvia she had once more evinced her good taste.

"If one could only cure her of her affectations she would be a charming companion for the great man, but as it is.... We must get some people for this afternoon," she broke off, going to the telephone.

Dorothy took more trouble over Sylvia's party than over anything since she chose the decorations of the flat; difficult though it was, she managed to collect several men whom she supposed to be intelligent, chiefly because they had less money than her other friends. It was like looking for gold in an alms-bag to find in their circle enough men to whose intelligence even Dorothy could subscribe, and she asked herself doubtfully what the great man would have thought of the result. Well, well—Sylvia might be critical, but she had no right to be as critical as that, and perhaps one or two of them were more intelligent than she thought.

Among the men invited that afternoon was Harry Tufton, who had just been sent down from Oxford. Anxious to show himself worthy of his election to the Bullingdon, he had let himself be driven from his wonted gravity and discretion by some ambitious demon, and, after mixing his wine with this fiery spirit, had painted either the dean's nose or the dean's door red—the story varied with his listeners' credulity. Hence his arrival in London, where he had made haste to invite Dorothy out to supper and give her some news of his friend Lord Clarehaven. She had been engaged that evening, and now she bethought herself of asking him to tea. It was a daring move, but somehow she believed that Tufton would appreciate it, and perhaps be impressed by her ability to keep friends with girls like Sylvia and Lily. Nevertheless, it certainly was daring to invite the very person who had seen with his own eyes of what Lily was capable; it was also a temptation to Sylvia's tongue.

Dorothy considered that her party was a success, and she was pleased to observe that Sylvia was evidently struck by the intelligence of a young Liberal journalist called Vernon Townsend. This young man, lately down from Oxford, was delighting the select minority who read a brilliant weekly called *The Point of View* with his hebdomadal destructiveness as a critic of the drama. The Aristotelian way in which he used to prove in two thousand words winged with scorn that "The River Girl" was not so good a play as "John Gabriel Borkmann" was a great consolation to his readers, who were mostly unacted playwrights. After a column of Townsend's smoke they were sure that they were in the van of progress, riding, one might say, in the engine-driver's cab upon a mighty express that was thundering away from mediocrity. If sometimes in the course of their journey the coal-dust of realism made them look a little dirty, that was a small penalty to pay for riding in front of the common herd.

"It must be jolly to run the funicular up Parnassus," said Sylvia to this young man. "And jolly to drink of the Pierian spring or from the well of truth without either of them leaving a nasty taste in the mouth."

"Very good," he allowed, and laughed with the serious attention that critics give to jokes. "But you must take in *The Point of View*."

"I will. From your description it must have all the feverish brilliance of a young consumptive. I suppose the air on the top of Parnassus is good for this Keats of weekly reviews?"

"That's an extremely intelligent girl," said Mr. Townsend to his hostess. "Why haven't I ever noticed her on the stage?"

Mr. Townsend went often to the Vanity because he was searching for talent; he had a theory that all good actresses and all good plays were born to blush unseen.

"It's a good theory," said Sylvia, "and of course you'll add the audience. One might extract a moral from the fact that they're much more careless about turning down the lights during the performance of a play in Paris than they are in London. Dorothy, Mr. Townsend assures me that I ought to be a great actress."

Dorothy smiled encouragingly and passed on to see that her guests were well supplied with cakes. Yes, the party was going well. Sylvia was entertaining other people and herself being entertained. Lily was sitting languorously back in a deep chair, listening to a young candidate for Parliament whose father had so successfully imposed a patent medicine upon his contemporaries that there seemed no reason why his son should not as successfully cure the body politic. Dorothy frankly admitted Lily's beauty when Olive commented upon it.

"She's like a lovely spray of flowers," said Olive.

Dorothy thought that this was rather an exaggerated simile, and she could not help adding that she hoped Lily would not fade as quickly.

Presently Tufton came up to his hostess and begged her to do him the honor of a little talk.

"Everybody is very happy. Charming little party. Yes," he assured her. "But you mustn't tire yourself. Let me get you an ice."

Dorothy was flattered by this almost obsequious manner, and it flashed upon her that he was trying to get in with her, not, as the girls at the theater would have put it, "get off" like most men.

"Your two friends from Oxford are much improved," he began. "Do you remember our little scene after lunch? I felt for you tremendously. It's good of you to carry your old friends along with you on the path to success."

"You think I'm going to be successful?"

"You *are* successful. In confidence, you'll be encouraged to hear that Richards expects a lot from you. Yes, he told my father. You've not seen Clarehaven lately?" Dorothy shook her head, and Mr. Tufton nodded gravely; behind those solemn indications of cerebral activity two twin souls rubbed noses.

"Of course I haven't seen him just lately. You heard of my little joke? It had quite a 'varsity success. Yes, I painted the dean's door. Well, somebody had to pull the evening together, and I tossed up with Ulster—the Duke of Ulster—you haven't run across him? No? Awful good chap. Yes. 'Look here, Harry,' he said to me, 'something's got to be done. Which of us two is going to paint Dickie's door vermilion?' Dickie is the dean. 'Toss you,' said I. 'Right,' said he. 'Woman,' said I, and lost. So I got a bucket of paint and splashed it around, don't you know. Everybody shouted, 'Jolly old Tuffers,' and the authorities handed me my passports. But, after all, what earthly use is a degree to me?"

Dorothy looked a wise negative and brought the conversation back to Clarehaven.

"I suppose you'll be seeing him again very soon now?"

Mr. Tufton nodded. "And I can prophesy that you'll be seeing him again very soon."

She shrugged her shoulders.

"You mustn't be cynical," he warned her.

"Can one help it?"

"You've no reason to be cynical. I suppose Clarehaven is almost my most intimate friend, and I can assure you that you have no reason to be cynical. Difficulties there have been, difficulties there will be, but always remember that I'm your friend whatever happens."

And most of all her friend, Dorothy thought, if she happened to become a countess.

After this tea-party Sylvia and Lily often came to Halfmoon Mansions; when in July Dorothy and Olive took a cottage at Sonning they were often invited down there for picnics on the Thames. The other girls at the theater could not understand why it was necessary to look beyond Maidenhead for repose and refreshment from singing in a punt every night; and although such of them as were invited to Sonning enjoyed themselves, they always went back to town more firmly convinced than ever that Dolly Lonsdale was a most mysterious girl. Yet it ought not to have been impossible to understand the pleasure of hurrying away from the Vanity to catch the eleven forty-five at Paddington, and of alighting from the hot train about a quarter to one of a warm summer night to be met by a scent of honeysuckle in the station road, to see the white flowers in their garden and the thatched roof of their cottage against the faintly luminous sky, and, while they paused for a moment to fumble in their bags among the powder-puffs and pocket-mirrors for the big key of their door, to listen to the train's murmur still audible far away in the stillness of the level country beyond.

"I ought always to live in the country," said Dorothy, gravely.

But in August rehearsals for "The Duke and the Dairymaid" began, and the cottage at Sonning had to be given up. The new production at the Vanity included a trio between the ducal tenor and two subsidiary dairymaids, to be one of whom Dorothy was chosen by the management. She might fairly consider that her new part was exactly three times as good as that she had played in the sextet; moreover, her salary was doubled, and by what could only be considered a stroke of genuine luck Queenie Molyneux, who would certainly have been chosen for the other dairymaid, was lured away to the rival production of "My Mistake" at the Frivolity Theater. Millie Cunliffe, who took her place, had a finer mouth than Queenie's, which was too large and expressive for anything except lines like those with which she led the Pink Quartet at the Frivolity; but Millie had not such a beautiful mouth as Dorothy, and it was not nearly so apt at singing or speaking; her ankles, too, were not so slim and shapely as Dorothy's, nor were they made for dancing like hers. So Dorothy enjoyed a vogue with gods and mortals, and was now plainly visible to the naked eye in the constellation of musical comedy.

IV

The departure of Queenie Molyneux to the Frivolity had a more intimate bearing on Dorothy's future than the mere removal of a rival of the footlights to a safe distance: it gave her back Clarehaven.

That Savoy supper-party last Easter had not seemed likely at the time to lead to a situation even as much complicated as Dorothy's ambition to marry an earl. When Arthur Lonsdale escorted Queenie home afterward, he had probably counted upon such a climax to the entertainment; but he must have been astonished to hear from his friend next morning that Dorothy was not to be won lightly by a Savoy supper nor kept with the help even of the tolerably large income that friend enjoyed. From the moment that the immediate gratification of Clarehaven's passion was denied him, Lonsdale must have divined a danger of the affair's turning out serious, and he had obviously done all he could to discourage him from frequenting Dorothy's unresponsive company; she learned, indeed, from various sources that he was devoting his leisure to curing Clarehaven. Then suddenly the melody of Queenie's Pink Quartet enchained him, and he was always to be seen at the Frivolity. Long days cramming for the Foreign Office were followed by long evenings at the Frivolity and ... anyway, Queenie seemed to have decided she liked Lonsdale better than wealth. But if the melody of the Pink Quartet in "My Mistake" was an eternal joy, so, too, was the melody of the trio in "The Duke and the Dairymaid"; henceforth Clarehaven from his stall could nightly feed his passion for Dorothy without being subjected to the mockery and tutelage of his former companion. What between lunches at Verrey's and suppers at the Savoy it was not surprising that before the leaves had fallen from the London plane-trees he should have hung a necklace of pearls round her neck. Unfortunately, though Clarehaven showed his appreciation of Dorothy by figuratively robbing his coronet of its pearls, he did not go so far as to offer her the coronet itself; and when he suggested that she should leave Halfmoon Street for an equally pleasant flat round the corner, she was naturally very indignant and asked him what kind of a girl he thought she was.

"You don't care twopence about me," he said, woefully.

"How can I let myself care about you?" she countered. "You ought to know me well enough by this time to be sure that I would never accept such an offer as you've just made me. I know that you can't marry me. I know that you have your family to consider. In the circumstances, isn't it better, my dear Tony, that we should part? I'm dreadfully sorry that our parting should come after your proposal rather than before it. But horribly as you've misjudged me, somehow I can't bear you any ill will, and in token of my forgiveness I shall always wear these pearls. Pearls for tears, they say. I'm afraid that sometimes these old sayings come only too true."

"Yes, but I can't get along without you," protested Clarehaven.

She smiled sadly.

"I'm afraid you can get along without me in every way except one, only too easily."

"Why did you lead me on, if you weren't in earnest?"

"Lead you on?"

"You asked me back to the flat. You gave me every encouragement. Obviously somebody is paying for this flat, so why shouldn't I?"

"Lord Clarehaven!" exclaimed Dorothy, with the stern grandeur of an Atlantic cliff rebuffing a wave. "You have said enough."

She rang the bell and asked Effie, the maid whose attentions she shared with Olive, to show his lordship the door. His poor lordship left Halfmoon Mansions in such perturbation that he forgot to slip the usual sovereign into Effie's hand, and she cordially agreed with her mistress when he was gone that kind hearts are indeed more than coronets. Dorothy's simple faith in her own abilities had received such a shock that she began to cry; but it was restored by a sudden suspicion that she possessed a latent power for tragedy that might take her out of the squalid world of the Vanity into the ether of the legitimate drama. She had never suspected this inner fountain that grief had thus unsealed, and she let her tears go trickling down her cheeks with as much pleasure as a small boy who has found a watering-can on a secluded garden path.

"Don't carry on so, miss," Effie begged. "Men are brutes, and that's what all us poor women have to learn sooner or later. Don't take on about his lordship. A fine lordship, I'm sure. Give me plain Smith, if that's a lordship. Look at your poor eyes, miss, and don't cry any more."

Dorothy did look at her poor eyes, and immediately compromised with her emotions by going out and ordering a new dress. When she came back Olive, who had been given a heightened account of the scene by Effie, was exquisitely sympathetic; and the great man, when he was informed of Clarehaven's disgraceful offer, was full of good worldly advice and consolation.

"I think you can rely upon your powers of catalysis, Dorothy," he said.

She did not think her failure to understand such a strange word reflected upon her education, and asked him what it meant.

"In unchemical English, as unchemical as your own nice light-brown hair, *you* won't change; but if I'm not much mistaken you'll play the very deuce with Master Clarehaven's mental constitution."

This was encouraging; if Dorothy's faith in her beauty and abilities had been slightly shaken by Clarehaven's omission to marry her, the loss was more than made up for by an added belief in her own importance and in the beauty of her character.

Among the men who sometimes came to the flat was a certain Leopold Hausberg, a financier reputed to be already fabulously rich at the age of thirty-five, but endowed with an unfortunately simian countenance by the wicked fairy not invited to his circumcision. He possessed in addition to his wealth the superficial geniality and humor of his race, and was not accustomed to find that Englishwomen were better able than any others to resist Oriental domination. Hausberg had not concealed his partiality for Lily, and Dorothy, in her desire to accentuate her own virtue, told Sylvia, soon after Clarehaven's proposal, that it would be useful for Lily to have a rich friend like that. Sylvia flashed at her some objectionable word out of Shakespeare and would not be mollified by Dorothy's exposition of the difference between her character and Lily's, although Dorothy took care to remind her of a remark she had once made when they were on tour together about the inevitableness of Lily's decline.

Dorothy had good reason, therefore, to feel annoyed with Sylvia when she found out presently that Sylvia was apparently working on Leopold Hausberg to do exactly what she herself had been so rudely scolded for suggesting. As much fuss was being made about Lily's behavior as if she had refused the dishonorable attentions of an earl; yet with all this ridiculous pretense Sylvia was taking care to do for Lily what she was either too stupid or too hypocritical to do for herself. If Lily's happiness lay in the devotion of vulgar young men, she might at least get the money she wanted for them out of Hausberg without letting a friend do her dirty work. When the continually cheated suitor approached Dorothy with complaints about the way Sylvia was managing the business she listened sympathetically to his hint that Sylvia was trying to keep Lily from him until she had made enough money for herself, and she took the first opportunity of being revenged upon Sylvia for the horrid Shakespearian epithet by telling her what Hausberg had said.

One Saturday night in November Olive and Dorothy came home immediately after the performance to rest themselves in preparation for a long drive in the country with the great man, who seldom had an opportunity for motoring and had made a great point of the enjoyment he was expecting to-morrow. They had not long finished supper when there was a furious ringing at the bell, and Hausberg, in a state of blind anger, was admitted to the flat by the frightened maid.

"By God!" he shouted to Dorothy. "Come with me!"

She naturally demurred to going out at this time of night, but Hausberg insisted that she was deeply involved in whatever it was that had put him in this rage, and in the end, partly from curiosity, partly from fear, she consented to accompany him. While they were driving along, Hausberg explained that he had at last persuaded Lily to abandon Sylvia and accept an establishment in Lauriston Mansions, St. John's Wood. He had furnished the flat regardless of expense, and this afternoon, when Lily was supposed to have been moving in, he had been sent the latch-key and bidden to present himself at midnight.

"Very well," said Hausberg between his teeth. "Wait until you see what...." You wait...." he became inarticulate with rage.

They had reached Lauriston Mansions and, though it was nearly one o'clock in the morning, a group of figures could be seen in silhouette against the lighted entrance, among which the helmets of a couple of policemen supplied the traditional touch of the sinister.

"Haven't you got it out yet?" Hausberg demanded of the porter, who replied in a humble negative.

"What *are* you talking about?" Dorothy asked, and then with authentic suddenness she felt the authentic nameless dread clutching authentically at her heart. Why, *it* must be a dead body; grasping Hausberg's arm and turning pale, she asked if Lily had killed herself.

"Killed herself?" echoed Hausberg. "Not she. I'm talking about this damned monkey that your confounded friends have left in my flat."

The porter came forward to say that there was a gentleman present who had a friend who he thought knew the address of one of the keepers of the monkey-house at the Zoo, and that if Mr. Hausberg would give orders for this gentleman to be driven in the car to his friend's address no doubt something could be done about expelling the monkey. The gentleman in question, a battered and crapulous cab-tout, presented himself for inspection, and one of the policemen offered to accompany him and impress the reported keeper with the urgency of the situation. While everybody was waiting for the car to return, the lobby of the flat became like the smoking-room of a great transatlantic steamer where travelers' tales are told, such horrible speculations were indulged in about the fierceness of the monkey.

"So long as it ain't a yourang-gatang," said one, "we haven't got nothing to be afraid of. But a yourang-gatang's something chronic if you can believe all they say."

"A griller's worse," said another.

"Is it? Who says so?"

"Why, any one knows there ain't nothing worse than a griller," declared the champion of that variety. "A griller 'll bite a baby's head off the same as any one else might look at you. A griller's worse than chronic; it's ferocious."

"Would it bite the head off of an yourang-gatang?" demanded the first theorist, truculently.

"Certainly it would; so when he's let out you'd better get behind George here so as to hide your ugly mug."

This caused a general laugh, and the upholder of the orang-utan seemed inclined to back his favorite with an appeal to force, until the porter interposed to prevent a squabble.

"Now, what's the good in arguing if it's a griller or a yourang-gatang?" he demanded, in a nasal whine. "All I know is it got my poor trouser leg into a rare old yourang-atangle when I was 'oppin it out of the front hall."

"Is there much damage done?" Hausberg asked.

"Damage?" repeated the porter. "Damage ain't the word. It looks as if there'd been a young volcano turned loose in the flat."

"But what I don't understand," Dorothy began, primly, "is why I have been brought into this."

Various ladies in light attire from the upper flats were beginning to peer over into the well of the staircase, and Dorothy was wondering if she were not being compromised by this midnight adventure.

"Let's get the monkey out first," said Hausberg, "and then I'll tell you why."

After listening for another three-quarters of an hour to disputes between the various supporters of the gorilla and the orang-utan, which extended to a heated argument about the comparative merits of Mr. Balfour and Mr. Chamberlain, the car came back, and the intruder, which was announced to be a chimpanzee, was ejected by the keeper, and, after an attempt to hand it over to the police, shut up till morning in a boot-hole.

The flat presented a desolate spectacle when Dorothy and Hausberg entered it; the chimpanzee had smashed the ornaments, ripped up the curtains, tore the paper from the walls, and wrenched off all the lamp-brackets; he had then apparently been seized with a revulsion against the bananas and nuts strewn about the passage for his supper and had gnawed the porter's hat.

"Now," said Hausberg, sternly, to the owner of the hat, who was tenderly nursing it, "just tell this lady exactly what has happened here."

"Well, sir, about twelve o'clock this morning a gentleman drove up to the mansions with a crate and said he was a friend of Mr. Hausberg's and had brought him a marble Venus for a present, and I was to put it in the hall of the flat. I particularly remember he said a Venus, because I thought he said a green'ouse, which surprised me for the moment, and I asked him if he didn't, mean a portable aquarium, which is what my wife's brother has in the window of his best parlor."

"Go on, you fool!" Hausberg commanded. "We don't want to hear about your wife's brother."

"Well, I accepted delivery of this Venus and between us we got this Venus——"

"Don't go on rhyming like that," said Hausberg. "Tell the story properly in plain prose."

"Between us—I mean to say me and the lift-boy together—we deposited in the hall this crate which had a tin lining for the chim-pansy to breathe with according to instructions duly received. When I turned up my nose at this Venus, which smelled very heavy, the gentleman, who didn't give his name, explained that you was intending to use it for a hat-stand, and told us not to wait, as he'd unpack the crate hisself. I looked at him a bit hard, but he give me something for me and the boy between us before we come down-stairs again, and I thought no more about it. The gentleman drove off about ten minutes afterward with a friendly nod, and I was just sitting down to my dinner in the domestic office on the ground floor when the people underneath—of course you'll understand I'm referring to the flat now—the people underneath came down and complained that something must have happened over their heads, as the noise was something shocking and bits of the ceiling was coming down, or they said it would be coming down in two two's if the noise wasn't stopped. Well, of course up I went to investigate, and when I opened the door and seed all the wall-paper hanging in strips I thought something funny must have occurred, and I felt a bit nervous and began swallering. Then all of a sudding, before I knew where I was, something had me by the trouser leg, and if I'd of been a religious man I'd of said right out it was the devil himself; but when I seed it was a great hairy animal I run for the front door and slammed it to behind me, it being on the jar for a piece of luck, because if it hadn't of been on the jar my calf was a goner."

"Why didn't you send for me at once?"

"Well, sir, how was I to know you hadn't put the chim-pansy there for the purpose?"

"Do you think I take flats for chimpanzees?" demanded Hausberg.

"No, sir, I don't, but if you'll pardon me, there's a lot of queer things goes on in these mansions, and I've learned not to interfere before I'm asked to, and sometimes not then. Only last week Number Fourteen got the D. T.'s on him and threw a sewing-machine at me when his young lady called me up to see what could be done about quieting him down. And now this here monkey has cost me a pair of trousers and a new hat with the name of the mansions worked on the front which I shall have to replace, and I only hope I sha'n't be the loser by it."

"Get out," snarled Hausberg.

He was in such a rage that he looked more like a large monkey than ever while he was striding in and out of every dismantled room; and Dorothy realized the extreme malice of the joke that had been played upon him.

"You know who did this?" he said to her, wrathfully.

She shook her head.

"Do you mean to tell me you don't know that it was your friend Lord Clarehaven?"

"Rubbish!" said Dorothy. "Why should he shut a chimpanzee in *your* flat?"

"Your friend Clarehaven," Hausberg went on, "and that little swine Lonsdale are responsible for this; but when I tell you that they drove down this afternoon to Brighton with Lily and that cursed friend of hers—"

"How do you know?" she interrupted, with some emotion.

"You don't suppose I set a girl up in a flat without having her watched first, do you? When I buy," said Hausberg, "I buy in the best market. Here's the detective's report."

He handed her a half-sheet of note-paper written in a copperplate hand with a record of Lily's day, ending up with the information that she and her friend Sylvia Scarlett, accompanied by the Earl of Clarehaven and the Honorable Arthur Lonsdale, had driven down to Brighton immediately after lunch and reached the Britannia Hotel at five o'clock, "as confirmed per telephone."

"Well," said Hausberg, grimly, "Lily has been paid out by losing my protection, but, by God! I'll get even with the rest of them soon or late."

"You don't really think that I had anything to do with this?" asked Dorothy. "Why, I haven't seen either Clarehaven or Lonsdale for a month! I didn't even know that they had met Sylvia and Lily. They didn't meet them in Halfmoon Street. Why do you drag me here at this hour of the night?"

Hausberg seemed convinced by her denials, and his manner changed abruptly.

"I'm sorry I suspected you as well. I might have known better. I see now that we've both been made to look foolish. What can I do to show you I'm sorry for behaving like this? We're old pals, Dorothy. I was off my head when I came round here and they told me the trick that had been played on me. Damn them! Damn them! I'll—But what can I do to show you I'm sorry?"

"You'd better invest some money for me," said Dorothy, severely.

"How much do you want?"

"No, no," she said. "I've got two hundred and fifty pounds that I want to invest; only, of course, I must have a really good investment."

"That's all right," he promised. "I'll do a bit of gambling for you."

They had left the flat behind them and were walking slowly down-stairs when suddenly from one of the doors on the landing immediately below a man slipped out, paused for a moment when he heard their footsteps descending, thought better of his timidity, hurried on down, and was out of sight before they reached the landing.

"Good Heavens!" Dorothy ejaculated, seizing her companion's arm.

"I'm afraid I've made you jumpy," he said. "Poor old Dorothy, I shall have to find a jolly good investment to make up for it."

Hausberg was quite his old suave self again; it was Dorothy who was pale and agitated now.

"It was nothing," she murmured; but it was really a great deal, because the man she had seen was Mr. Gilbert Caffyn, the secretary of the Church of England Purity Society.

Dorothy did not enjoy her motor drive that Sunday. It was pale-blue November weather with the sun like a topaz hanging low in the haze above the Surrey hills, but the knowledge that Clarehaven all this month, perhaps even for longer, had been carrying on with Lily and Sylvia when she had taken such care to keep them apart tormented her beyond any capacity to enjoy the landscape or the weather. Heartless treachery, then, was the result of being kind to old friends—and oh, what an odious world it was! There would have to be a grand breaking of friendships presently—yes, and a grand dissolution of family ties as well, for, at any rate, in the midst of this miserable and humiliating affair she had at least been granted the consolation of catching out her father, which might be useful one day. Olive wondered, when the great man left them after supper, why Dorothy had been so gloomy on the drive. She had told the story of the chimpanzee so well, and the great man had laughed more heartily over it than over anything she could remember. Why was Dorothy so sad? Was there something she had left out? Surely on Hausberg's mere word she was not thinking anything horrid about Sylvia's going for a drive with Clarehaven? They had probably just driven down to Brighton for dinner to laugh over the chimpanzee.

"I shall see Sylvia once more," said Dorothy, "and that will be for the last time."

"But I'm sure you'll find Hausberg has made everything appear in the worst light," Olive protested. "I'm sure Sylvia would never snatch a man away from any girl."

"I don't understand how you can go on being friends with me and yet defend her," said Dorothy.

Olive begged her dearest Dorothy to wait for Sylvia's explanation before she got angry with herself, and on Monday afternoon Sylvia of her own accord came to the flat.

"I know everything," said Dorothy, frigidly.

"Then for Heaven's sake tell me what Hausberg said when he opened the door and saw the chimpanzee. Did he say, 'Are you there, Lily?' and did the chimpanzee answer with a cocoanut?"

"Chimpanzee," repeated Dorothy, wrathfully. "You who call yourself my friend deliberately set out to ruin my whole life, and when I reproach you with it you talk about chimpanzees!"

"Don't be silly, Dorothy," Sylvia scoffed. "Hausberg wanted a lesson for saying I was living on Lily, and with Arthur Lonsdale's help I gave him one."

"And what about Clarehaven?" asked Dorothy. "Did he help you?"

"Oh, that foolish fellow wanted a lesson, too. So I took him down to Brighton and gave him a jolly good one, though it wasn't so brutal as Hausberg's."

"Thanks very much," said Dorothy, sarcastically. "In future when my—my—"

"Your man. Say it out," Sylvia advised.

"When a friend of mine requires a lesson I prefer to give it him myself."

"My dear Dorothy," exclaimed Sylvia, with a laugh, "you're not upsetting yourself by getting any ridiculous ideas into your head about Clarehaven and myself? I assure you that—"

"I don't want your assurances," Dorothy interrupted. "It doesn't matter to me what you do with Clarehaven, except that as a friend of mine I think you might have been more loyal."

"Don't be foolish. I'm the last person to do anything in the least disloyal."

"Really?" sneered Dorothy.

"Clarehaven simply came down to Brighton to talk about you. He's suffering from the moth and star disease. Though you won't believe me, I was very fond of you, Dorothy dear; I am still, really," she added, with a little movement of affection that Dorothy refused to notice. "But I do think you're turning into a shocking little snob. That's the Vanity *galère*. No girl there could help being a snob unless she were as simple and sweet as Olive."

"Perhaps you'd like to steal Olive from me, too?" Dorothy asked, bitterly.

"I tell you," the other answered, "it's not a question of stealing anybody. I kept Clarehaven up all night drinking whiskies-and-sodas while I lectured him on his behavior to you. We sat in the sitting-room. If you want a witness, ask the waiter, who has varicose veins and didn't forget to remind us of the fact."

"I suppose Lonsdale and Lily were sitting up with you at this conference? Do you think I was born yesterday? Well, I warn you that I shall tell Queenie Molyneux what's happened."

"If you do," said Sylvia, "I've an idea that Lonsdale will be only too delighted. I fancy that's exactly what he wanted."

"This is all very sordid," said Dorothy, loftily. Then she told Sylvia that she never wished to see her again, and they parted.

Dorothy insisted that Olive ought also to quarrel with Sylvia, but, much to her annoyance, Olive dissented. She said that in any case the dispute had nothing to do with her, and actually added that in her opinion Sylvia had behaved rather well.

"I'm sure she's speaking the truth," she said.

Dorothy thought how false all friends were, and promised that henceforth she would think about no one except her own much-injured self.

"One starts with good resolutions not to be selfish," she told Olive, "and then one is driven into it by one's friends."

Sylvia's story seemed contradicted next day by the arrival of Clarehaven in a most complacent mood, for when Dorothy asked how he had enjoyed his week-end he did not seem at all taken aback and hoped that her Jew friend had enjoyed his.

"I wish I could make you understand just how little you mean to me," she raged. "How dare you come here and brag about your—your— Oh, I wish I'd never met you."

"If you don't care anything about me," he said, "I can't understand why you should be annoyed at my taking Sylvia Scarlett down to Brighton. I don't pretend to be in love with her. I'm in love with you."

Dorothy interrupted him with a contemptuous gesture.

"But it's true, Dorothy. I'm no good at explaining what I feel, don't you know; but ever since that day I first saw you in St. Mary's I've been terrifically keen on you. You drove me into taking up Sylvia. I don't care anything about Sylvia. Why, great Scot! she bores me to death. She talks forever until I don't know where I am. But I must do something. I can't just mope round London like an ass. You know, you're breaking my heart, that's what you're doing."

"You'd better go abroad," said Dorothy. "They mend hearts very well there."

"If you're not jolly careful I shall go abroad."

"Then go," she said, "but don't talk about it. I hate people who talk, just as much as you do."

Within a week Lord Clarehaven had equipped himself like the hero of a late nineteenth-century novel to shoot big game in Somaliland, and on the vigil of his departure Arthur Lonsdale came round to see Dorothy.

"Look here. You know," he began, "I'm the cause of all this. Hard-hearted little girls and all that who require a lesson."

"Yes, it's evident you've been spending a good deal of time lately with Sylvia," said Dorothy.

"Now don't start backfiring, Doodles. I've come here as a friend of the family and I don't want to sprain my tongue at the start. Poor old Tony came weeping round to me and asked what was to be done about it."

"It?" asked Dorothy, angrily. "What is *it*? The chimpanzee?"

"No, no, no. *It* is you and Tony. If you go on interrupting like this you'll puncture my whole speech. When Tony skidded over that rope of pearls and you froze him with a look, he came and asked my advice about what to do next. So I loosened my collar like Charles Wyndham and said: 'Make her jealous, old thing. There's only one way with women, which is to make them jealous. I'm going to make the Molyneux jealous. If you follow my advice, you'll do the same with the Lonsdale.'"

Dorothy nearly put her fingers in her ears to shut out any more horrible comparisons between herself and Queenie, but she assumed, instead, a martyred air and submitted to the gratification of her curiosity.

"Well, just about that fatal time," Lonsdale continued, "Tony and I went for a jolly little bump round at Covent Garden and bumped into Sylvia and Lily *en pierrette*, as they say at my crammer's, where they're teaching me enough French to administer the destinies of Europe for ten years to come. Where were we? Oh yes, *en pierrette*. 'Hello, hello' I said. 'Two jolly little girls *en pierrette*, and what about it? Well, we had two or three more bumps round, and Tony was getting more and more depressed about himself, and so I said, 'Why don't we go down to Brighton and cheer ourselves up?' 'That's all right,' said Sylvia, 'if you'll help me put a jolly old chimpanzee in a fellow's flat.' I said, I'll put a jolly old elephant, if you like.' You see, the notion was that when Hausberg opened the door of the flat he should say, 'Are you there, Lily?' It was all to be very amusing and jolly."

"And what has this to do with Clarehaven?" asked Dorothy.

"Wait a bit. Wait a bit. I'm changing gears at this moment, and if you interrupt I shall jam. You see, my notion was that Tony should buzz down to Brighton with us and ... well ... there's a nasty corner here.... I told you, didn't I, that the only way with hard-hearted little girls is to make them jealous? And the proof of the pudding, as they say, is in the eating, what? Anyway, no sooner did Queenie hear I'd eloped with an amorous blonde than we made it up. Look here, the road's clear now, so let's be serious. Tony's madly in love with you. It's no use telling me you're a good little girl, because look round you. Where's the evidence? I mean to say, your salary's six pounds a week. So, I repeat, where's the evidence? You may dream that you dwell in marble halls on six pounds a week, but you can't really do it."

"If Lord Clarehaven has sent you here to insult me," said Dorothy, "he might at least have had the courage to come and do it himself."

"You're taking this very unkindly. On my word of honor I assure you, Doodles, that Tony's trip to Brighton ended in talk. I know this, because I heard them. In fact, I summoned the night porter and asked him to stop the beehive next door."

"This conversation is not merely insulting," said Dorothy, "it's very coarse."

"I see you're prejudiced, Doodles. Now Queenie was also prejudiced; in fact, at one point she was so prejudiced that she jabbed me with a comb. But I calmed her down and she gradually began to appreciate the fact that not only is there a silver lining to every cloud, but that there is also a cloud to most silver linings. Bored with mere luxury, she realized that a good man's love— soft music, please—should not be lightly thrown away; and now, to be absolutely serious for one moment, what about commissioning me to buzz down to Devonshire and tell Tony that there's no need for him to go chasing the okapi through equatorial Africa?"

"All this levity may be very amusing to you, Mr. Lonsdale, but to me it is only painful."

"Well, of course, if you're going to take my friendly little run round the situation like that, there's nothing more to be said."

"Nothing whatever," Dorothy agreed.

Lonsdale retired with a shrug, and a day or two later Lord Clarehaven's departure for Mombasa was duly recorded in the *Morning Post*. Dorothy's self-importance had been so deeply wounded by the manner in which Lonsdale had commented upon her position in the world that for some time she could scarcely bear to meet people, and she even came near to relinquishing the publicity of the stage, because she began to feel that the nightly audience was sneering at her discomfiture. The gift of a set of Russian sables from Hausberg and the news that her investments were prospering failed to rouse her from the indifference with which she was regarding life. All that had seemed so rich in the flat now merely oppressed her with a sense of useless display. The continual assurances she received that only the melodious trio had saved "The Duke and the Dairymaid" from being something like a failure gave her no elation. Her silks and sables were no more to her than rags; her crystal flasks of perfumes, and those odorous bath-salts, in which the lemon and the violet blended so exquisitely the sharp with the sweet, had lost their savor; even her new manicure set of ivory-and-gold did not pass the unprofitable hours so pleasantly as that old ebony set of which she had been so proud in West Kensington, it seemed a century ago. Lonsdale by his attitude had made her feel that the luxury of her surroundings was not the natural expression of a personality predestined to find in rank its fit expression, but merely the stock-in-trade of a costly doll.

It was Tufton who provided Dorothy with a new elixir of life that was worth all the scent in Bond Street, and a restorative that made the most pungent toilet vinegar insipid as water.

"I don't think you ought to take it so badly," he said. "Shooting the rhino for the sake of a woman is better than throwing the other kind of rhino at her head. It shows that he's pretty badly hit."

"The rhino?" asked Dorothy, with a pale smile.

"No, no," protested Tufton, shocked at carrying a joke too far. "Clarehaven. Wait till he comes back. If he comes back as much in love as he went away you'll hear nothing more about flats round the corner. Curzon Street is also round the corner, don't forget, and my belief is that you'll move straight in from here."

"You're a good pal, Harry."

"Well, I don't think my worst enemy has ever accused me of not sticking to my friends."

This was true; but then Mr. Tufton did not make friends lightly. Old walls afford a better foothold to the climber than new ones.

When Dorothy pondered these words of encouragement she cheered up; and that night John Richards, who had watched her performance from the stage-box, told his sleeping partner that he intended to bring her along in the next Vanity production.

"She gets there," he boomed. "Goo' gir'! Goo' gir'!"

V

Dorothy indulged her own renewed *joie de vivre* by investigating the glimpse of her father's private *joie de vivre* vouchsafed to her that night in St. John's Wood, and without much difficulty she found out that for the last two years he had been maintaining there a second establishment, which at the very lowest calculation must be costing him £400 a year. It was not remarkable that he had wanted to obtain a higher rate of interest on his wife's capital. His daughter debated with herself how to play this unusual hand, and she decided not to lead these black trumps too soon, but to reserve them for the time when they might threaten her ace of hearts and that long suit of diamonds. At present she was not suffering the least inconvenience from her family, and since she went to live in Halfmoon Street it had not been her habit to visit Lonsdale Road more often than once a month. These visits, rare as winter sunshine in England, were not much warmer: the family basked for a while in the radiance of Dorothy's rich clothes, but they soon found that clothes only give heat to the person who wears them, and since Dorothy did not encourage them to follow the sun like visitors to the azure coast, they made the best of their own fireside and avoided any risk of taking cold by depending too much on her deceptive radiance.

Meanwhile, Hausberg had turned Dorothy's £250 into £500 by nothing more compromising than good advice; and by March, to celebrate her twenty-first birthday, the £500 had become £2,000. Not even then did Hausberg ask anything from her in return; occasionally a dim suspicion crossed her mind that a profound cause must lie underneath this display of good will, and she asked herself if he was patiently, very patiently, angling for her; but when time went by without his striking, the suspicions died away and did not recur. Moreover, her financial adviser was engaged in dazzling Queenie Molyneux with diamonds, to the manifest chagrin of Lonsdale, who had let the liaison between himself and Queenie come to mean much more to him than he had ever intended that evening at the Savoy. In the end his mistress was so much dazzled by the diamonds that she put on rose-colored spectacles to save her eyes and, looking through them at Hausberg, decided to accept his devotion. Lonsdale took the theft of his love hardly; whatever chance he might have had of entering the Foreign Office disappeared under an emotional strain that in so round and pink a young man was nearly grotesque. This seemed to Dorothy a suitable moment to repay evil with good, and when, shortly afterward, she saw the disconsolate lover gloomily contemplating a half-bottle of Pol Roger '98 on a solitary table at the Savoy she went over to him and offered to be reconciled.

He squeezed Dorothy's hand gratefully, sighed, and shook his head.

"I can't keep away from the old place. Every night we used to come here and—" The recollection was too much for him; he could do nothing but point mutely to the half-bottle.

"That makes you think," he said, at last. "After the dozens of bottles we've had together, to come down to that beastly little dwarf alone."

"And you've failed in your examination, too?" inquired Dorothy, tenderly rubbing it in.

"Just as well, Doodles, just as well. I should be afraid to attach myself even to an embassy at present."

The band struck up the music of the Pink Quartet.

"Good God!" he exclaimed. "This is too much. Here, Carlo, Ponto, Rover—What's your name?"

The waiter leaned over obsequiously.

"Here, take this fiver with my compliments to Herr Rumpelstiltzkin and ask him to cut out that tune and give us the 'Dead March' instead."

"Why not the 'Wedding March'?" asked Dorothy, maliciously.

"I give you my solemn word of honor," said Lonsdale, "that if only Queenie—well, I think I can get up this hill on the top speed—if I were the first, I *would* marry Queenie. You know, I'm beginning to think Tony made rather an ass of himself, buzzing off like that to Basutoland or wherever it is. By the way, has it ever struck you what an anomaly—that's a good word—I got that word out of a *précis* at my crammer's. It's a splendid word and can be used in summer and winter with impunity, what? Has it ever struck you what an anomaly it is that you can get a license to shoot big game and drive a car, but that you can't get a license to shoot Hausbergs? Well, well, if Queenie had your past and your own future and could cut out some of the presents, by Jove! I would marry her. I really would."

Dorothy said to herself that she had always liked Arthur Lonsdale in spite of everything, and when he asked her now if her friends were not waiting for her she told him that they could wait and gratified the forsaken one by sitting down at his table.

"Of course, when Queenie and I parted," he went on, "she made it absolutely clear to me that this fellow Hausberg meant nothing to her; in fact, between ourselves, she rather gave me to understand that things might go on as they were. But you know, hang it! I can't very well do that sort of thing. The funny thing is that the more I refuse, the more keen she gets. I mean to say it is ridiculous, really, because of course she can't be very much in love with *me*. To begin with, well, she's about twice my height, what? No, I think I shall have to go in for motor-cars. They used to be nearly as difficult to manage as women not so long ago, but they seem to be answering to civilization much more rapidly. It's a pity somebody can't blow along with some invention to improve women. Skidding all over the place, don't you know, as they do now ... but I cannot understand why Hausberg should have fixed on Queenie. I always thought he was after you, and I'm not sure he isn't. Did you turn him down?"

"He has only been helping me with some investments."

"I never heard of a Jew helping people with their investments just for the pleasure of helping."

"I had money of my own to invest," Dorothy explained. "Family money."

"Lonsdale money, in fact, eh?" laughed the heir of the house.

"Well, if you really want to know, it is Lonsdale money. Money left in trust for me by my grandmother, who was a Lonsdale. I know you laugh at this, but it's perfectly true."

"Oh no, I don't laugh at you," said Lonsdale. "I never thought you were a joke. In fact, I asked the governor if he could trace anything about your branch in the family history. But the trouble with him is that he's not very interested in anything except politics. Frightfully narrow-minded old boy. He's been abroad most of his life, poor devil. He's out of touch with things."

Dorothy thought that if her Lonsdale ancestry could appear sufficiently genuine to induce the heir of the family to consult his father about it there was not much doubt of its impressing the rest of the world. It happened that among the party with which she was supposed to be supping that night was a young Frenchman with some invention that was going to revolutionize the manufacture of motor-cars. She decided to introduce him to Lonsdale, and a month or two later she had the gratification of hearing that Lord Cleveden had been persuaded to allow his son the capital necessary to begin a motor business in which the Frenchman, with his invention, was to be one of the partners, and a well-known professional racing-motorist another. The firm expressed their gratitude to Dorothy not only by presenting her with a car, but also by paying her a percentage on orders that came through her discreet advertisement of their wares. If Clarehaven came back now and asked Lonsdale what she had been doing since he left England, surely he would no longer try to damn the course of their true love.

Just after Dorothy and Olive had left town for their holiday in July the great man died suddenly, and, naturally, Olive was very much upset by the shock.

"Never mind," said Dorothy. "Luckily I've made some money, so we needn't leave the flat."

"I wasn't thinking of that point of view," Olive sobbed. "I was thinking how good he'd always been to me and how much I shall miss him."

"Well, now you can tell me who he was," Dorothy suggested, consolingly.

"No, darling, oh no; this is the very time of all others when I wouldn't have anybody know who he was."

Dorothy, however, searched the papers, and she soon came to the conclusion that the great man was none other than the Duke of Ayr. Such a discovery thrilled her with the majesty of her retrospect, and she fancied that even Clarehaven would be a little impressed if he knew who Olive's friend was:

John Charles Chisholm-Urquhart, K.T., 9th and last Duke of Ayr; also Marquess and Earl of Ayr, Marquess and Earl of Dumbarton, Earl of Kilmaurs and Kilwinning, Viscount Dalry and Dalgarven, Viscount of Brackenbrae, Lord Urquhart, Inverew, and Troon, Baron Chisholm, Earl Chisholm, Baron Hurst, Baron Urquhart of Coylton, Lord Urquhart of Dumbarton, and Baron Dalgarven.

The last Duke of Ayr! Nobody in the world to inherit one of all those splendid titles! Not even a duchess to survive him!

The press commented just as ruefully as Dorothy upon the extinction of another noble house. Dukes and dodos, great families and great auks, one felt that they would soon all be extinct together.

"It's a great responsibility to marry a peer," Dorothy thought.

She gently and tactfully let Olive know that she had found out the identity of the great man, and they went together to stand for a minute or two outside Ayr House, where the hatchment, crape-hung, was all that was left of so much grandeur and of such high dignities and honors. Nor did Dorothy allude to the duke's omission to provide for Olive in his will, though, being a bachelor without an heir, he might easily have done so. No doubt death had found him unprepared; but the funeral must have been wonderful, with the pipers sounding "The Lament" for Chisholm when the coffin was lowered into the grave.

"I'm very glad they're closing 'The Duke and the Dairymaid' this week," said Dorothy. "I should hate to see that title now on every 'bus and every hoarding."

The Vanity's last production had not been such a success as either of its two predecessors, and many people about town began to say that if John Richards was not careful the Frivolity was going to cut out the Vanity. Therefore in the autumn of 1905 a tremendous effort was made to eclipse all previous productions with "The Beauty Shop." Early in August John Richards sent for Dorothy, gave her a song to study, and told her to come again in a week's time to let him hear what she made of it. To print baldly the words of this great song without the melody, without the six beauties supporting it from the background, without the entranced scene-shifters and the bewitched audience, without even a barrel-organ to recall it, is something like sacrilege, but here is one verse:

When your head is in a whirl.
And your hair won't curl,

And you feel such a very, very ill-used girl.
Chorus. Little girl!

Then that is the time—
Chorus. Every time! Every time!

To visit a Bond Street Beauty Shop.
Chorus. To visit our Bond Street Beauty Shop.

And when you come out,
And you're seen about
In the places you formerly frequented—
Chorus. On the arm of her late-lamented.

Why every one will cry,
Oh dear, oh lord, oh my!
There's Dolly with her collie!
All scented and contented!
Chorus. She's forgotten the late-lamented.

For Dolly's out and about again,
She doesn't give a damn for a shower of rain.
Here's Dolly with her collie!
And London!   *Chorus.* Dear old London!
London is itself again!

"Goo' gir' said Mr. Richards when Dorothy had finished and the dust in his little office in the cupola of the Vanity had subsided. "Goo' gir'. I thi' you'll ma' a 'ice 'ihel hit in that song."

The impresario was right: Dorothy did make a resounding hit; and a more welcome token of it than her picture among the letterpress and advertisements of every illustrated paper, the dedication of a new face-cream, and the christening of a brand of cigarettes in her honor, was the reappearance of Clarehaven with character and complexion much matured by the sun of Africa, so ripe, indeed, that he was ready to fall at her feet. She received him gently and kindly, but without encouragement; he was given to understand that his treatment had driven her to take refuge in art, the result of which he had just been witnessing from the front of the house. Besides, she told him, now that Olive's friend was dead, she must stay and look after her. People had misjudged Olive and herself so much in the past that she did not intend to let them misjudge her in future. She was making money at the Vanity now, and she begged Lord Clarehaven, if he had ever felt any affection for her, to go away again and shoot more wild animals. Cupid himself would have had to use dum-dum darts to make any impression on Dorothy in her present mood.

Such nobility of bearing, such wounded beauty, such weary grace, could only have one effect on a man who had spent so many months among hippos and black women, and without hesitation Clarehaven proposed marriage. Dorothy's heart leaped within her; but she preserved a calm exterior, and a sad smile expressed her disbelief in his seriousness. He protested; almost he declaimed. She merely shook her head, and the desperate suitor hurried down to Devonshire in order to convince his mother that he must marry Dorothy at once, and that she must demonstrate, either by visit or by letter, what a welcome his bride would receive from the family. Clarehaven lacked eloquence, and the dowager was appalled. Lonsdale was telegraphed for, and presently he came up to town to act as her emissary to beg Dorothy to refuse her son.

"It'll kill the poor lady," he prophesied. "I know you're not wildly keen on Tony, so let him go, there's a dear girl."

"I never had the slightest intention of doing anything else. You don't suppose that just when I've made my first success I'm going to throw myself away on marriage. You ought to know me better, Lonnie."

Lonsdale was frankly astonished at Dorothy's attitude; but he was glad to be excused from having to argue with her about the unsuitableness of the match, because he did sincerely admire her, and, moreover, had some reason to be grateful for her practical sympathy at the time of his break with Queenie Molyneux. He went away from Halfmoon Street with reassurances for the countess.

It was at this momentous stage in Dorothy's career that Mr. Caffyn, awed by the evidence of his daughter's fame he beheld on every side, chose to call for her one evening at the stage-door with a box of chocolates, in which was inclosed a short note of congratulation and an affectionately worded request that she would pay the visit to her family that was now long overdue. Dorothy pondered for a minute her line of action before sending down word that she would soon be dressed and that the gentleman was to wait in her car. When she came out of the theater and told the chauffeur to drive her to West Kensington, Mr. Caffyn expressed his pleasure at her quick response to his appeal. They drove along, talking of matters trivial enough, until in the silence of the suburban night the car stopped before 17 Lonsdale Road.

"Good-by," said Dorothy.

"You'll come in for a bit?" asked her father, in surprise.

"Oh no; you'll be wanting to get to bed," she said.

"Well, it's very kind of you to drive me back," Mr. Caffyn told her, humbly. "Very kind indeed. You'll be interested to know that this is a much nicer motor than the Bishop of Chelsea's. He was kind enough to drive me back from the congress of Melanesian Missions the other day, and so I'm acquainted with his motor."

"He didn't drive you to Lauriston Mansions, did he?" Dorothy asked.

The sensitive springs of the car quivered for a moment in response to Mr. Caffyn's jump.

"What do you mean?" he stammered.

"Oh, I know all about it," his daughter began, with cold severity. "It's all very sordid, and I don't intend to go into details; but I want you quite clearly to understand once and for all that communication between you and me must henceforth cease until I wish to reopen it. It's extremely possible, in fact it's probable, in fact I may say it's certain that I'm shortly going to marry the Earl of Clarehaven, and inasmuch as one of the charms of my present position is the fact that I have no family, I want you all quite clearly to understand that after my marriage any recognition will have to come from me first."

Mr. Caffyn was too much crushed at being found out in his folly and hypocrisy to plead his own case, but he ventured to put in a word for his wife's feelings and begged Dorothy not to be too hard on her.

"You're the last person who has any right to talk about my mother. Come along, jump out, father. I must be getting back. I've a busy day to-morrow, with two performances."

The sound of Mr. Caffyn's pecking with his latch-key at the lock was drowned in the noise of the car's backing out of Lonsdale Road. Dorothy laughed lightly to herself when she compared this interview with the one she had had not so many months ago about the £500, which, by the way, she must send back to her mother if Hausberg advised her to sell out those shares. No doubt, such a sum would be most useful to her father with his numerous responsibilities.

"And now," she murmured to herself, "I see no reason why I shouldn't meet Tony's mother."

VI

Dorothy had not been entirely insincere with Lonsdale in comparing marriage with success to the detriment of marriage. Success is a wonderful experience for the young, in spite of the way those who obtain it too late condemn it as a delusion; few girls of twenty-one, luxuriously independent and universally flattered, within two years of going on the stage would have seen marriage even with an earl in quite such wonderful colors as formerly. Fame may have its degrees; but when Dorothy, traveling in her car, heard errand-boys upon the pavement whistling "Dolly and her Collie" she had at least as much right to feel proud of herself as some wretched novelist traveling by tube who sees a young woman reading a sixpenny edition of one of his works, or a mother whose dribbling baby is prodded by a lean spinster in a tram, or a hen who lays a perfectly ordinary egg and makes as much fuss over it as if it were oblong.

It was certain that if Dorothy chose she could have one of the two principal parts in the next Vanity production and be earning in another couple of years at least £60 a week. There was no reason why she should remain in musical comedy; there was no reason why she should not take to serious comedy with atmosphere and surreptitious curtains at the close of indefinite acts; there was no reason why some great dramatist should not fall in love with her and invert the usual method of sexual procedure by laying upon her desk the offspring of their spiritual union. The possibilities of the future in every direction were boundless.

At the same time even as a countess her starry beams would not necessarily be obscured. As Countess of Clarehaven she might have as many pictures of herself in the illustrated papers as now; she could not give her name to face-creams, but she might give it to girls' clubs: one countess had even founded a religious sect, and another countess had ... but when one examined the history of countesses there was as much variety as in the history of actresses. And yet as a Vanity countess would it not be most distinguished of all not to appear in the illustrated papers, not to found sects and dress extravagantly at Goodwood? Would it not be more distinguished to live quietly down in Devonshire and make no more startling public appearances than by sometimes opening a bazaar or judging a collection of vegetables? Would it not be more distinguished to be the mother of young Lord Clare and Lady Dorothy Clare, and Lady Cynthia Clare, and the Honorable Arthur Clare.... Dorothy paused; she was thinking how improper it was that the younger sons of an earl should be accorded no greater courtesy than those of a viscount or a baron, when his daughters were entitled to as much as the daughters of a duke or a marquess. And after all, why shouldn't Tony be created a marquess? That was another career for a countess she had omitted to consider—the political hostess, the inspiration and amanuensis of her husband's speeches to the House of Lords. Some infant now squalling in his perambulator would write his reminiscences of a great lady's *salon* in the early years of the twentieth century, when the famous Dorothy Lonsdale stepped out of the public eye, but kept her hold upon the public pulse as the wise and beautiful Marchioness of Clarehaven. The second Marquess of Clarehaven, she dreamed; and beneath this heading in a future Debrett she read below, "Wife Living of the

First Marquess. Dorothy (Marchioness of Clarehaven)"; if Arthur Lonsdale married well, that marchioness might not object to one of her younger daughters marrying his eldest son. Dorothy started. How should she herself be recorded in Debrett? "Dorothy, daughter of Gilbert Caffyn"? Even that would involve a mild falsification of her birth certificate, and if her sister Dorothy married that budding young solicitor from Norbiton they might take action against her. She hurriedly looked up in Debrett and *Who's Who* all the other actresses who had married into the peerage. In Debrett their original names in their stark and brutal ugliness were immortally inscribed; but in *Who's Who* their stage names were usually added between brackets. "The Earl of Clarehaven, *m.* 1905 Norah *d.* of G. Caffyn (known on the stage as Dorothy Lonsdale)." Ugh! At least she would not advertise the obvious horror of her own name so blatantly. She would not be more conspicuous than "Norah (Dorothy) *d.* of G. Caffyn." But how the girls at the theater would laugh! The girls at the theater? Why should the girls at the theater be allowed any opportunity of laughter—at any rate in her hearing? No, if she decided to accept Tony she should obliterate the theater. There should be no parade about her marriage; she would be married simply, quietly, and ruthlessly.

At the Vanity, Dorothy and her collie were a ravishing success; but she was a better actress off the stage than she was on, and she had soon persuaded herself that she really was still uncertain whether to accept Clarehaven's hand or not. The minor perplexities of stage name and real name, of town and country life, of publicity and privacy as a countess, magnified themselves into serious doubts about the prudence of marrying at all, and by the month of December Clarehaven was nearly distracted by her continuous refusals of him. The greater favorite she became with the public the more he desired her; and she would have found it hard to invent any condition, however flagrantly harsh, that would have deterred him from the match. Tufton almost went down on his knees to implore her to marry the lovesick young earl, his greatest friend; and even Lonsdale talked to Dorothy about her cruelty, and from having been equipped a month ago with invincible arguments against the match, now told her that in spite of everything, he thought she really ought to make the poor lad happy.

"He's as pale as a fellow I bumped in the back last Thursday, cutting round Woburn Square on the wrong side," he declared.

"No, he's not so sunburnt as he was," Dorothy agreed.

"Sunburnt? He's moonburnt—half-moonburnt—starburnt! But sunburnt! My dear Doodles, you're indulging in irony. That's what you're doing."

"I don't see why I should marry him when his mother hasn't even written me a letter. I don't want his family to feel that he's disgracing them by marrying me. If Lady Clarehaven will tell me with her own lips that she'll be proud for her son to marry me, why, then I'll think about it."

"No, really, dash it, my dear girl," Lonsdale expostulated. "You're being unreasonable. You're worse than a Surrey magistrate. Let the old lady alone until you're married and she has to make the best of a bad bargain."

"Thanks very much," Dorothy said. "That's precisely the attitude I wish to guard myself against."

Lonsdale's failure to soften Dorothy's heart made Clarehaven hopeless; he reached Devonshire to spend Christmas with his family in a mood so desperate that his mother began to be nervous. The head-keeper at Clare Court spoke with alarm of the way his lordship held his gun while getting over stiles.

"Maybe, my lady, that after lions our pheasants seem a bit tame to his lordship, though I disremember as I ever saw them wilder than what they be this year—but if you'll forgive the liberty, my lady, a gun do be as dangerous in Devonshire as in Africa, and 'tis my belief that his lordship has summat on his mind, as they say."

A shooting accident upon a neighboring estate the very day after this warning from the keeper determined Lady Clarehaven to put her pride in her pocket and write to Dorothy.

CLARE COURT, DEVON,
January 2, 1906.

DEAR MISS LONSDALE,—I fear you must have thought me most remiss in not writing to you before, but you will, perhaps, understand that down here in the country the notion of marrying an actress presents itself as a somewhat alarming contingency, and I was anxious to assure myself that my son's future happiness was so completely bound up in such a match that any further opposition on my part would be useless and unkind. Our friend Arthur Lonsdale spoke so highly of you and of the dignity of your attitude that I was much touched, and I must ask you to forgive my lack of generosity in not writing before to tell you how deeply I appreciated your refusal to marry my son. I understand now that his departure from England a year ago was due to this very cause, and I can only bow before the strength of such an affection and withdraw my opposition to the marriage. I am assuming, perhaps unjustifiably, that you love Tony as much as he loves you. Of course, if this is not so, it would be an impertinence on my part to interfere in your private affairs, and if you write and tell me that you cannot love Tony I must do my best as a mother to console him. But if you do love him, as I can't help feeling that you must, and if you will write to me and say that no barrier exists between you and him except the old-fashioned prejudice against what would no doubt be merely superficially an ill-assorted union, I shall welcome you as my daughter-in-law and pray for your happiness. I must, indeed, admit to being grievously worried about Tony. He has not even bothered to keep up the shooting-book, and such extraordinary indifference fills me with alarm.

Yours sincerely,
AUGUSTA CLAREHAVEN.

Dorothy debated many things before she answered this letter; but she debated longest of all the question of whether she should write back on crested note-paper or simple note-paper. Finally she chose the latter.

7 HALFMOON MANSIONS,
HALFMOON STREET, W

January 6, 1906.

DEAR LADY CLAREHAVEN,—Your letter came as a great joy to me. I don't think I have ever pretended that I did not love Tony with all my heart, and it was just because I did love him so much that I would not marry him without his mother's consent.

My own Puritan family disowned me when I went on the stage, and I said to myself then that I would never again do anything to bring unhappiness into a family. I should prefer that if I marry Tony the wedding should be strictly quiet. I cannot bear the way the papers advertise such sacred things nowadays. Having had no communication with my own family for more than two years, I do not want to reopen the painful memories of our quarrel. My only ambition is to lead a quiet, uneventful life in the depths of the country, and I hope you will do all you can to persuade Tony to remain in Devonshire. You will not think me rude if I do make one condition beforehand. I will marry him if you will promise to remain at Clare Court and help me through the difficult first years of my new position. Please write and let me have your promise to do this. You don't know how much it would help me to think that you and his sisters will be at my side. Perhaps you will think that I am assuming too much in asking this. I need not say that if you find me personally unsympathetic I shall not bear any resentment, and in that case Tony and I can always live in Curzon Street. But I do so deeply pray that you will like me and that his sisters will like me. Your letter has given me much joy, and I only wait for your answer to leave the stage (which I hate) forever.

Yours sincerely,
DOROTHY LONSDALE.

The dowager was won. By return of post she wrote:

MY DEAR DOROTHY,—Thank you extremely for your very nice letter. Please do exactly as you think best about the details of your wedding. You will receive a warm welcome from us all.

Yours affectionately,
AUGUSTA CLAREHAVEN.

During these negotiations Olive had been away at Brighton getting over influenza, and Dorothy decided to join her down there and be married out of town to avoid public curiosity. She had telegraphed to Clarehaven to leave Devonshire, and Mr. Tufton was enraptured by being called in to help with advice about the special license.

"My dear Dorothy," he assured her, enthusiastically, "you deserve the best— the very best."

"I don't want any one at the Vanity to know what's going to happen."

Tufton waved his hands to emphasize how right she was.

"It'll be a terrible blow to the public," he said, "and also to John Richards. You were his favorite, you know. Yes. And think of the beautiful women he has known! But you're right, you mustn't consider anybody except yourself."

"It's rather difficult for me to do that," Dorothy sighed.

"I know. I know. But you must do it. Clarehaven and I will come down with the license, and then ... my dear Dorothy, I really can't tell you how pleased I am. Do, do beg the dowager not to change that pergola. But I shall be down, I hope, some time in the spring."

"Of course."

"And what about Olive?" he asked.

"Poor Olive," she sighed. "And only last week she lost dear little San Toy. Yes, she'll miss me, I'm afraid, but she'll be glad I'm going to be so happy."

"All your friends will be glad."

"And now, Harry, please get me a really nice hansom, because I must simply tear round hard for frocks and frills."

Dorothy spent most of the money that Hausberg had made for her on old pieces of family jewelry; she also ordered numerous country tweeds; of frills she had enough.

A few days later Clarehaven, accompanied by Tufton and the special license, reached Brighton, where he and Dorothy were quietly married in the Church of the Ascension. Lady Clarehaven thought, when she drove back to the rooms to break the news to Olive, how few of the passers-by would think that she had just been married. She commented upon this to Tony, who replied with a laugh that Brighton was the last place in England where passers-by stopped to inquire if people were married.

"Tony," she said, with a pout, "I don't like that sort of joke, you know."

"Sorry, Doodles."

"And don't call me Doodles any more. Call me Dorothy."

Olive was, of course, tremendously surprised by her friend's announcement; but she tried not to show how much hurt she was by not having been taken into her confidence beforehand.

"I wanted it to be a complete secret," Dorothy explained. "And I didn't want all the papers in London to write a lot of rubbish about me."

"Darling, you can count on me as a pal to help you all I know. You've only got to tell me what you want."

Dorothy pulled herself together to do something of which she was rather ashamed, but for which she could perceive no alternative.

"Olive, I hate having to say what I'm going to say, and you must try to understand my point of view. I never intend to go near the stage-door of a theater again. I don't want to know any of my friends on the stage any more. If you want to help me, the best way you can help me is not to see me any more."

Clarehaven came into the room at this moment, and Dorothy rose to make her farewells.

"Good-by, Olive," she said. "We're going down to Clare Court to-morrow, and I don't expect we shall see each other again for a long time."

"I say," Clarehaven protested. "What rot, you know! Of course you'll meet again. Why, Olive must come down and recover from her next illness in Devonshire. We shall be pining for news of town by the spring, and—"

Lady Clarehaven looked at her husband, who was silent.

"Have you wired to your mother when we arrive to-morrow?" she asked.

"You're sure you won't drive down?"

"In January?" Dorothy exclaimed.

"Well, I've told the car to meet us at Exeter. That will only mean a seventy-mile drive—you won't mind that—and we'll get to Clare before dark."

"Forgive these family discussions in front of you," said Dorothy to her friend. Then shaking her hand formally, she went out of the room.

During the drive up to town, while Clarehaven was sitting back playing with his wife's wrist and looking fatuously content, he turned to her once and said:

"Dorothy, you *were* rather brutal with poor old Olive."

She withdrew her hand from his grasp, and not until he ceased condoling with Olive did she let him pick it up again.

"And oh dear, oh lord, oh my!" he exclaimed, "we must have the jolly old collie down at Clare."

"The collie?" she repeated. "What collie?"

"Your collie." He began to whistle the bewitching tune.

"Please don't. One hears it everywhere," she said, fretfully. "Olive will look after the dog. She's just lost her Pekinese."

CHAPTER IV

I

ABOUT the time that the fifth Earl of Clarehaven upset the lares and penates of his house by marrying a Vanity girl the people of Great Britain, having baited with red rags the golden calf of Victorianism until the poor beast had leaped from its pedestal and disappeared in the flowing tide, were now accepting from a lamasery of Liberal reformers the idol of silver speech, forgetting either that silver tarnishes more quickly than gold or that new brooms sweep clean, but soon wear out. However, the new era lasted for quite a month, and long enough for the Dowager Countess of Clarehaven to reach the conclusion that her son's marriage was a sign of the times. Poets extract consolation for their private woes and joys from observing that nature sympathizes with them. When they are fain to weep, the skies weep with them; April's weather follows the caprice of the girl next door; even great Ocean laughs when his little friend the rhymester gets two guineas for a sonnet. What is permitted to a poet will not be denied to a countess, and if the dowager considered her chagrin to be a feather in the mighty wing of revolution—to the widows of Conservative peers down in Devonshire the return of the Liberal party in 1906 seemed nothing less than revolution—she should not, therefore, be accused of exaggeration.

When in 1880 Lady Augusta Fanhope married the fourth Earl of Clarehaven she brought neither beauty nor wealth to that dissolute and extravagant man of thirty-five, who as a subaltern in the Blues had earned a kind of fame by the size of his debts and by the length of his whiskers. Soon after he succeeded to the title fashion made him cut short the whiskers; but his debts increased yearly, and if he had not died during his son's minority there would have been little left for that son to inherit. Nobody understood why he married Lady Augusta, herself least of all. Even when he was still alive she had taken refuge in the Anglican religion; when he died she presented a memorial window by Burne-Jones to Little Cherrington church. By now, when he had been dead ten years and his son was bringing an actress to rule over Clare Court, the dowager had come to regard her late husband as a saint. Fashion had trimmed his whiskers; time had softened his memory; the stained-glass window had done the rest.

"I'm glad your father never lived to see these dreadful Radicals sweeping the country," she said to her daughters on this January day that before it faded into darkness would bring such changes to Clare. What the dowager really meant to express was her relief that the last earl was not alive to meet his daughter-in-law; he ought not to have been easily shocked, but marriage with an actress would certainly have shocked him greatly, and his language when shocked was bad. The effect of Dorothy's letter had already worn a little thin; the dowager's pre-figuration of her approximated more closely every moment to an old standing opinion of actresses she had formed from a large collection of letters and photographs left behind by her husband, which she had lacked the courage to burn unread. Her daughters Arabella and Constantia argued that this Dorothy must be a "top-holer" to make their brother so desperate. Last month he had taken them for several long walks and waxed so eloquent over her beauty and charm and virtue that they had accepted his point of view; with less to lose than their mother and unaware of their father's weakness, they saw no reason why an actress should not make Tony as good a wife as anybody.

"But love is blind," said the dowager. None knew the truth of this better than she. "And in any case, dear children, beauty is only skin-deep."

"Luckily for us, mother," said Arabella.

"I think you exaggerate your plainness," the dowager observed. "You do not make the least attempt to bring out your good features. You, dearest Bella, have very nice ankles; but if you wear shoes like that and never pull up your stockings their slimness escapes the eye. And you, Connie, have really beautiful ears; but when you jam your cap down on your head like that you cause them to protrude in a way that cannot be considered becoming."

The girls laughed; they were too much interested in country life to bother about their appearance. Boots were made to keep out moisture and get a good grip of muddy slopes: caps were meant to stay on one's head, not to show off one's ears. Besides, they were ugly; they had decided as much when they were still children, and, now that they were twenty-one and nineteen, would be foolish to begin repining. Arabella's ankles might be slim, but her teeth were large and prominent; her eyes were pale as the wintry sky above them; her hands were knotted and raw; her nose stuck to her face like a piece of mud thrown at a fence; her hair resembled seaweed. As for Constantia, her nose was much too large; so was her tongue; so were her hands; her eyes were globular, like marbles of brown agate; everything protruded; she was like a person who has been struck on the back of the head in a crowd.

"The question is," said Arabella, "are we to drive over to Exeter to meet them? Because if we are I must tell Crowdy to see about putting us up some sandwiches."

"Well, unless you're very eager to go," the dowager pleaded, "I should appreciate your company. Were I left quite alone, I might get a headache, and I am so anxious to appear cheerful. I think we ought to assume that Dorothy will be as nervous as we are. I think it would be kind to assume that."

"I vote for letting Deacock take the car by himself," Constantia declared. "I always feel awkward at meeting even old friends at a station, and it'll be so awfully hard to talk with the wind humming in my ears."

When the noise of the car had died away among the knolls and hollows of the great park the dowager turned to her daughters:

"It's such a fine day for the season of the year that perhaps I might take a little drive in the chaise."

It was indeed a fine day of silver and faint celeste, such a one as in January only the West Country can give. The leafless woods and isolated clumps of trees breathed a dusky purple bloom like fruit; the grass was peacock green. The dowager, moved by the brilliance of the landscape and the weather to a complete apprehension of the fact that she was no longer mistress of Clare, had been seized with a desire to take a last sentimental survey of her dominion. Although her daughters had made other plans for the morning, they willingly put them aside to encourage such unwonted energy. While the pony was being harnessed, the dowager took Arabella's arm and walked up and down the pergola that ran like a battlement along a spur of the gardens and was the most conspicuous object to those approaching Clare Court through the park.

"It's too late to change it before Dorothy comes," she decided, mournfully. "But I do hope that there will be no more taking of Mr. Tufton's advice. I'm sure that curved seat he persuaded me to put at the end was a mistake. People deposit seats in gardens without thinking. Nobody will ever sit there. It simply means that one will always have to walk round it. So unnecessary! I do hope that Dorothy will give orders to remove it."

"Connie," Arabella exclaimed, with a joyful gurgle, "don't you love the way mother practises the idea of Dorothy? She used to be just the same when we were expecting a new governess."

Her sister, who was munching an apple, nodded her agreement without speaking.

The dowager was about to propose a descent by the terraces to visit her water-lily pool (which would have involved a tiresome climb up again for nothing, because the rose-hearted water-lilies of summer were nothing now but blobs of decayed vegetation) when the wheels of the chaise crackled on the drive and the girls insisted that if she were going to have enough time for an expedition before lunch she must start at once.

Clare Court viewed from the southeast appeared as a long, low house of gray stone with no particular indication of its age for the unprofessional observer, to whom, indeed, the chief feature might have seemed the four magnolias that covered it with their large glossy leaves, the rufous undersides of which, mingling with the stone, gave it a warmth of color that otherwise it would have lacked. The house was built on a moderate elevation, the levels of which were spacious enough to allow for ornamental gardens on the south side of the drive; these had been laid out in the Anglo-Italian manner with pergolas and statuary, yews instead of cypresses, and box-bordered terraces leading gradually down to the ornamental pool overhung on the far side by weeping willows. The kitchens and servants' quarters on either side of the house were masked by shrubberies and groves of tall pines, in the ulterior gloom of which the drive disappeared on the way to the stables and the home farm.

The dowager got into the chaise, and the pony, a dapple gray of some antiquity, proceeded at a pace that did not make it difficult for the two girls, who by now had summoned to heel half a dozen dogs of various breeds, to keep up with it on foot.

"Shall we turn aside and look at the farm?" Constantia suggested, where the road forked.

"No, I think I'd like to drive down to the sea first of all," said the dowager.

"Bravo, mother!" both her daughters applauded.

The dogs, understanding from their mistresses' accents that some delightful project was in the air, began to bark loudly while they scampered through the scraggy rhododendrons and put up shrilling blackbirds with as much gusto as if they were partridges. The drive kept in the shadow of the pines for about two hundred yards, until where the trees began to grow smaller and sparser it emerged upon a spacious sward that between bare uplands went rolling down to the sea a mile away. To one looking back Clare Court now appeared under a strangely altered aspect as a gray pile rising starkly from a wide lawn and unmellowed by anything except the salt northwest wind; even the dowager and her daughters, who had lived in it all these years, could never repress an exclamation of wonder each time they emerged from the dim pinewood and beheld it thus. On the other side of the house there had been sunlight and a rich prospect of parkland losing itself in trees and a carefully cultivated seclusion. Here was nothing except a line of gray-green downs undulating against space, in a dip of which was the shimmer of fusing sky and sea. Except at midsummer the pines were tall enough to cut off the low westering sun from the house, and on this January day from where they were standing in pale sunlight the gray pile seemed frozen. The sense of desolation was increased by a walled-up door in the center of the house, above which angelic supporters sustained the full moon of Clare on a stone escutcheon. The first baronet had failed to establish his right to the three chevronels originally borne by that great family and had been granted arms that accorded better with the rococo taste of his period.

"I've always wanted to plant a hedge of those hydrangeas with black stalks in front of the pines," said the dowager, pensively, "but unless they come blue they wouldn't look nice, and perhaps they wouldn't be able to stand the wind on this side. But the effect would be lovely in summer. Blue sky! Blue sea! Blue hydrangeas! Dark pine-trees and vivid grass! It really would be a wonderful effect. Of course, it may be that Tony's wife will be quite interested in flowers. One never can tell. Come along, Clement." Clement was the pony, so-called because he was such a saint.

The drive now skirted the edge of the downs in a gradual descent to Clarehaven, a small cove formed by green headlands as if earth had thrust out a pair of fists to scoop up some of the sea for herself. The ruins of two round towers were visible on both headlands; on the slopes of the westernmost stood a little church surrounded by tumble-down tombstones that, even as the bodies of those whom they recorded had become part of the earth on which they lived, were themselves growing yearly less distinguishable from the outcrops of stone that no mortal had set upon these cliffs. Two cottages marked the end of the drive, which lost itself beyond them in a rocky beach that was strewn with fragments of ancient masonry. At sight of the chaise several children had bolted into the cottages like disturbed rabbits, and presently a couple of women tying on clean aprons came out to greet the countess and offer the hospitality of their homes. Their husbands, one of whom was called Bitterplum, the other less picturesquely Smith, were mermen of toil, fishers in summer and for the rest of the year agricultural laborers.

"It's very kind of you, Mrs. Smith, and of you, too, Mrs. Bitterplum," said the dowager, "but I can only stay a few minutes. What a beautiful day, isn't it? You must get ready to welcome his lordship, you know. He'll be bringing her ladyship to see you very shortly. Are Bitterplum and Smith quite well?"

"Oh ess, ess, ess," murmured the wives, wiping their mouths with their aprons. Then Mrs. Smith volunteered:

"Parson Beadon's to the church."

At this moment a black figure appeared from the little building, and after experiencing some difficulty in locking the church door behind him hurried down the path to meet the important visitors. Mr. Beadon, the rector of Clarehaven-cum-Cherringtons, was a tall, lean man, the ascetic cast of whose countenance had been tempered by matrimony as the indigestible loaf of his dogma had been leavened by expediency. Although Lord Clarehaven was patron of the living that included Great Cherrington, its church warden was a fierce squire who owned most of the land round; here Mr. Beadon was nearly evangelical, with nothing more vicious than a surpliced choir to mark the corruption of nineteen hundred years of Christianity. At Little

Cherrington, where the dowager worshiped and where she had her stained-glass window of the fourth earl, he indulged in linen vestments as a dipsomaniac might indulge in herb beer; but at Clarehaven, with none except Mrs. Bitterplum and Mrs. Smith to mark his goings on, he used to have private orgies of hagiolatry, from one of which he was now returning.

After Mr. Beadon had greeted the dowager and the two girls he asked, anxiously, if Tony had arrived, and confided with the air of a very naughty boy that he had been holding a little celebration of St. Anthony with special intention for the happiness of the marriage. St. Anthony was not on the dowager's visiting-list, having no address in the Book of Common Prayer; but she could hardly be cross with the rector for observing his festival, inasmuch as he had the same name as her son. Mr. Beadon was a good man whose services at Little Cherrington were exactly what she wanted and who had, moreover, written an excellent history of Clarehaven and the Devonshire branch of the Clare family. At the same time, the bishop was also a good man, and she devoutly hoped that the Bohemianism of Mr. Beadon's services at Clarehaven would not take away what was left to his episcopal appetite from the claims of diabetes.

"One of Mrs. Bitterplum's children has been serving me," said Mr. Beadon. "Yes, it was an impressive little—Eucharist." He had brought his lips together for Mass, and Eucharist came out with such a cough that the dowager begged him not to take cold. Mrs. Bitterplum brought him out a cup of chocolate, a supply of which he kept in her cottage to assuage the pangs of hunger after his long walk and arduous ritual on an empty stomach. He swallowed the chocolate quickly, not to lose the pleasure of company back to Little Cherrington; but with all the heat and hurry of his late breakfast he could not stop talking.

"Mrs. Bitterplum is always kind enough—yes—curious old West Country name...."

Arabella and Constantia had turned away to hide their smiles.

"I have failed hitherto to trace its origin. No.... Oh, indeed yes, when you're ready, Lady Clarehaven. Good day to you, Mrs. Smith. Good day, and thank you, Mrs. Bitterplum."

The pony's head had been turned inland, and Mr. Beadon talked earnestly to the dowager while the chaise was driving slowly back. The topic of the marriage led him along the by-paths of family lore in numerous allusions to the historical importance of the various spots where the dowager lingered during her last drive as mistress of Clare; but the rector's discourse was so much intruded upon by gossip of nothing more than parochial interest that it will be simpler to give a direct abstract of the family history.

In the middle of the thirteenth century a younger member of the great family of Clare whose demesnes stretched east and west from Suffolk to Wales fell in with one of those pirate Mariscos that from Lundy Island swept the Bristol Channel for ships laden with food and wine; in the course of his seafaring he had discovered a cove on the north coast of Devonshire that struck him as an excellent center for piracy on his own account, notwithstanding that his chief patron had recently been hanged, drawn, and quartered. He fortified his cove with round towers at either entrance and thus created Clarehaven, where his descendants for a hundred years or more levied toll on passing traffic and made an alliance with the gentleman pirates of Fowey, whom in the reign of Edward III they helped to drive back the discomfited men of Kent from the west. The baser sort of pirates that in time came to haunt Lundy made the less professional exploits of the Clares no longer worth while, and before the close of the fourteenth century they had for many years abandoned the sea and were reaping a more peaceful harvest from the land. During the great days of Elizabeth the old spirit was reincarnate in one or two members of the family, who fared farther than the Bristol Channel and rounded fiercer capes than Land's End; but when in the early years of the seventeenth century a great storm drove the sea to overwhelm Clarehaven, there was not more to destroy than a few cottages belonging to the fishermen that were now all that remained of the medieval pirates. Then came the Great Rebellion, when Anthony Clare, Esquire, mustered his grooms and fishermen to meet Sir Bevil Grenville marching from Cornwall for the king. Finding large Roundhead forces at Bideford between him and Sir Bevil, he retired again to the obscurity of North Devon until the glorious Restoration, when with a relative he appeared in Parliament as member for the borough of Clarehaven, and was created a baronet by Charles II for his loyalty. Sir Anthony, with a borough in his pocket and two thousand acres of land on which to develop agriculture and choose a site for a house, abandoned what was left of the old pirate's keep and began to build Clare Court. He chose an aspect facing the sea, but died before the house was finished; Sir Gilbert, his son, being more interested in digging for badgers than for foundations, suspended building and contented himself with half a house. Sir Anthony, the third baronet, took after his great-grandfather and dreamed of sailing north to help the Earl of Mar in 1715. He must often have stood in that now walled-up doorway under the escutcheon of his house and gazed northward between the uplands to the sea; luckily for his successors the days were long past when a Clare could go on board his own ship lying at anchor in Clarehaven as snug as a horse in his stable. Sheriffmuir was far from Devon, but the news of that ambiguous battle reached the baronet before he had taken a rash step forward for a lost cause. Every night for thirty years he was carried to bed drunk, and, though he was never too drunk to sip from a goblet which had not been previously passed across a finger-bowl to the king over the water, he was too drunk and gouty to come out in '45. The nephew who succeeded him two years later worked hard for the second George to atone for his uncle's disaffection, and the family came to be favorably regarded at court. Sir William was a bachelor and hated the sea. When not at St. James's he used to live in Clare Lodge, a trim, red-brick house he had built for himself about a mile eastward of the family mansion, overlooking the hamlet of Little Cherrington and many desirable acres of common land.

Mr. Beadon was discoursing of Sir William when the dowager paused to admire the view from Clare Lodge. An excellent tenant had lately vacated it, and she was wondering how long it would be before she and the girls should be living there. She turned her attention once more to the rector's mild criticism of Sir William, who had not attempted to make Clarehaven a real borough, but who had bought Little Cherrington, and inclosed all the acres he coveted. When he died in 1764, his cousin Anthony enjoyed a tolerably rich inheritance, to which he added by marrying a Miss Arabella Hopley with a dowry of £10,000. This lady, by the death of her brother in a hunting accident, some years later became heiress of Hopley Hall and three thousand acres of good land adjoining the Clare estate; Sir Anthony loyally sent the two members for his borough, which by now was reduced to three or four cottages moldering at the tide's edge, to vote for the government; and on being rewarded in the year 1796 with the barony of Clarehaven, he decided to finish Clare Court. Before his succession he had spent a good deal of time at the famous health resort of Curtain Wells, and he was not satisfied with the sea view that did not include sunshine; it was he who pulled down the kitchens and stables behind and built the present front of Clare Court. His son Gilbert was prominent during the Napoleonic wars for seeing that his tenantry kept a lookout for Bonaparte; and by putting down smuggling he performed a vicarious penance for the deeds of his ancestors. It was he who completed Clare Court; and in 1816, ten years before his death, he was created Earl of Clarehaven and Viscount Clare, a peer of that United Kingdom lately achieved by Pitt with such a mixture of glory and shame. To mark his appreciation of the divine favor the first earl built at Little Cherrington a chapel-of-ease to Clarehaven church, the congregation of which by that time was the three electors of the borough. He then bought the living of Great Cherrington, and presented this shamrock of a cure to his natural son, who became rector of Clarehaven-cum-Cherringtons. This gentleman paid a curate £40 a year to look after the three churches and was last seen in an intoxicated condition on the quay of Boulogne harbor.

The present incumbent, who was anxious that the dowager should not object to a step up he proposed to take next Easter by introducing colored vestments at Little Cherrington and linen vestments at Great Cherrington for those very early services that fierce Squire Kingdon would never get up to attend, perhaps alluded to the history of his predecessor in order to emphasize his own superiority. It was all very discreetly done, even to selecting the moment when the two girls were examining a shepherd's sick dog and therefore out of hearing.

"How different from the late lord," Mr. Beadon sighed. "Mrs. Beadon"—the rector paid tribute to his outraged celibacy by never referring to her as his wife—"Mrs. Beadon often wonders why I don't write a special memoir of him."

The dowager gazed affectionately at the chlorotic window by Burne-Jones.

"Perhaps his life was too quiet," she said. "I think the window is enough."

"*Claro non clango*. But when Mr. Kingdon dies," said the rector, tartly, "I understand that Mrs. Kingdon will erect an organ to *his* memory."

They passed out of the church and stood looking down into the lap of the fair landscape outspread before them, talking of other ancestors: of Richard, the second earl, who married the daughter of a marquis and saw Clarehaven disfranchised in 1832, by which time the borough was so rotten that there was nothing perceptible of it except a few seaweed-covered stones at low tide; it was he who destroyed a couple of good farms to provide himself with a park worthy of his rank, which he inclosed with a stone wall and planted trees, the confines of which his descendants now tried proudly to trace in the wintry haze. Lest any want of patriotism should be imputed to the second earl, Mr. Beadon reminded his listeners of how Geoffrey, the third earl, did his duty to his country, first as a member of Parliament for one of the divisions of Devonshire, when he showed the Whigs that the disfranchisement of his borough was not enough to keep a Clare out of Parliament, and afterward as Lord Lieutenant of the county; his duty to his sovereign by acting as Vice-Chamberlain to her Majesty's household. Of his son Gilbert, the fourth earl, enough has been said; though it may be added here that he sold Hopley Hall and many acres besides.

"On the whole, though, I think he was right," said Mr. Beadon. "These Radicals, you know."

"Come and have lunch with us," the dowager invited.

It would be the last independent hospitality she could offer at Clare Court.

II

While the dowager was presiding over lunch at Clare for the last time, while her daughters were getting more and more openly excited about the arrival of their sister-in-law, and while even Mr. Beadon partook of their excitement to such an extent that he ate much less than usual, Dorothy was sitting down to lunch in the restaurant-car of the Western express. Her old life was being left behind more rapidly and with less regret than the country through which the train was traveling. Happiness always widens the waist of an hour-glass. Dorothy was so happy in being a countess that on this railway journey time and space passed with equal speed; and she looked so happy that all those who recognized her or were informed by one of the waiters who she was commented upon her radiant air. They decided with that credulous sentimentality imported into Great Britain with Hengist and Horsa that she must be very deeply in love with her husband; no one suspected that she might be more deeply in love with herself. The head waiter, anxious to pay his own humble tribute to the happy pair, removed the vase of faded flowers from the table they occupied and put in its place another vase of equally faded flowers. If he could have changed the lunch as easily, no doubt he would have done so, but train lunches are as immemorial as elms, and it would have taken more than the marriage of a Vanity girl to a Devonshire nobleman to persuade the Great Western Railway Company that sauce tartare is not the only condiment, and that there are more fish in the sea than the anemic brill.

In days now mercifully forever fled Dorothy had often admired with a touch of envy the select minority of the human race that seemed able to obtain from the staff of a great railway station all the attention it wanted. Now she had entered that select minority, and perhaps nothing brought home more sharply the fact that she was a countess than the attitude of the station-master at Exeter.

"Welcome back to the West, my lord," he said to Clarehaven, who thanked him for his good wishes with the casual rudeness that minor officials of all countries find so attractive in their acknowledged patrons.

A perspiring woman with a little boy in her arms clutched the station-master's sleeve and begged to be informed if the express that was now lying along the platform like a great sleek snake was the slow train to whatever insignificant market-town she was bound. It was annoying for the station-master to have his little chat with Lord Clarehaven interrupted like this, especially by a woman who seemed under the impression that he was a porter. However, the official possessed a store of nobility from which to oblige an importunate inferior, and majestically he condescended to reveal that the slow train would leave in half an hour from the obscure platform it haunted. The station-master was forthwith invited to look after a much-dinted tin box while the perspiring and anxious creature's little boy was accommodated in the cloak-room; before he could protest she had darted off.

"Wonderful what they expect you to do for them, isn't it?" he laughed, with the lordly magnanimity that once inspired the English nation with confidence in the capacity of its chosen representatives to rule the world. At this moment a porter announced that his lordship's car was in the station-yard.

"Be under no apprehensions about your baggage, my lord," said the station-master. "I shall expedite it myself. Be under no apprehensions," he repeated; "it will certainly reach Cherrington Lanes to-night."

The porter, who was as eager as his chief to show his appreciation of being employed at a railway station patronized by Lord and Lady Clarehaven, overstepped the bounds of good will by picking up the perspiring woman's tin box in order to place it in the car. Luckily his chief perceived the horrible mistake in time and bellowed at him to take it out and leave it on the pavement outside the station. Then raising his cap, a gesture reserved for noblemen and irritation of the scalp, the station-master bowed Lord and Lady Clarehaven upon their way.

"Car going well, Deacock?"

"Not too well, my lord."

"Make the old thing hum, because I want her ladyship to reach Clarehaven before dark."

The chauffeur touched his cap, and the car answered generously to his efforts in spite of continual criticisms leveled against it by the owner.

"We must get a Lee-Lonsdale," he said to his wife.

"That would be very nice for Lonnie," she agreed. "Mine, of course, was more a car for town. So I sold it."

She did not add that her own Lee-Lonsdale had provided her with a bracelet of rubies.

"The setting is new," she had said to Tony when she showed him this heirloom. "But the stones are old."

And who should have contradicted her?

The green miles were rolled up like a length of silk; milestones fluttered like paper in the wake of the car; and by five o'clock they were driving through the lodge gates. Mrs. Crawley with nine little Crawleys, the fruit of Mr. Crawley's spare time from the peach-house at Clare, flung a few primroses into the car and cheered their new lady. Dorothy thought the primroses were very pretty and stood up to nod her thanks; she did not realize that even an earl's estate in Devonshire might find it hard to produce so many primroses in the month of January; but she looked so beautiful standing up in the car that Mrs. Crawley felt the exertions of her large and ubiquitous family were well rewarded. The car leaped forward again, followed by shrill cheers that lingered upon the evening air and echoed many times in Dorothy's heart. The spellbound hush of landed property held earth in thrall, and the countess wished to enjoy it.

"Not too fast through the park," she begged.

The car slowed down; at the top of the first incline from which the house was visible it stopped to give Dorothy a moment in which to admire her great possessions. The whole sky was plumed with multitudinous small clouds rosy as the ruffled throats of linnets in spring; on the summit of the last long incline before them Clare Court with its gardens and terraces and gleaming pergola dreamed in the enchantment of the wintry sunsets; in the dark groves on either side the trunks of the pines glowed like pillars of fire. Nothing broke the stillness except a mistlethrush singing very loud from an oak-tree close at hand, and when the bird was silent the lowing of a cow far away on some other earth, it seemed. Suddenly from woodland near the drive came a sound like pattering leaves; a line of fallow deer rippled forth and broke into startled groups that nosed the air now vibrant with the noise of dogs approaching.

"How lovely!" Dorothy exclaimed. "You never told me there were deer," she added, reproachfully, as if the absence of deer had been the one thing that all this time had kept her from accepting Clarehaven's hand. "And how divine it must be here in summer."

"Well, if you hadn't been such a timid little deer, we might have been here, anyway, last October."

Dorothy might have retorted that if Clarehaven had not been so bold a hart she might have been here the summer before last; but she did not remind him of that little flat round the corner, because the herd dashed off to a more remote corner of the park at sight of several dogs scampering down the drive with loud yaps of excitement, and Tony's sisters running behind. Dorothy jumped out of the car to meet her relations for the first time, glad to encounter them like this with dogs barking and so much of the conversation directed to keeping them in order, for she had half expected in that preludial hush to behold the dowager materializing from the misty dusk like a gigantic genie from an uncorked jar.

"Only two hours from Exeter. Pretty good for the old boneshaker, what?" said Tony. "Deacock drove her along like a thoroughbred."

The chauffeur touched his cap and, smiling complacently, leaned over to pat the tires of the car.

"Mother's waiting at the house," said Arabella. "She would have driven down in the chaise to meet Dorothy, but she didn't know exactly when you'd be here and was so afraid of catching cold just when she most wanted not to."

There followed a stream of gossip about the health of various animals, and about the way Marlow, the head-keeper, was looking forward to shooting Cherrington Long Covert, and how much afraid he had been that Tony would not be back before the end of the month, and how glad he was that he was back, in the middle of which Constantia informed Dorothy that there was a meet at Five Tree Farm two days hence and asked her if she was going to hunt for the rest of the season. Arabella kicked her sister so clumsily that Dorothy noticed the warning, and with a sudden impulse to risk all, even death, in the attempt, she replied that of course she intended to hunt for the rest of the season. Tony began to protest, but she cut him short.

"My dear boy, when I lived with my grandmother I always hunted. And I've kept up riding ever since."

"Well, that's topping," exclaimed Connie.

"Yes, that really is topping," echoed Arabella.

"But alas! I don't shoot," Dorothy confessed, "so if it won't bore you too much you'll have to give me lessons."

"Oh, rather," began Connie, immediately. "Well, you see, the most important thing is not to look across your barrels. I find that most people—Well, for instance, supposing you put up a woodcock...."

"I say, Connie, shut up, shut up," Tony exclaimed. "You can't begin at once. You'll put our eyes out in the car with that stick."

The shooting-lesson was postponed; and clambering into the car, in another five minutes they had all reached the house. Dorothy's first emotion at sight of the dowager was relief at finding that she was quite a head shorter than herself. In spite of Napoleon, height is, on the whole, an advantage to human beings in moments of stress. Dorothy had involuntarily imagined her mother-in-law as a tall, beaked woman with a cold and flashing eye, in fact with all the attributes the well-informed novelist usually awards to dowagers. This dowdy little woman, whose slight resemblance to a beaver was emphasized by wearing a cape made of that animal's fur, had to stand on tiptoe to greet her daughter-in-law, and it was unreasonable to be frightened of a woman who in an emotional crisis had to stand on tiptoe. Nevertheless, Dorothy was sincerely grateful for her kindly welcome, and took the first opportunity of whispering some of her hopes and fears for the future to her mother-in-law, who invited her, after tea, to come up-stairs to her den and have a little talk. When they entered the small square room in an angle of the house twilight was still sapphire upon the window-panes, one of which looked out over the park and the other mysteriously down into the grove of pines. Fussing about with matches, the dowager explained apologetically that she preferred always to trim and light her own lamp.

"One gets these little fads living in the depths of the country."

"Of course," Dorothy agreed, planning with herself some similar fad for the near future.

The lamp was lighted; the windows changed from sapphire to indigo as the jewel changes when it is no longer held against the light; in the golden glow the walls of the room broke into blossom, it seemed. Dorothy, reacting from Mr. and Mrs. Caffyn's taste in domestic decoration, had supposed that all well-bred and artistic people devoted themselves to plain color schemes such as she had elaborated in the Halfmoon Street flat; but here was a kind of decoration that, though she knew instinctively it could not be impeached on the ground of bad taste, did astonish her by its gaudiness. Such a prodigality of brilliant red-and-blue macaws, of claret-winged pompadouras and birds of paradise swooping from bough to bough of such brilliant foliage; such sprawling purple convolvuluses and cleft crimson pomegranates on the trellised screen; such quaint old china groups on the mantelpiece; such tumble-down chairs and faded holland covers; and everywhere, like fruit fallen from those tropic boughs, such vividly colored balls of wool.

"Oh," exclaimed Dorothy, divining in a flash of inspiration how to make the most of her totem, "it's exactly like my grandmother's room!"

"I am fond of my little den," said the dowager, "and as long as you so kindly want me to stay on at Clare I hope you won't turn me out of it."

Dorothy expostulated with a gesture; she would have liked to show her appreciation of the room in some perfect compliment, but she could think of nothing better than to suggest sharing it, a prospect that she did not suppose would attract her mother-in-law.

"I feel a dreadful intruder," she sighed.

"My dear child, please. I might have known that Tony would have chosen well for himself, and I do hope you understand—I tried to explain to you in my letter—how old-fashioned and out of the world we are down here. My husband was a very quiet man, and for the last ten years of his life a great invalid. The result was that I scarcely appreciated how things had changed in the world, and I foolishly fancied that Tony was just as much of a country cousin as myself. His sudden departure to Africa like that came as a great shock to me. One scarcely realizes down here that there is such a place as Africa." Heaven and her wall-paper were the only scenes of tropical luxuriance in the imagination of which the dowager indulged herself. "And, of course, my mother was very much upset at the idea of the marriage."

Dorothy started. Was there, then, a super-dowager to be encountered?

"I see that Tony has not told you about her. Chatfield Hall, where my brother lives, whom you will learn to know and love as Uncle Chat, is only fifteen miles from Clare."

Dorothy did not know how to prevent her mother-in-law's perceiving her mortification; to think that in her long study of Debrett she had omitted to make herself acquainted with what was therein recorded of the family of Fanhope! Really she did not deserve to be a countess!

"My mother," went on the dowager, "who as you've no doubt guessed is now an extremely old lady, was inclined to blame me for Tony's choice. She has always been accustomed to expect a good deal from her children. Even Uncle Chat has never yet ventured to introduce a motor-car to Chatfield. So you must not be disappointed if at first she's a little brusk. Poor old darling, she's almost blind, but her hearing is as acute as ever, and oh dear, I am so glad you have a pretty voice."

"Did you think I should have a cockney accent?" Dorothy asked.

"Well, to be frank, the contingency had presented itself," the dowager admitted. "And I am so glad you don't use too much scent. I know everybody uses scent nowadays, but my mother, whose sense of smell is even more acute than her hearing, abominates scent. It does seem so ironical that she should have kept her sense of smell and almost lost her sight. You mustn't be frightened by her; but if you are you must remember that we're all frightened by her, which ought to be a great consolation. I thought we would drive over and see her to-morrow. It would be nice to feel that the ice was broken."

"Even if I do get rather wet," Dorothy laughed.

The dowager smiled anxiously; she was not used to extensions of familiar phrases, and her daughter-in-law's remark made her sharply aware that a stranger was in the house.

"You think you'd rather wait a day or two before you go?" she suggested.

"Oh no, I think we ought to go and see Lady Chatfield as soon as possible," said Dorothy.

"I'm so glad you agree with me."

"I'm rather sensitive where mothers are concerned," said Dorothy.

She felt that now was her moment to win the dowager immovably to her side. There was something in the atmosphere of this gay little room, some intimacy as of a garden long tended by a gentle and lonely soul, that invited a contribution from one who was privileged to enter it like this. Dorothy felt that the room needed "playing up to." The medium that tempted her was the fairy-tale; a room like this was meant for fairy-tales.

"I told you, didn't I, that this room reminded me of my grandmother's room, and what you tell me about Lady Chatfield reminds me a little of her character. My grandmother was a Lonsdale, a descendant of a younger branch of the Cleveden Lonsdales. Her husband was an Irish landowner called Doyle who was involved somehow with political troubles. I don't quite know what happened, but he lost most of his money and died quite suddenly soon after my mother was born. My grandmother came back to England with her little daughter and settled down in Warwickshire, her native county. When my mother was quite young—about twenty—she fell in love with my father, who was reading for Holy Orders in the neighborhood. My grandmother opposed the match, but my mother ran away, and my father, instead of becoming a clergyman, took up rescue work in the slums."

"A fine thing to do," the dowager commented, approvingly.

"Yes, but unfortunately my grandmother was very proud and very unreasonable. She never forgave my mother, although she had me to live with her until I was eleven, when she died. I was brought up in the depths of the country and ever since I have always longed to get back to it. I used to ride with friends of my grandmother. One of them was the Duke of Ayr. Did you ever meet him? He died the other day, but of course I hadn't seen him for many years."

"I did meet him long ago," said the dowager. "He was a great influence for good in the country."

"Oh, a wonderful man," Dorothy agreed. "Well, the few family heirlooms my grandmother still possessed were left to me, together with a small sum of money, which I'm sorry to say my father spent. That was my excuse for going on the stage. I told him that it was his fault and his fault only that I had to earn my own living. But the rescue work had affected his common sense. He turned me out of the house. I lived for a whole year on fifty pounds. But I was determined to succeed, and when I met Tony and he asked me to marry him I refused, because I had grown proud. You can understand that, can't you? Tell me, dear Lady Clarehaven, that you can understand my anxiety to prove that I could be a success. Besides, when I was a child the estrangement between my mother and my grandmother had greatly affected my imagination. I didn't want to find myself the cause of estranging another mother from her son. Have you forgiven me? Do you think that you will ever love me?"

The dowager wept and declared that as soon as her own mother was pacified she should make it her business to reconcile Dorothy with hers.

"Oh no," cried Dorothy, "that's impossible. My father must learn a little humility first. When he has learned his lesson I will be reconciled with my family, but meanwhile haven't you a place in your heart for me?"

The dowager, so far as it was possible for a small woman to perform the action with one so much taller than herself, clasped Dorothy to her heart.

"How I wish my husband were alive to be with us this evening," she exclaimed.

It was probably as well that he was not; if he had been, neither age nor decency would have intervened to prevent the fourth earl from making love to his daughter-in-law. The fifth earl interrupted any further exchanges of confidences by bursting into the room to protest against his wife's desertion.

"Your mother has been so sweet to me, Tony," she said.

"Of course she has," he answered. "She knows what I've had to go through to bring off this coup."

"Indeed," the dowager confessed, "I never suspected he had such determination. Dear old boy, it only seems yesterday that he was such a little boy, and now—" She broke off with a sigh and patted him on the shoulder.

"Your mother and I have just decided that it would be best if I am presented to Lady Chatfield to-morrow," Dorothy announced.

"What?" cried Clarehaven. "No. Look here! Steady, mother! I'm absolutely against that. I'm sorry to appear the undutiful grandson and all that, but really, don't you know, I must discourage her a bit. I didn't bring Dorothy down to Clare to be buzzing over to Chatfield all the time. We'll get Uncle Chat over here to dinner one night, and that'll be quite enough."

The dowager looked appealingly at her daughter-in-law, who at once took matters into her own hands.

"Don't be absurd, Tony. Of course we shall go to-morrow."

He would have continued to protest, but his wife fixed him with those deep-brown eyes of hers.

"Now, don't go on arguing, there's a dear boy, or your mother will think we do nothing but quarrel."

Tony was silent, and the dowager regarded her daughter-in-law with open admiration. She had never seen one of the males of Clare or Fanhope quelled so completely since the days when she was a little girl and saw her own fierce old mother quell her husband.

That night in the bridal chamber of Clare the fifth earl chose a not altogether suitable costume of pink-silk pajamas in which to give utterance to his plans for the future. If Dorothy had been beautiful in the dowager's bower, she was much more fatally beautiful now in a dishabille of peach bloom and with her fawn-colored hair glinting in the candle-light against the dark panels of this ancient and somber room. When Clarehaven began to walk up and down in the excitement of his projects she went slowly across to a Caroline chair with high wicker back, sitting down in which she waited severely and serenely until he had finished. Tony might prance about in his pajamas, but he was no more free than a colt which a horse-breaker holds in tether to be jerked down upon his four legs when he has kicked his heels long enough.

"I didn't marry you," her husband was protesting, "to come and live down here and be ruled by Grandmother Chatfield. I don't give a damn for my grandmother; she's a meddlesome old woman who ought to have been dead ten years ago. As for Uncle Chat, he bores me to death. He can only talk about cigars and pigs. Look here, Doodles, we're going to stay here three or four more days, and then we're off to the Riviera. We'll make Lonnie come with us and drive down through France—topping roads—and I want to try the pigeons at Monte. After that I thought we'd go to Cairo, or perhaps we might go to Cairo first and take Monte on the way back. Anyway, Curzon Street will be ready by the beginning of May. I'm having it devilishly comfortably done up. I didn't tell you about that; it's going to be the most comfortable house in London. I tried every chair myself in Waring's. I'm sorry I had to bore you at all with my family, but I'm awfully fond of my mother, and I knew she wouldn't be happy till she'd seen you, and all that. Well, now it's done, and we can buzz on again as soon as possible."

"Any more plans?" asked Dorothy.

"No, I thought we'd go up to Scotland for August, and after that I don't see why we shouldn't have a good shoot here in September. But I haven't thought much about next autumn."

"That's where I'm cleverer than you," said his wife. "I've not only thought about next autumn, but about next week, and about next year, and the year after that, and the year after that, too. Listen, old thing. When you first met me you wanted to put me in a little flat round the corner, didn't you? Please don't interrupt me. You couldn't understand then why I wouldn't accept your offer; I don't think you really understand very much better even now. London for me doesn't exist any longer. How you can possibly expect me to go away from this glorious place, which I already love as if I'd lived here all my life, to tear about the Continent with you as if I wasn't your wife at all, I don't know. If you don't realize what you owe to your name, I realize it. I don't choose that people should say: 'There goes that ass Clarehaven who married a girl from the Vanity. Look at him!' I don't choose that people should point you out as my husband. I choose to be your wife, and I intend that all your family—and when I say your family I mean your mother's family, too—shall go down on their knees and thank God that you did marry a Vanity girl, and that a Vanity girl knew what she owed to her country in these dreadful days when common Radicals are trying to destroy all that we hold most sacred. I want you to take your place in the House of Lords, when you've lost that trick of talking to everybody as if they were waiters at the Savoy. Why, you don't deserve to be an earl!"

"My dear thing, you mustn't attach too much importance to a title. You must remember...."

"Are you trying to correct my tone?" she asked, coldly. "Because, let me tell you that all this false modesty about your position is only snobbery dressed out in a new disguise. Anyway, I didn't marry you to be criticized."

"Oh well, of course, if you insist on staying down here for the present I suppose I must," said Tony. "Anyway, I dare say we can have some jolly parties to cheer the place up a bit."

"No, we sha'n't have any jolly parties—at any rate yet awhile," said Dorothy. "I don't intend to begin by turning Clare gardens into bear gardens."

"Good Heavens! what is the matter with you?" he demanded. "What has my mother been saying?"

"Your mother hasn't been saying anything. I said all these things over to myself a thousand thousand times before I married you."

"Well, why didn't you tell me some of your ideas before you did marry me?" he muttered.

"Do you regret it?" she asked, standing up.

"Don't be a silly old thing, Doodles. Of course I don't regret it. But having married the loveliest girl in London, I should like to splash around a bit with you. My tastes are bonhomous. I'd always thought.... Dash it, I love you madly, you know that. I'm proud of you."

"Aren't you proud that the loveliest girl in London is willing to be loved by you only? God! my dear boy, you ought to be grateful that you've got me to yourself."

She held out her arms, and it was not remarkable that in those arms and with those lips Clarehaven forgot all about driving along the topping roads of France in a Lee-Lonsdale car. When his wife released him from the first real embrace she had ever given him he staggered like one who has been enchanted.

"Dash it...." he murmured, blinking his eyes to quench the fire that burned them. "I'm not very poetical, don't you know—but your kisses—well, really, do you know I think I shall take to reading poetry?"

III

The next morning Dorothy paced the picture-gallery of Clare that ran the whole length of the north side of the house. She had several ordeals to pass in the few days immediately ahead, and she derived much help from the contemplation of her predecessors at Clare. Gradually from the glances of those tranquil dames, some of whom for more than two centuries had gazed seaward through the panes of those high narrow windows mistily iridescent from a thousand salt gales, Dorothy caught an attitude toward life; from their no longer perturbable expressions, from their silent testimony to the insignificance of everything in the backward of time, she acquired confidence in herself. What was old Lady Chatfield except a picture, and how could she harm an interloper even more vulnerable than an actress? She should try this afternoon to think of the super-dowager as one of the long row of noble dames and console herself with the thought that in another hundred years the fifth Countess of Clarehaven would be accounted the loveliest of all the ladies in this gallery. Who was there to outmatch her? Even the first countess, with all Romney had yielded from his magic store of roses, would have to admit she was surpassed by her successor.

"But who shall paint my portrait?" Dorothy asked herself. "Romney should be alive now. There's no painter as good as he for my style of beauty. And how shall I be painted? If I manage to ride to hounds as triumphantly as I hope I shall, I might be painted in a riding-habit. The black would set off my hair and my complexion and my figure. I don't want everybody at the Academy to say that my dress is so wonderful, as if without a dress I should be nothing. Thirty years from now I will be painted again in some wonderful dress. But oh, if only I don't fail at the meet on Monday! If only—if only...."

At lunch Tony suggested that he should drive Dorothy to Chatfield in the car and that his mother and sisters should go in the barouche. The dowager reminded him how much his grandmother objected to motor-cars at Chatfield and urged that it was unfair on Dorothy to irritate the old lady wantonly.

"I never heard such nonsense," Tony exclaimed. "She'll soon be expecting us to row over to Chatfield in the Ark. Well, I sha'n't go at all. You and Dorothy had better drive over together in the victoria."

The dowager threw out a signal of distress to her daughter-in-law, who said firmly but kindly that they would all drive over together in the drag.

"We shall look like a village treat," muttered Tony, sulkily.

"But I'm anxious to see the country," said Dorothy. "And you drive much too fast in the car for me to see anything. I don't want to arrive blown to pieces."

Naturally in the end Dorothy had her way about going in the drag, and she wondered what Tony could have wished better than to swing through the gates of Chatfield Park and pull up with a clatter at the gates of Chatfield Hall. The very sound of the footman's feet alighting on the gravel drive was like a seal upon the dignity of their arrival. Uncle Chat came out to greet them, a round, red-faced man with short side-whiskers, dressed in a pepper-and-salt suit. He had been a widower for ten years, but his wife before she died—slowly frightened to death by her mother-in-law, as malicious story-tellers said—had left him two sons and two daughters. Paignton, the eldest boy, was a freshman at Trinity, Cambridge, and was at present away on a visit; Charles, the second boy, was still at home, with Eton looming in a day or so; Dorothy liked his fresh complexion and the schoolboy impudence that not even his grandmother had been able to squash. She told him that she was going to hunt on Monday for the first time for several years, and he promised to be her equerry and show her some gaps that might be welcome.

"But it's not difficult country," he assured her. "Not like Ireland."

"No. My great-grandfather was killed by an Irish wall," she said.

Tony looked up at this. Perhaps he was thinking that if she rode as recklessly as she talked she really would be killed out hunting. Of the other easy members of the family Mary and Maud were jolly girls still in the thrall of a governess, while Lady Jane, Tony's aunt, was milder even than his mother, and, having now been for over fifty years at the super-dowager's beck and call, had the look of one who is always listening for bells.

The super-dowager herself lived in a self-propelling invalid chair in which, though she was reputed to be blind, she propelled herself about the ground floor of Chatfield with as much agility as the mole, another animal whose blindness is probably exaggerated. Beyond occasionally knocking over a table, she did more damage with her tongue than with her chair and kept the kitchen in a state of continuous alarm. One of her favorite pastimes was to coast down the long corridor that divided them from the rest of the house, and, pulling up suddenly beside the cook, to accuse her of burning whatever dish she was preparing. The only servants at Chatfield who felt at all secure were those high-roosting birds, the housemaids.

"Who's making all this noise?" demanded the super-dowager, advancing rapidly into the hall soon after the Clarehaven party had arrived, and scattering the group right and left.

"Tony has brought his wife to see you," said her daughter. "They only reached Clare last night."

"Tony's wife?" repeated the old lady. "And who may she be? Chatfield, if Paignton marries an actress you understand that I leave here at once? I've made that quite clear, I hope?"

"If you have, Lady Chatfield," said Dorothy, "I'm sure that Paignton won't marry an actress."

"Who's that talking to me?"

At this moment Arabella and Constantia, who, because their noses were respectively too small and too large, easily caught cold, sneezed simultaneously.

"Augusta," said the super-dowager.

"Yes, mamma."

"Don't tell me that's not Bella and Connie, because I know it is. Can nothing be done about their taking cold like this? They never come here but they must go sneezing and sniffing about, until one might suppose Chatfield was draughty."

Considering that for her peregrinations the super-dowager insisted upon every door of the ground floor's being left open, one might have been justified in supposing so.

"Where's that girl?" demanded the old lady. "Why doesn't she come close? Has she got a cold, too?"

"No, no," laughed Dorothy, "I haven't got a cold."

"Your voice is pleasant, child," said the super-dowager. "Augusta, her voice is pleasant. Chatfield, her voice is pleasant. Clarehaven, come here. Your wife has a pleasant voice."

"Of course she has," said the grandson. "You ought to have heard her sing 'Dolly and her Collie.'"

If looks could have killed her husband, Dorothy would have been the third dowager present at that moment; but strange to say, the old lady seemed to like the idea of Dorothy's singing.

"She *shall* sing me 'Dolly and her Collie'; she shall sing it to me after tea. Come, let's have tea," and, giving a violent twirl to her wheel, the old lady shot forward in advance of the party toward the drawing-room, beating by a neck the footman at the door, who in order to avoid dropping the tray had to perform a pirouette like a comic juggler.

"Why did you make me look such a fool?" Dorothy muttered to Tony at the first opportunity.

"My dear girl, believe me, I'm the only person who knows how to manage the silly old thing."

Dorothy was miserable all through tea, wondering if the super-dowager was really in earnest about making her sing. She wondered what the servants would think, what her mother-in-law would think, what her uncle would think, what her new cousins would think, what the whole county of Devon would think, what all England would think of her humiliation. Perhaps the old lady was not in earnest. Perhaps it was merely a test of her dignity. Were ever sandwiches in the world so dry as these?

"What's that?" the super-dowager was exclaiming. "Certainly not! Nobody can hear this song except myself. I should never dream of allowing a public performance at Chatfield. This is not a performance. This is a contribution to my miserable old age."

The old lady swooped about the room like a hen driving intruding sparrows from her grain; when all were banished she swung rapidly backward and commanded Dorothy to begin. Poor Dorothy tried to explain how the effect of the song had depended upon the accessories. There had been the music, for instance.

"Never mind about the music," said the super-dowager.

"And there was a chorus of six."

"Never mind about the chorus."

"And then I haven't got my dog."

"Never mind about the dog."

Dorothy, who had thought that she had put "Dolly and her Collie" behind her forever, had to stand up and sing to Lady Chatfield as she had sung to Mr. Richards in the cupola of the Vanity not so many months ago.

"The words are rubbish," said the old lady. "The tune is catchy, but not so catchy as the tunes they used to write. Your voice is pleasant. Come nearer to me, child. They tell me you're handsome. Yes, well, I can almost see that you are. And I'm glad of it, for the Clares are an ugly race."

Considering that the super-dowager was directly responsible for Tony's mother, and therefore partially responsible for Arabella and Constantia, this opinion struck Dorothy as lacking proportion.

"Beauty is required in the family. You understand what I mean? Let's have none of these modern notions of waiting five or six years before you do your duty. Produce an heir."

The old lady said this so sharply that Dorothy felt as if she ought to put her hand in her pocket and produce one then and there.

"Call Tony in to me. Tony," she said, "you're an ass; but not such an ass as I thought you were."

"Good song, isn't it, grandmother?" he chuckled.

"Don't interrupt me. I said you were only not such an ass as I thought. You're still an ass. Your wife isn't. You understand what I mean? Produce an heir. Now I must go to bed." She swept out of the room like a swallow from under the eaves of a house.

On the way back to Clare, Bella and Connie could not contain their delight at the success Dorothy had made with their grandmother. Tompkins, the Chatfield butler, had confided in Connie just before she left that her ladyship had been heard to hum on entering her bedroom—an expression of superfluous good temper in which she had not indulged within his memory. The old lady was always cross at going to bed, probably because she could not wheel it about like her chair. Nor was grandmother the only victim to Dorothy's charm: Uncle Chat had been full of compliments; Charles and the girls had declared she was a stunner; Aunt Jane had corroborated Tompkins's story about humming.

The dowager, who always came away from Chatfield with a sense of renewed youth, though sometimes, indeed, feeling like a naughty little girl, was almost sprightly on the drive back to Clare. She had expected to be roundly scolded by her mother, and here she was going away with her pockets full of nuts, as it were; the little anxieties of daily life dropped from her shoulders, and when the drag met a very noisy motor in a narrow stretch of road she sat perfectly still and listened to the coachman's soothing clicks with profound trust in his ability to calm the horses.

"By the way, I hope you won't mind the suggestion, dear," she said to Dorothy, "but I think it would be nice to arrange a little dinner-party for Saturday night—just our particular neighbors, you know—Mr. and Mrs. Kingdon, Mr. and Mrs. Beadon, Mr. Hemming the curate, Doctor Lane, and Mr. Greenish of Cherrington Cottage."

Tony groaned.

"What could be nicer?" said Dorothy. "But...."

"You're going to say it sounds rather sudden. Yes—well, it will be sudden. But it struck me that it would be much nicer if we were a little sudden. You see, your wedding was rather sudden, and our neighbors will appreciate such a mark of intimacy. No doubt the Kingdons and the Beadons will have called this afternoon, and I thought that if you don't object I would send out the invitations myself and make it a sort of wedding breakfast. I know it all sounds very muddled, but my inspirations nearly always turn out well. I should like to feel on Sunday that we were all old friends. Besides, if you're really going to hunt on Monday, it will be nice for you to meet Mr. Kingdon, who is master of the Horley."

"I think it's a delightful idea," Dorothy exclaimed. "Thank you so much for suggesting it."

"This is going to be a terrible winter and spring," Clarehaven groaned.

"Tony, please don't be discouraging," said his mother. "I'm feeling so optimistic since our visit to Chatfield. Why, I'm even hoping to reconcile Mr. Kingdon and Mr. Beadon. Not, of course, that they're open enemies, but I should like the squire to appreciate the rector's beautiful character, and it seems such a pity that a few lighted candles should blind him to it. Mr. Kingdon will take in Dorothy; the rector will take me; you, Tony dear— please don't look so cross—ought to take in Mrs. Kingdon, who's a great admirer of yours—such a nice woman, Dorothy dear, with a most unfortunate inability to roll her r's—it's so sad, I think. Then the doctor will take in Mrs. Beadon; Mr. Greenish, Arabella; and Mr. Hemming, Connie."

"I like Tommy Hemming," said Connie. "He's a sport."

"I should call him a freak," Clarehaven muttered.

"We ought to do some riding to-morrow and Friday," his sister went on, quite unconcerned by his opinion of the curate. "I think Dorothy ought to ride Mignonette on Monday. She's a perfect ripper—a chestnut."

Dorothy liked the name, which reminded her of her own hair, and certainly had she chosen for herself she would have chosen a chestnut for the meet at Five Tree Farm. The dowager's forecast was right—both the Kingdons and the Beadons had called upon the new countess, and the dowager pattered up-stairs to her bird-bright room to send out invitations for Saturday.

"You see what you've let yourself in for," said Tony to his wife that night. "However, you'll be as fed up as I am when you've had one or two of these neighborly little dinners. And look here, Doodles, seriously I don't think you ought to hunt. I'm not saying you can't ride, but you ought to wait till next season, at any rate. You may have a nasty accident, and—well, yes, I'm the one to say it, after all—you may make a priceless fool of yourself."

"Do you think so?" Dorothy asked. "Do you think I made a priceless fool of myself when I sang to your grandmother this afternoon? If I can carry that off, I can certainly ride after a fox. Kiss me. You mean well, but you don't yet know what I can do."

A former Anthony kissed away kingdoms and provinces; this Anthony kissed away doubts and fears and scruples as easily.

Dorothy dressed herself very simply for the neighborly little dinner-party. She decided that white would be the best sedative for any tremors felt by the neighbors at the prospect of finding their society led by an actress; and she made up her mind to cast a special spell upon the M. F. H. and so guard herself from the consequences of any mistake she might make at the meet. There was nothing about Mr. Kingdon that diverged the least from the typical fox-hunting squire that for two hundred years has been familiar to the people of Great Britain. His neck was thick and red; his voice came in gusts; and he recounted as good stories of his own the jokes in *Punch* of the week before last. What deeper sense in Squire Kingdon was outraged by the rector's ritualism it would be hard to say, for his body did not appear to be the temple of anything except food and drink; perhaps, like the bull that he so much resembled, an imperfectly understood nervous system was wrought upon by certain colors. The congregation of Great Cherrington would scarcely have been stirred from their lethargic worship to see the squire with lowered head charge up the aisle, when Mr. Beadon began to play the picador with a colored stole, and toss Mr. Beadon over his shoulders into the font. Mrs. Kingdon was to her husband as a radish is to a beet-root. The weather is a bad lady's maid, and the weather had made of Mrs. Kingdon's complexion something that ought to have infuriated her husband as much as Mr. Beadon's colored stoles. In spite of her hard and highly colored appearance, she was a mild enough woman, given to deep sighs in pauses of the conversation, when she was probably thinking about the rolling of her r's and regretting that three of her children had inherited this impotency of palate or tongue.

"We must all pull together," she said to Dorothy, who expressed her anxiety to find herself lugging at the same rope as Mrs. Kingdon against whatever team opposed them.

"Very true, Mrs. Kingdon," the rector observed. "I wish the squire was always of your opinion."

"Mr. Beadon can never forget that he is a clergyman," whispered Mrs. Kingdon when the rector passed on.

Yet the monotone of Mr. Beadon's clericality had once been illuminated when he had broken that vow of celibacy to which he had attached such importance in order to marry Mrs. Beadon. In the confusion of the Sabine rape Mrs. Beadon might have found herself wedded, but that any man in cold blood and with many women to choose from should have deliberately chosen Mrs. Beadon passed normal comprehension. Her husband treated her in the same way as he treated the crucifix from Oberammergau that he kept in a triptych by his bed. He would admire her, respect her, almost worship her, and then abruptly he would shut her up with a little click. Mrs. Beadon was much thinner even than her husband; while she was eating, the upper part of her chest resembled a musical box, her throat a violin played pizzicato, the accumulated music of which expressed itself during digestion in remote trills and far-off scales. She was seldom vocal in conversation, but voluble in psalms and hymns; she performed many kind actions such as blowing little boys' noses on the way to school, and though she did not blow Dorothy's nose, she squeezed her hand and confided that the news of Lord Clarehaven's marriage had meant a great deal to her.

"Oh, so much!" she had time to repeat before her husband closed the doors of the triptych.

Mr. Hemming, the curate, was a muscular and, did not his clerical collar forbid one to suppose so, a completely fatuous young man. When he was pleased about anything he said, "Oh, cheers!" When he was displeased he shook his head in silence. Mr. Beadon told Dorothy that he was a loyal churchman, and certainly once in the course of the evening he came to the rescue of his rector, who had been pinned in a corner of the room, by asking the squire, why he wore a pink coat when he hunted. The squire replied that such was the custom for an M. F. H., and Mr. Hemming, with a guffaw, said that it was also the custom for a fisher of men to wear sporting colors. This irreverent attempt to put fishing on an equality with fox-hunting naturally upset the squire, and the dowager's hopes, of an early reconciliation between him and the rector were destroyed.

Of the other two guests, Doctor Lane was a pleasant, elderly gentleman whose chief pride was that he still read *The Lancet* every week. One felt in talking to him that a man who still read *The Lancet* after twenty-five years of Cherrington evinced a sensitiveness to medical progress that was laudable and peculiar. He was a widower without children and devoted what little leisure he had to the study of newts, salamanders, and olms; a pair of olms, which a friend had brought him back from Carniola, he kept in a subterranean tank in his garden, enhancing thereby in the eyes of the village his reputation as a physician. The last guest, Mr. Greenish, was a well-groomed bachelor of about forty, one of that class who suddenly appear for no obvious reason in remote country villages and devote themselves to gardening or other forms of outdoor life, who are useful about the parish, and who often play billiards well. They may be criminals hiding from justice;

more probably they are people who have inherited money late in life from aunts, and who, having long dreamed of retiring into the country, do so at the first opportunity. Mr. Greenish did not hunt, but he was a good shot, and Clarehaven found him the least intolerable of his immediate neighbors.

It cannot be said that Dorothy found it difficult to shine at such a party; indeed, she was such a success that when the evening came to an end no doubt remained in the dowager's mind that to-morrow morning Little Cherrington church would have double its usual congregation to see the new countess. In fact, Mr. Kingdon was so much taken with her that he announced his own intention of worshiping at Little Cherrington, and the rector regretted that he had not known of this beforehand in order that he might have seized the opportunity, in the absence of the squire, to test the congregation of Great Cherrington with a linen chasuble. As a matter of fact, on the way home he plotted with Mr. Hemming to do this, and was successful in passing off the vestment on the congregation as a flaw in the curate's surplice.

Dorothy looked particularly attractive that Sunday in her coat and skirt of lavender box-cloth, for the fashion of the moment was one that well showed off a figure like hers. The rector's sermon on a text from the Song of Solomon alluded with voluptuous imagery to the romance of the married state, and, being entirely unintelligible to the congregation, was considered round the parishes to be one of the best sermons he had ever preached. If only to-morrow, thought Dorothy, when she walked out of the churchyard through a crowd of uncovered rustics, she could leave the hunting-field as triumphantly. Her rides on the preceding days with Clarehaven and the girls had been successful. They had all congratulated her, and any lingering anxiety in her husband's mind seemed to have passed away. As the moment drew near, however, Dorothy began to be nervous about breaches of hunting etiquette, and she spent Sunday afternoon in turning over the pages of bound volumes of *Punch* in order to extract from the weekly hunting joke hints what not to do. A succession of irate M. F. H.'s, purple in the face and shaking crops at presumptuous cockneys, haunted her dreams that night; when she woke to a moist gray morning, for the first time in her life she felt really nervous. It was in vain that she sought to reassure herself by recalling past triumphs on the stage or by telling herself how easily she had dealt with Lady Chatfield. Failure in either of those cases would not have been irremediable; but let her make no mistake, before to-day's dusk she should have settled the whole of her future life. If she made a fool of herself she should never escape from being pointed out as a Vanity girl; if she succeeded, the Vanity girl would be forgotten, and by sheer personal prowess she might lead the county. It was a tribute to Dorothy's complexion that not even on this rather shaky morning did she feel the need for rouge. Five Tree Farm was only three miles from Clare Court, and the meets there, being considered the best of the season, always had very large fields. She was disappointed that Tony was not in pink, but he told her he did not care enough about hunting to dress up for it.

"That's what I like about shooting," he said, "there isn't all this confounded putting it on."

The master cantered up and congratulated Dorothy on her first appearance with the Horley Hunt.

"We're going to draw Dedenham Copse first," he informed her, and cantered off again, shouting loudly to two unfortunate young men with bicycles who were doing no harm at all, but whom he persisted in abusing as "damned socialists." Suddenly, hounds gave tongue with changed, almost intolerable eager note; there was a thud of hoofs all round her; confused cries; the sound of a horn shrilling to the gray sky....

"Wonderful morning for scent," she heard somebody say, and flushed because she thought a personal remark had been passed about herself; but before she had time to worry who had said it and why it had been said Mignonette was nearly leading the field.

"Dorothy," shouted her husband, "for God's sake don't get too far in front. Hold your mare in a bit. And for God's sake don't ride over hounds."

But Dorothy paid no attention to him and was soon galloping with the first half-dozen. By her side appeared Charlie Fanhope.

"Topping run," he breathed. "I say, you're looking glorious. Awful to think I shall be on the way to Eton this time to-morrow."

She smiled at him; from out of the past came the memory of an old colored Christmas supplement on the walls of the nursery in Lonsdale Road. A girl and a boy on rocking-horses, brown and dapple-gray, the boy wearing a green-velvet cap and jacket, the girl befrilled and besashed, were both plunging forward with rosy smiles. Underneath it had been inscribed: "Yoicks! Tally-ho!" While her mare's heels thudded over the soft turf, Dorothy kept saying to herself, "Yoicks! Yoicks! Yoicks!" Charlie Fanhope, riding beside her, was as fresh and rosy as the boy in the picture.

"You can't take that gate, can you?" he was saying.

Before her like a ladder rose a five-barred gate. At the riding-school in Knightsbridge Dorothy had jumped obstacles quite as high; but those had been obstacles that collapsed conveniently when touched by the heels of her horse.

"I say I don't think you can take that gate," Charlie Fanhope repeated, anxiously. "I'll open it. I'll open it."

But Dorothy in a dream left all to Mignonette; remembering from real life to grip the pommel, to keep her wrists down, and to sit well back, she seemed to be uttering a prolonged gasp that was carried away by the wind as a diver's gasp is lost in the sound of the water. Where was her cousin? Left behind to crackle through one of those gaps he knew of. Yoicks! Yoicks! Yoicks! They were in a wide, down-sloping meadowland intensely green, and checkered with the black and red riders in groups; hounds were disappearing at the bottom of the slope in a thick coppice. Nursery pictures of Caldecott came back to Dorothy when she saw the squire with his horn and his mulberry-colored face and his huge bay horse go puffing past to investigate the check, which lasted long enough for Dorothy to receive many felicitations upon her horsewomanship.

"My word! Doodles," said her husband, cantering up to her side. "You really are a wonder, but for the Lord's sake be careful."

"I told you that you didn't yet really know me," she murmured; before he could reply, from the farthest corner of the coppice came the whip's "Viewhalloo." Hounds gave tongue again with high-pitched notes of excitement as of children playing. Forrard away! For-rard! They were off again with the fox gone away toward Maidens' Common, and before the merry huntsmen the prospect of the finest run in Devonshire. Thirty minutes at racing speed and never a check; wind singing; hoofs thudding; a view of the fox; Dorothy always among the first half-dozen riders.

They killed some twelve miles away from Clare in Tangley Bottom, and nobody would have accused the master, when he handed Dorothy the brush, of being influenced by the countess's charming company at dinner on Saturday night. Best of all in a day of superlatives, Clarehaven had taken a nasty toss; his wife had him in hand as securely as she had Mignonette.

"Glorious day," Connie sighed when at last they were walking through the gates of the park.

"Glorious," echoed Dorothy.

A faint flush low on the western sky symbolized her triumph. And though one or two malicious women said that it was a pity Lord Clarehaven should have married a circus girl, the legend never spread. Besides, they had not been introduced to the Diana of Clare, who soon had the county as securely in hand as her horse and her husband.

Dorothy, tired though she was, felt the need of confiding in somebody the tale of her triumph. She was even tempted to write to Olive. In the end she chose her mother; perhaps the kindness of the dowager had stirred a dormant piety.

She wrote:

MY DEAR MOTHER,—I am sorry I could not come and see you before I got married, but you can understand how delicate and difficult my position was, and how much everything depended on myself. No doubt, later on when I am thoroughly at home in my new surroundings, it will be easier for us to meet again. I don't know if father told you that I did explain to him my motives in treating you all rather abruptly. Or did he never refer to a little talk we once had? You will be glad to hear that I am very, very happy. My husband adores me, my mother-in-law has been more than kind, and my sisters-in-law equally so. On Thursday we drove over to Chatfield Hall to see my husband's grandmother, old Lady Chatfield, who is famous for speaking her mind, and of course not at all prejudiced in my favor by my having been on the stage. However, we had a jolly little talk together and everybody is delighted with the impression I made. On Saturday we had a small dinner-party. The rector, who is very High Church and would not, therefore, appeal to father, was there. Mr. Kingdon, the squire, would be more his style. There was also a Mr. Greenish, who promised to teach me gardening. Quite a jolly evening. Yesterday morning all the villagers cheered when I came out of church, and to-day I hunted with the Horley. I was rather a success. I hope you got the check for £500 I sent you, and that you will buy yourself something nice with it. It isn't exactly a present, but in a way it counts as one, doesn't it? You must try to be a little more firm with father in future. Don't forget that though I may seem heartless I am not really so. I hope you will write to me sometimes. You should address the envelope to The Countess of Clarehaven, but if you speak about me to your friends you should speak about me as Lady Clarehaven.

Your loving daughter,
DOROTHY CLAREHAVEN.

IV

For two years Dorothy's life as a countess went quietly along, gathering in its train a number of pleasant little memories that in after years were to mean something more than pleasure. The major difficulties of her new position were all encountered and defeated in that first week; thenceforward nothing seriously disturbed her for long. In the autumn of the year in which Clarehaven married, the dowager, after consulting Dorothy, decided that his restlessness was finally cured and that the danger of his wanting to tear about the Continent in Lee-Lonsdale cars no longer threatened the family peace. In these circumstances the dowager thought it would be tactful to move into Clare Lodge with Arabella and Constantia.

She should not be too far away if her daughter-in-law had need of her, and by moving that little way off she should do much to prevent her son's chafing against the barriers of domesticity. It would be easier for Dorothy to act as hostess of the shooting-parties that were arranged for the autumn if she were apparent as the only hostess. In the administration of the village the two countesses shared equally—the dowager by superintending the making of soup and gruel for sick villagers, Dorothy by assisting at its distribution. The rector won Dorothy's heart by his readiness to discuss with her the history of the great family into which she had married, and by preparing a second edition of his *Clarehaven and the Clares* for when it should be wanted, affixing against the fifth earl's name an asterisk, like a second star of Bethlehem, that should direct the wise reader to this foot-note:

...The present Earl in January, 1906, delighted his many friends and well-wishers in the county by wedding the beautiful Miss Dorothy Lonsdale, a distant connection of that Lord Cleveden who is famous as a most capable administrator in the land of the golden wattle and upon "India's coral strand."

She for her part won Mr. Beadon's heart by often attending his services at Clarehaven, and not merely by attending herself, but by insisting upon Mrs. Bitterplum's and Mrs. Smith's attending, too. This arrangement suited everybody, because the dowager at Little Cherrington was able to worship her stained-glass window without a sense that, whatever she might be before God's throne, she was now of secondary importance in the church. The step up that the rector had promised himself for Easter was effected without an apoplexy from Mr. Kingdon, possibly because the white stole did not inflame his taurine eye. At Whitsuntide, however, when a red stole appeared, his face followed the liturgical sequence, and there was a painful scene in the churchyard on a hot morning in early June. Dorothy, on being appealed to by the rector, drove over to Cherrington Hall that afternoon and remonstrated with Mr. Kingdon on his inconsiderate behavior. She pointed out that Mrs. Beadon was in an interesting condition at the moment and that if Mr. Kingdon had his prejudices to consider, Mr. Beadon had his conscience; that it was not right for the squire to add fuel to the ancient rivalry between Great and Little Cherrington; and finally that inasmuch as the bishop was shortly coming to stay at Clare for a confirmation, it would be unkind to pain his sensitive diocesan spirit with these parochial disputes. Dorothy's arguments may not have convinced the squire, but her beauty and condescension penetrated where logic was powerless, and Mr. Beadon was allowed to preach for more than twenty bee-loud Sundays after Trinity wearing a grass-green stole round his neck and with never a word of protest from the squire. Nor were the Sundays within the octaves of St. Peter or St. James, of St. Lawrence or St. Bartholomew, profaned by the squire's objections to the tribute of red silk that Mr. Beadon paid to the blood of the martyrs. His wife celebrated her husband's victory by producing twins at Lammastide, and everybody in the neighborhood said that the religious tone of Cherrington was remarkably high.

In September Dorothy had her first shooting-party, to which, among others, Arthur Lonsdale and Harry Tufton were invited. Tony had been in camp with his yeomanry regiment during most of August; he seemed glad to be back at Clare; the shooting was good; the visits of his old friends from London did not apparently disturb him. Notwithstanding Connie's lessons, Dorothy never became a good shot; she really hated killing birds. However, she encouraged Clarehaven to go on with his favorite sport, and herself hunted hard all the season. She was much admired as a horsewoman, and the fact that she had not so long ago been a Vanity girl was already as dim as most old family curses are. In early spring Tony suggested that it would be a good idea to go up to town for the season.

"A very good idea," she agreed. "Bella and Connie ought to be presented." Dorothy spoke as calmly as if she had been presented herself. "It's a pity I can't present them," she added, "but I should not like to be presented myself. I don't think that actresses ought to be presented, even if they do retire from the stage when they marry. Sometimes an individual suffers unjustly; but it's better that one person should suffer than that all sorts of precedents should be started. Of course, your mother will present them."

"But look here, I thought we'd go up alone," Tony argued. "I told you I'd had the house done up very comfortably. I don't think the girls would enjoy London a bit."

"They may not enjoy it," said Dorothy, "but they ought to go."

May and June were spent in town in an unsuccessful attempt to induce many eligible bachelors even to dance with Arabella and Constantia, let alone to propose to them. Dorothy condoled with the dowager on Arthur Lonsdale's bad taste in not wanting to marry Arabella; Arthur himself was lectured severely on his obligations, and she could not understand why he would not stop laughing, particularly as Lady Cleveden herself had been in favor of the match. Dorothy went to the opera twice a week; but she refused to go near the Vanity. Once she drove over to West Kensington to see her mother, whose chin had more hairs than ever, but who otherwise was not much changed. The rest of the family alarmed her with the flight of time. Gladys and Marjorie were the Agnes and Edna of four years ago; Agnes and Edna themselves were getting perilously like the Norah and Dorothy of four years ago; Cecil was a medical student smoking bigger pipes than Roland, who himself had grown a very heavy black mustache. The countess managed to avoid seeing her father, and when her mother protested his disappointment she said that he would understand. Mrs. Caffyn was too much awed by having a countess for a daughter to insist, and she assured her that not only did she fully appreciate her reasons for withdrawing from open intercourse with her family, but that she approved of them. The countess gave her a sealskin coat for next winter, kissed her on both cheeks, and disappeared as abruptly from West Kensington as Enoch from the antediluvian landscape.

The responsibility of two plain sisters became too much for Clarehaven; after Ascot he admitted that he should be thoroughly glad to get back to Clare, which was exactly what his wife had hoped.

While Dorothy was studying with the rector the lives of obscure saints and the histories of prominent noblemen, she took lessons with the doctor in natural history and with Mr. Greenish in horticulture. Mr. Greenish enjoyed sending off on her account large orders to nursery gardeners all over England for rare shrubs that he had neither the money nor the space to buy for himself. Both at the Temple Show and at Holland House he had been continually at Lady Clarehaven's elbow with a note-book; and the glories of next summer in the Clare gardens made bright his wintry meditations. Mr. Greenish himself looked rather like a tuber, and it became a current joke that one day Dorothy would plant him in a secluded border. The dowager was delighted by her daughter-in-law's hobby, for which, though it ran to the extravagance of ordering the whole stock of a new orange tulip at a guinea a bulb, not to mention twenty roots of sunset-hued *Eremurus warer* at forty shillings apiece, and a hundred of topaz-hung *Eremurus bungei* at ten shillings, she had nothing but enthusiasm.

"My golden border will be lovely," Dorothy announced.

"It will be unique," Mr. Greenish added. "Lady Clarehaven is specializing in shades of gold, copper, and bronze," he explained to the dowager.

"These roots oddly resemble echinoderms," said Doctor Lane, looking at the roots of the *Eremurus*.

"I should have said starfish," Mr. Greenish put in.

"Starfish *are* echinoderms," said the doctor, severely.

"Wonderful!" the dowager exclaimed, with the eyes of a child looking upon the fairies. She herself never rose to the height of her daughter-in-law's Incalike ambitions; but her own Japanese tastes (expensive enough) were gratified. Those black-stemmed hydrangeas were ordered by the hundred to bloom by the edge of the pines, and Dorothy presented her with twenty-four of M. Latour-Marlias's newest and most expensive hybrid water-lilies. Nor did the hydrangeas come pink; they knew that they were being employed by a noble family and preserved the authentic blue of their patrons' blood. As the rector hoped before he died that popular clamor in the Cherringtons would compel him to flout his bishop by holding an open-air procession upon the feast of Corpus Christi, so Dorothy aspired to convert the two villages from vegetables to flowers. She knew, however, that it would be useless to attempt too much at first in this direction, and at Mr. Greenish's suggestion she decided to open her campaign by organizing a grand entertainment for the two Cherringtons, Clarehaven, and the several villages and hamlets in the neighborhood. Uncle Chat was called in to help with his advice, and while Tony was in camp she made her preparations. Marquees were hired from Exeter; the countryside pulsated with the spirit of competition. Dorothy drew up the bills herself with a nice compromise between the claims of age and strict precedence in her list of patrons.

CLAREHAVEN AND CHERRINGTON AGRICULTURAL FÊTE AND FLOWER SHOW

Saturday, August 31, 1907

UNDER THE PATRONAGE OF

The Earl of Chatfield; the Earl and Countess of Clarehaven; Lavinia, Countess of Chatfield; Augusta, Countess of Clarehaven; the Viscount Paignton; the Lady Jane Fanhope; the Lady Arabella Clare; the Lady Constantia Clare; the Lady Mary Fanhope; the Lady Maud Fanhope; George Kingdon, Esq., J.P., M.F.H., and Mrs. Kingdon; the Rev. Claude Conybeare Beadon, M.A., and Mrs. Beadon; Dr. Eustace Lane; Horatio Greenish, Esq.

Prizes for live stock, including poultry, pigeons, and rabbits.

Prizes for collections of mixed vegetables.

A special prize offered by the Earl of Chatfield for the best collection of runner-beans.

A special and very *valuable* prize offered by the Countess of Clarehaven for the best collection of *flowers* from a cottage garden.

A special prize offered by the Dowager Countess of Clarehaven for the best collection of wild flowers made by a village child within a four-mile radius of Clare Court.

A special prize offered by Doctor Lane for a collection of insect pests set and mounted by the scholars of Cherrington Church Schools and Horley Board Schools.

The Countess of Clarehaven has kindly consented to give away the prizes.

The band of the Loyal North Devon Dragoons (by kind permission of Colonel Budding-Robinson, M.V.O., and officers) will play during the afternoon.

Swings, roundabouts, cocoanut-shies, climbing greasy pole for a side of bacon offered by H. Greenish, Esq., sack-races, egg-and-spoon races, hat-trimming competition for agricultural laborers.

ILLUMINATIONS AND FIREWORKS

Entrance, one shilling. After five o'clock, sixpence. After eight, threepence. Children free.

REFRESHMENTS

It was a blazing day, one of those typical days when rustic England seems to consist entirely of large cactus dahlias and women perspiring in bombazine. Tony, to Dorothy's annoyance, had declined to open the proceedings with a speech, and with Uncle Chat also refusing, Mr. Kingdon had to be asked to address the competitors. He bellowed a number of platitudes about the true foundations of England's greatness, told everybody that he was a Conservative—a Tory of the old school. He might say amid all this floral wealth a Conservatory. Ha-ha! He had no use for new-fangled notions, and, by Jove! when he looked round at the magnificent display that owed so much to the energy and initiative of Lady Clarehaven, by Jove! he couldn't understand why anybody wanted to be anything else except a Conservative.

"No politics, squire," the village atheist cried from the back of the tent, and Mr. Kingdon, who had been badly heckled by that gentleman at a recent election meeting, descended from the rostrum.

When the time came to distribute the awards Dorothy sprang the little surprise of which only Mr. Greenish was in the secret, by making a speech herself. She spoke with complete self-assurance and, as the *North Devon Courant* said, "with a gracious comprehension of what life meant to her humbler neighbors."

"Fellow-villagers of the two Cherringtons and of Clarehaven," she began, evoking loud applause from Mr. and Mrs. Bitterplum and Mr. and Mrs. Smith, who between them had raised the largest marrow, for which they would shortly receive ten shillings as a token of England's gratitude, "in these days when so much is heard of rural depopulation I confess that looking round me at this crowded assembly I am not one of the alarmists. I confess that I see no signs of rural depopulation among the merry faces of the little children of our healthy North Devon breed. I regret that the committee did not include in its list of prizes another for the best collection of home-grown children." (Loud cheers from the audience, in the middle of which one of the little Smiths of Clarehaven had to be led out of the tent because there was some doubt whether in chewing one of the prize dahlias he had not swallowed an earwig.) "Meanwhile, I can only marvel at the enthusiasm and good will with which you have all worked to make our first agricultural fête the success it undoubtedly has been. I am told by people who understand these things that no finer runner-beans have ever appeared than the collection of runner-beans for which, after long deliberation by the judges, Mr. Isaac Hodge of Little Cherrington has been awarded the prize." (Cheers.) "I will not detain you with eulogies of the potatoes shown by our worthy neighbor, Mr. Blundell of Great Cherrington. Nor shall I detain you by singing the praises of the really noble beet-roots from the garden of Mr. Adam Crump of Horley Hill. But I should like to say here how much I regret that the collections of flowers fell so far below the standard set by the vegetables. We must remember that without beauty utility is of little use. This autumn I shall be happy to present flower seeds to all cottage gardens who apply for them. Mr. Greenish has kindly consented to act as my distributer. Next year I shall present five pounds and a silver cup for the best exhibit from these seeds. And now nothing remains for me except to congratulate once more the winners on their well-deserved success, and the losers on a failure that only the exceptional quality of the winning exhibits prevented being a success, too."

Amid loud cheers Dorothy pinned rosettes to the lapels of the perspiring competitors, shook hands with each one, to whom she handed his prize wrapped in tissue-paper, and, bowing graciously, descended from the dais.

"Now if I can make a speech like that at a flower-show," she said to her husband that evening, "why can't you speak in the House of Lords?"

The fact of the matter was that Dorothy was beginning to worry herself over Clarehaven's lack of interest in the affairs of his country. Since they had been married the only additional entry in Debrett under his title was the record of his being a J.P. for the county of Devon. Dorothy felt that this was not enough; he should be preparing himself by his demeanor in the House of Lords to be offered at least an under-secretaryship when the Radicals should be driven from power.

"All right," said Tony. "But I can't very well play the hereditary legislator and all that if you insist upon keeping me down in the country."

"When does Parliament reassemble?" she asked.

"Oh, I don't know. Some time in the autumn, I suppose."

"Very well, then, we'll go up to town on one condition, which is that you will make a speech. If you haven't spoken within a week of the opening I shall come back here."

Tony, in order to get away from Devonshire, was ready to promise anything, but at the end of October, on a day also memorable in the history of Clare for the largest battue ever held in those coverts, Dorothy told her husband that she was going to have a baby.

He flushed with the slaughter of hundreds of birds, she flushed with what all this meant to her and him and England, faced each other in the bridal chamber of Clare that itself was flushed with a crimson October sunset.

"Tony, aren't you wildly happy?"

"Why, yes ... of course I am ... only, Doodles, I suppose this means you won't go up to town? Oh well, never mind. Gad! you look glorious this evening." He put his arms round her and kissed her.

"Not that way," she murmured. "Not that way now."

V

The pride and joy that Dorothy felt were so complete that she would take no risk of spoiling them by allowing her husband to intrude upon her at such a time. This boy of hers—there was no fear in her sanguine and circumspect mind that she might produce a daughter—was the fruit of herself and the earldom. To this end had she let Clarehaven make love to her, and if now she should continue to allow him such liberty she should be cheapening herself like a woman of pleasure. If at first she had rejoiced in her own position as a countess, all that self-satisfaction was now incorporated in this unborn son to be magnified by him into nobility and all that was expressed by nobility in its fullest sense. The thrill that every woman, however much she may dread or resent it, feels at the first prospect of maternity was for Dorothy heightened beyond any comparison that would not be blasphemous. On this small green earth would walk a Viscount Clare that, having taken flesh from a Vanity girl, should be the savior of his country. It no longer mattered that her husband was blind to the duties of his rank when she held in her womb, not some political pawn-broker like Disraeli, but an incarnation of the benign genius of aristocracy, a being that would indeed ennoble herself. Yet the father of this prodigy regarded him merely as an unwelcome hindrance to his plan for spending the winter in London. If it were not for the duty she owed to a great house to produce other children, and so by every means in mortal power save the family from extinction, she should never again live with Tony as his wife. What had been all their kisses except the prelude to this event? Did he with his boots and his guns suppose that as a man he counted with this unborn son within her? Poor vain fool, not to have comprehended that every conjugal duty, every social obligation, every movement of her head, every flash of her eye, every offer of her hand since she came to Clare had been consecrated to this great issue. Yet his flimsy imagination, which, were it never so flimsy, might at such a moment have managed to spur his body to kneel in awe of the future, had thought of nothing except to make love as lightly as he had made incessant love to her ever since they were married. Love! What did she care for that kind of love? Only for this result, only because she had believed that perfect fruit comes from perfect blossom, had she yielded to him all of herself with passion, sometimes with ecstasy. And now her reward was at hand. The wild autumnal gales might sweep round the ancient house, but at last it was secure; she, Dorothy Lonsdale, had secured it.

There was no hunting, of course, for Dorothy this season, not even in so mild a form as cubbing, and, amorous of solitude, she often used to walk by herself to Clarehaven; there, on one of those green headlands that had withstood the sea when the fortifications of Clare had crumbled in the foaming tide, she would sit by the hour, drinking in from the salt blast strength and endurance for this son of hers dedicate from the womb to his country and to his order. On those wild days the little church, which belonged to the dim origins of the family and had been built by sea-rovers to abide in their hearts while they were seafaring, became a true shrine for her. She would take refuge there from the fury of the storm, and there sit in an ancient chair bleached and worm-eaten, her eyes fixed upon that east window stained by nothing save spindrift and scud from the sea. The wind would howl and shriek, would rattle at the hasps of the narrow windows like hands entreating shelter, would drum and whistle and moan by the old oaken doors, while Dorothy sat in a stillness of gray light, herself radiant with that first beauty of coming motherhood before the weary months of waiting have begun to drag the cheeks. There for hours she would sit, her eyes shining, her neck blue-veined with blood coursing to reinforce the second life that was in the making, her complexion not paragoned by the petal of any rose in all the roses that ever had or ever would bloom at Clare.

Everything in the little church had taken on a luminous gray from the open space of light by which it was surrounded. The altar was of granite; the candlesticks of pewter; the crucifix of silver. Wise with all his follies, the rector had chosen this church to express whatever, still untainted by expediency or snobbery, was left of his inmost aspirations, and here he had allowed nothing to affront the stark simplicity of such architecture. Here there were no chrysanthemums in brazen vases, only sprigs of sea-holly gathered by children on the salt edge of the downs, sea-holly from the fled summer that preserved the illusion of having been gathered yesterday. The benches had not been varnished; year by year they had slowly assumed that desiccated appearance of age which gives to wood thus mellowed a strangely immaterial look, a lightness and a grace, rough-hewn though it be, that varnished wood never acquires. In this building, wrought, it seemed, by labor of wind and cloud, of air and rain, Dorothy's coloring exceeded richness; when the yellow winter sun shone through the landward windows the effulgence mingled with the hue of her cheeks to incarnadine the very air around her and blush upon the stones beyond. How often had she sat thus in meditation upon nothing except the power and strength of her unborn son! Could her husband wait beside her in this church where his pirate ancestors, dripping with sea-water, had thanked God for their deliverance and for booty stacked upon the beach below? Not he! He would be trying to play with her wrist all the time, pecking at her with kisses like a canary at a lump of sugar.

Dorothy had no desire to make a secret of her condition; she was only too anxious that everybody who could appreciate its importance should be made aware of it. Yet there was nothing in her of the gross femininity that takes a pleasure in accentuating the outward signs of approaching motherhood and, as if it had done something unusual, rejoices in a physical condition that is attainable by all women. Dorothy's pride lay in giving an heir to a great family, not in adding another piece of carnality to the human race. Compared with most women, the grace and beauty with which she expressed her state was that of a budding daffodil beside a farrowing sow. So little indeed did Tony realize her condition that in January, on the anniversary of their wedding, he half jestingly rallied her on simulating it to keep him down in Clare. He added other reasons, which offended her so deeply that for the rest of these months she demanded a room to herself. Dorothy knew that by loosening the physical hold she had over him she was taking a risk, but she staked everything in the future upon the birth of this son, and she declined to imperil his perfection upon earth by unpleasant thoughts in these crucial months of his making. Perhaps, if she had been patient and taken a little trouble to explain her point of view more fully to Tony, he might have understood, but she was so intent upon aiding this other life within her that she could not spare a moment to educate her husband.

The super-dowager of Chatfield had kissed her grandson's wife on Christmas Eve, and when at Candlemas the old lady died Dorothy was sad to think she had not lived to kiss her son. The manner of her death was characteristic. February had come in with a spell of balmy weather, and Lady Chatfield, according to her habit on fine days, insisted upon going out to sun herself in front of the house. In this occupation she was often annoyed by hens invading the drive; to guard herself against their aggression she used always to be armed with several bundles of fagots, which she kept at her side to fling at the aggressive birds. Her son had often begged that she would allow the hens to be kept far enough away from the house to secure her against their trespassing; but the old lady really enjoyed the sport and passed many contented hours shooting at them like this with fagots. Unfortunately, that Candlemas morning, either she had come out insufficiently provided with ammunition or the birds were particularly venturesome. When the luncheon-bell rang there was not a fagot left, and a quantity of hens were clucking with impunity round her still form. At such a crisis her self-propelling chair must have refused to work for the first time; with ammunition exhausted, transport destroyed, communications cut, and the enemy advancing from every point, the old lady had died of exasperation. The dowager, grieved by what in her heart she felt was an unseemly way of dying and faintly puzzled how to picture her mother in the heavenly courts, spent a good deal of time in Little Cherrington church, praying that she would be humble in Paradise. The dowager's childlike and apprehensive fancy played round an apocalyptic vision of her mother criticizing the sit of a halo, or poking with a palm-branch just men in the eye. She confided some of these fears to Mr. Beadon, who tried to impress upon her his own conceptions of Eternal Life, gently and respectfully rebuking her for the materialism of which she was guilty. Dorothy found something most admirable in the super-dowager's death; she wished her own unborn son might inherit his great-grandmother's pertinacity and defiance for the time when, like intrusive poultry, democracy should invade the privileges of his order.

The dowager's loss of her mother was followed in March by a blow that upset her more profoundly. During a fierce gale a large elm-tree in Little Cherrington churchyard was blown down and in its fall broke the Burne-Jones window that commemorated the fourth earl. It was no great loss to art, but the effect upon the dowager was tremendous. The shock of seeing the irreverent winds of March blowing through that colored screen she had set up between herself and the reality of her husband destroyed the figment of him that her pampered imagination had elaborated, and she remembered him as he was—an ill-tempered gambler, a drunken spendthrift, always with that fixed leer of ataxy for a pretty woman ... she remembered how once she had overheard somebody say that Clarehaven was now a rake without a handle. Her conscience was pricked; she must warn Dorothy of what the Clare inheritance might include.

"Dorothy dear," she implored. "I don't like to seem interfering, but I do beg you not to leave Tony alone too much. I fear for him. I—" with whispers and head-shakes she poured out the true story of her married life.

But Dorothy, with her whole being concentrated upon that unborn son, had no vigilance to waste on Tony. If he should go to the bad, let him go. The sins of the fourth earl and the follies of the fifth should all be forgotten in that paragon the sixth. At the same time, the dowager's story left its mark on

Dorothy; thenceforward, when she paced the long picture-gallery of Clare, she would often ask herself in affright what passions and vices, what weakness, shame, and folly, had been cloaked by those painted forms of ancestors. She would give him her flesh; but he must inherit from them also; from those unblinking eyes he must derive some of the gleams in his own. But it should be from his mother that he derived most ... then she caught her breath. If that were so he would have in him something of Gilbert Caffyn, of that hypocrite her father. When the dowager's window was broken air was let in upon Dorothy's painted screen as well. She was honest with herself on those mornings when she paced the long gallery; she made no more pretense of romantic origins; the Lonsdale bugle-horn was cracked and useless. By what she was should her son live, not by what she liked to think she might be. Some of the strength that she had summoned for him during those autumnal hours in the little church by the sea she begged now for herself; while she defied those frigid glances that ever watched her progress up and down, up and down that long gallery, she stripped herself of all sham glories and for the sake of him within her dedicated herself to truth. Lady Godiva, riding naked through the streets of Coventry, was not more heroic than Dorothy riding naked through her own mind for the sake of that Lucius-Clare-to-be called by courtesy Viscount Clare.

Dorothy had chosen Lucius for his name after that other viscount who was Secretary of State to Charles I, that Lucius Cary who was killed at Newbury and whose story she had happened upon while reading tales of the great dead. If Lucius, Viscount Clare, could be like Lucius, Viscount Falkland, what would West Kensington matter? What would the Vanity mean, or that flat round the corner? What would signify the plebeian soul of her father?

The only person at present to whom Dorothy confided the name she had chosen was Arabella. The two girls had been very sympathetic during those winter months, and had entirely devoted themselves to their sister-in-law. At first, when she had withdrawn herself every day to go and meditate in Clarehaven church, they had been shy of intruding upon her; but their interest in family affairs, from those of guinea-pigs to those of cottagers, had become so much a part of their ordinary life that they could not resist trying to obtain Dorothy's permission for them to be interested in hers. Connie, whose main object was to watch over Dorothy's physical well-being, was ready to give it as much devotion as she would have given to a favorite mare in foal or to a litter of blind retriever pups; Arabella, who had inherited some of the dowager's ability to dream, was content to sit for as long as Dorothy wanted her company and talk of nothing except the future greatness of her nephew. Connie brought pillows for Dorothy's back; Arabella brought her books, in one of which Dorothy read about that very noble gentleman, Lucius Cary.

In February Clarehaven went up to town, partly because shooting was over, partly because he did not want to attend his grandmother's funeral. His behavior was commented upon harshly by Fanhopes and Clares alike; barely two years after her marriage Dorothy found that she, who was supposed to have been going to bring the families to ruin and disgrace, was now regarded as their salvation. Whatever she said was listened to with respect, whatever she did was regarded with approval. Before her pregnancy, Dorothy's conceit would have been gratified by such deference; now it only possessed a value for her son's sake. She longed more than ever for general esteem; but she coveted it for him, that he might grow up with pride and confidence in his mother.

When primroses lightened the woods of Clare like an exquisite dawn between the dusk of violets and the deep noon of bluebells, Connie exercised her authority over her half of Dorothy, forbade so much reading indoors, and prescribed walks. Dorothy now haunted the recesses of the woodland; when Tony, who had received a number of reproachful letters for staying in town at such a time, came back, she was gentler with him than any of the others were.

Those days spent in watching the deer, already snow-flecked to match the dappled sunlight of the woods, had been so enriched by contemplation of the active grace and beauty of these wild things that Dorothy discovered in herself a new affection for Tony, an affection born of gratitude to him, because it was he who had given her all this. He came back on a murmurous afternoon of mid-May. Dorothy was sitting upon the summit of a knoll where a few tall beeches scarcely troubled the sunlight with their high fans of lucent green. Beneath her ran a meadow threaded with the gold of cowslips, and while she stared into cuckoo-haunted distances she heard above the buzzing of the bees the sound of his car. Starting up, she waved to him, so that he stopped the car and ran up the slope to greet her.

"Why, Doodles, what's the matter?" he exclaimed. "You've been crying."

He was embarrassed by her hot wet cheeks when she pressed them to his.

"No, they're happy tears," she said. "I was thinking of him and that one day all this will be his." She caught the landscape in a gesture. "All the autumn, Tony, I prayed for him to be great and strong, and all the winter that he might be great and good. Now I think I should be happy if he did nothing more remarkable than love this land—his land. Tony, don't you feel how wonderful it is that you and I should give somebody all this?"

Formerly, when Dorothy had talked about their son, the father had not been able to grasp that there would ever be such a person. Now in this month before the birth he experienced a sudden awe in regarding his wife. That embrace she had given him for welcome, her figure, the look in her eyes—they were strange to him; she was strange to him—a new mysterious creature that awed him as an abstraction of womanhood, not as a lovely girl that granted or refused him kisses.

"I say, Doodles, I feel an awful brute for going away like that."

She laughed lightly.

"You needn't. I was happier alone. Don't look so disconsolate. I'm glad you've come now."

"I didn't stay up for the Derby," he pleaded, in extenuation of his neglect.

She laughed again.

"Tony, you haven't yet heard his name. I've chosen Lucius."

"That's a rum name. Why Latin all of a sudden? Or if Latin, why not Marcus Antoninus, don't you know?"

"It's a name I like very much."

He looked at her suspiciously.

"Who did you know called Lucius?"

"Nobody. It's a name I like. That's all."

"You promise me you never knew anybody called Lucius?" He had caught her hand.

"Never."

"All right. You can have it."

But the nimbus round her motherhood was for the husband melted by the breath of jealousy. Let children come to interrupt their love, she would be his again soon; and what trumpery she made of those women with whom he had played in London as a lonely child plays with dolls.

Dorothy's confinement was expected about the middle of June. When the nurse arrived, for the first time in all these months she began to have fears. She never doubted that the baby would be a boy; but she had dark fancies of monstrosity and madness, and the nurse had all she could do to reassure her. The weather during the first week of the month was damp and gusty; after that gilded May-time it seemed worse than it really was. The rustling of the vexed foliage held a menace that the sharp whistle of the winter gales had lacked. However, by the middle of the month the weather had changed for the better, and the last day was perfect.

When Dorothy's travail began in the afternoon, the nurse asked for the mowing of the lawns to be stopped, because she thought the noise would irritate her patient. Dorothy, however, told her that she liked the noise; in the comparatively long intervals between the first pains the mower consoled her with its pretense of mowing away the minutes and thus of audibly bringing the time of her achievement nearer.

The car was sent off to Exeter for another doctor, notwithstanding Dorothy's wish that nobody except Doctor Lane should attend her. The old gentleman had much endeared himself by his lessons in natural history, and that he should crown his teaching by a practical demonstration of his knowledge struck her as singularly appropriate. Doctor Lane himself expressed great anxiety for assistance, because it looked as if the confinement was going to be long and difficult. So hard was her labor, indeed, that when the Exeter doctor arrived it was decided to give her chloroform.

"Nothing's the matter, is it?" she murmured, perceiving that preparations were going on round her. "Why doesn't he come? Nurse," she called, "if babies take a long time, it means usually that the head is very large, doesn't it?"

"Very often, my lady, yes. Oh yes, it does mean that very often. Try and lie a little bit easier, dear. That's right."

"I think I'm rather glad," said Dorothy, painfully. "Lord Salisbury had an enormous head."

"Fever?" whispered Doctor Lane, in apprehensively questioning tones. "Tut, tut!"

Dorothy tried to smile at the silly old thing; but the pain was too much for smiles.

There was another long consultation, and presently she heard Lord Clarehaven being sent for.

"What's the matter?" she asked, sharply. "I'm not going to die, am I? I won't. I won't. He mustn't be brought up by anybody else."

The nurse patted her hand. Outside some argument was going on, rising and falling like the lawn-mower.

"A pity it's so dark," Dorothy murmured. "The mower had stopped, and I liked the humming. All that talking in the corridor isn't so restful. What's the time?"

"About half past ten, my lady."

A mighty pain racked her, a rending pain that seemed to leave her with reluctance as if it had failed to hurt her enough. Her whole body shivered when the pain passed on, and she had a feeling that it was a personality, so complete was it, a personality that was only waiting in a corner of the room and gathering new strength to rend her again.

Delirium touched her with hot fingers. It seemed that her body was like the small triangle of uncut corn round which the reaper relentlessly hums. It was coming again; it would tear the fibers of her again; it was coming; the humming was nearer every moment. In an effort to check the incommunicable experiences of fever, she asked if it was not the lawn-mower that was humming.

"No, dear, it's the doctors talking to his lordship."

"What about?"

The humming ceased, for they gave her chloroform. When she came to herself she lay for a second or two with closed eyes; then slowly, luxuriously nearly, she opened them wide to look at her son. There was nobody.

"Where is he?" she gasped, sitting up, dizzy and sick with the drug, but with all her nerves strung to unnatural, uncanny perceptiveness.

The dowager was leaning over the bed and begging her to lie down.

"What's burning my face?" cried Dorothy.

"It must be my tears," her mother-in-law sobbed.

"Why are you crying? My boy, where is he? Where is he? Oh, tell me, tell me, please tell me!"

The dowager and the nurse were looking at each other pitifully.

"Dorothy, my poor child, he was born dead."

The mother shrieked, for a pain that cut her ten thousand times more sharply than all the pains of her travail united in a single spasm.

"It was a question, dear, of saving your life or losing the baby's."

"You're lying to me," Dorothy shrieked. "It was a monster! I know that. It was a monster, and it had to be strangled. Oh, Doctor Lane, Doctor Lane, why did you let them bring another doctor? You promised me you wouldn't."

"No, no," said the dowager. "It was a perfect little boy with such lovely little hands and toes. Everything perfect; but his head was too large, dear. It was a question of you or him, and of course Tony insisted that he should be sacrificed."

"Where is he? Tony!"

Her husband came in and knelt by the bed.

"Why did you do that? Why? Why didn't you let me die? He would have been so much better than me. Can't you understand? Can't you understand?"

Everybody had stolen from the room to leave them together; but when he leaned over to kiss her she struck him on the mouth.

"You only wanted me for one thing," she cried.

"Doodles, don't treat me like this. I can't express myself. I never imagined that anything could be so horrible. I was asked to decide. You don't suppose I could have lived with a cursed child who had killed you!"

"How dare you curse him?"

"Dorothy, we'll have another. Don't be so miserable."

Suddenly she felt that nothing mattered.

"Will we?" she asked, indifferently.

"And we'll go up to town this autumn."

"Yes, there's nothing to keep us here," she said, "now."

CHAPTER V

I

ONE HUNDRED AND TWENTY-NINE Curzon Street was the dowry that the third Marquess of Longlan provided for his daughter, Lady Caroline Lacey, on her marriage in 1818 with Viscount Clare, the only son of the second Earl of Clarehaven. It was a double-fronted Georgian house with a delicate fanlight over the door, from which a fan-shaped flight of steps guarded by a pair of tall iron flambeau-stands led down to the pavement. That famous old beau, the first marquess, had given an eye to the architecture, and, being himself a man of fine proportions, had seen to it that the rooms of his new house would set off his figure to advantage. Solid without being stolid, dignified but never pompous, graceful but nowhere flimsy, and for everybody except the servants, who lived like corpses in a crypt, convenient—the town residence of Lord Clarehaven was as desirable as those desirable young men of Assyria upon whom in their blue clothes Aholah doted not less promiscuously than house-agents have doted upon a good biblical word.

When the second earl took charge of his wife's dowry, the fashions of the Regency were in the meridian, and the house was decorated and furnished to suit the prevailing mode. Apart from the verse of the period, there have been few manifestations of art and craft more detestable either for beauty or for comfort than those of the Regency. Great bellying lumps of furniture as fat and foul as the First Gentleman himself, and with as much superfluity of ornament as the First Gentleman's own clothes, were introduced into 129 Curzon Street to spoil the fine severity of the Georgian structure. Ugly furniture was added by the third earl, whose taste—he was a vice-chamberlain of the royal household in the 'fifties—was affected by his position as a mind is affected by misfortune. The dowager during the esthetic ardors that glowed upon the first years of her married life hung a few green and yellow draperies in the drawing-room, and during the early 'nineties she stocked these with woolen spiders or with butterflies of silk and velvet; in fact, when the fifth earl took over the control of his town house it was filled from the cellars to the attics with the accumulated abominations of eighty-five barbarous years. No doubt he would never have noticed the ugliness of the furniture if the discomfort of it had not been so obtrusive; but when he was planning to live merrily with his bride in Curzon Street he invited Messrs. Waring & Gillow to bring the house up to date with its own period and the present, allowing them a free hand with everything except the chairs, beds, and sofas, of which it was stipulated that none was to rate form or style above comfort. On the whole the result was an improvement; and since there are always enough relays of new competitors in the race for originality, purchasers were soon found even for those triads of chairs that are still seen in mid-Victorian drawing-rooms like empty cruets upon the mantelpiece of a coffee-room, and Tony was able to get a good price for the furniture of Gillows, who were by now as thoroughly worm-eaten as their handicraft. The arrangement with the decorators being modified by Dorothy's unwillingness to live in London, he postponed the complete renovation of the house to that happy date in the future when he and she should agree that East West, town's best.

Now at Clare, when Dorothy was lying in bed, careless of everything, Tony invited her to choose patterns from the books of wall-papers and chintzes sent down by Messrs. Waring & Gillow. Finding his wife in no mood to choose anything, he decided to gratify as well as he was able the taste she had expressed five or six years ago in the Halfmoon Street flat. The result was a series of what are called "chaste color schemes," which after being debauched by numerous chairs upholstered in glossy scarlet leather became positively meretricious under the temptation of silver-cased blotters and almanacs; four months after Dorothy's confinement the transformation of 129 Curzon Street into the dream of a Vanity girl was complete. She was still in too listless a mood to do anything except give a tired assent to whatever her husband proposed; physically and emotionally she was worn out, and when a second agricultural fête and flower-show was billed for August 25, 1908, she scarcely had the heart to present in person the silver cup and five pounds for the best flowers grown from the seeds she had supplied with such enthusiasm. Every adjunct of the show accentuated her own failure; from the women with their new babies to the chickens and the parsnips, everything seemed a rebuke to her own sterility.

Dorothy's pride might often degenerate into mere self-confidence, but it had hitherto been her mainstay in life; her failure to produce that son had sapped the foundations of pride by destroying self-confidence; her dignity as Tony's wife had been assailed, and she began to fret about the shallowness of her feeling for her husband. She would have been able to support a blow that fell with equal heaviness upon both, because she would have rejoiced in proving to Tony that she was more courageous than he; but he, from want of imagination, had let her feel that she had made a fuss about nothing; his attitude had been such, indeed, that in resuming relations with him she could not dispel the morbid fancy that she was behaving like his kept mistress. Once, in her determination to define their respective views of marriage, she asked him how he could bear to make love to a woman who was apparently so cold; in his answer he implied that her coldness was rather attractive than otherwise.

"But if you thought I really hated you to come near me?" she pressed.

"You don't really," he replied, and she turned away with a sigh of exasperation at the astonishing lack of sensitiveness in the male.

"You're nervy and strung up just at present," he went on. "And perhaps it has been bad for you to have so much of me all the time. But when you go back to town and find that you're envied by other women...."

"Because I'm married to you?" she interrupted, sharply.

"No, no, Doodles, I'm not so conceited as all that. Envied because you will be the loveliest of them all. But other men will envy me because I've got you for a wife. I don't think you realize how lovely you are."

She did realize it perfectly; but she resented a compliment that was inspired by self-satisfaction.

"The pleasure in being married to me, then," she challenged, "is that you're keeping me from other men? You wouldn't mind if I told you that I hated you, that I only married you to have rank and money, that I hooked you in the way an angler hooks a fat trout?"

"I was quite content to be hooked," said Tony.

"If I were unfaithful to you?"

His eyes hardened for a moment, like those of a groom who is being defied by a jibbing horse.

"Try it, old thing," he advised, and the whistle that lisped gently between his set teeth made expressive the quick breaths of rage that such a question evoked.

It was the day after the flower-show; they were sitting on the curved seat at the end of the pergola. Dorothy's question had an effect upon the conversation as if a painter had begged them to sustain a certain attitude until he could perpetuate it by his art; the stillness of deep summer undisturbed by a bird's note or by a whisper of a falling leaf was like thick green paint from which their forms, hastily sketched in, faintly emerged. Tony's whistle had ceased and he was stroking his mustache as if the action could help him to realize that he was alive. There seemed no reason why they should not sit there forever, like the statues all round, or the ladies and lovers in a picture by Mr. Marcus Stone. It was Tony who broke the spell by getting up and announcing business with somebody somewhere.

Dorothy, left alone on the seat, watched his form recede along the pergola, and asked herself in perplexity what she wanted as a substitute for that well-groomed, easy, and assured piece of manhood. If she was trying to tell herself that she pined to love a man without thought of children or considerations of rank and fortune, she could always elope with the first philanderer that presented himself. But she could not imagine any man for whose sake she would sacrifice as much. To be sure, she was not yet twenty-five; there lay before her many long years, one of which a grand passion might shorten to an hour. But could she ever fall in love? It was not merely because she was hard and ambitious that she was not in love with Tony and that she could not imagine herself in love with anybody else. In all her life no man had presented himself whom she could imagine in the occupation of anything like the half of one's personality that being in love would imply. Indeed, if she looked back upon the men she had known, she liked Tony best personally, apart from the material advantages that being married to him offered. Perhaps the mood she was in was nothing more than a morbid fastidiousness caused by physical exhaustion; perhaps by going up to town and leading another sort of life she should be able to view marriage more naturally. She had always criticized other women for the ease with which they fell into a habit of indulging themselves with the traditional prerogatives of their sex. Her own path had always lain so obviously in front of her nose that she had been impatient of the incommunicable aspirations expressed by other women with sighs and yearning glances; to her such women had always appeared like the tiresome people who are proud of not possessing what they would call "the bump of locality." Such dubious and apprehensive temperaments had always irritated her; madness itself was for Dorothy the result of a carefully cultivated hysteria; even illness had always seemed to her only a fraudulent method of securing attention. Was she now to array herself in the trappings of conventional femininity? She bent her mind—and it was not a pliable mind—as straight as she was able, and told herself that even if she failed ultimately to produce an heir no one could question her fitness and willingness to produce an heir. Anything that went wrong in the marriage would not be her fault. As a wife she had justified herself; and if motherhood was to be denied her—oh well, what did all this matter? She was too much exhausted to keep her mind straight, and at the first relaxation of her will it jumped away from her control like the mainspring of a watch, the quivering coils of which, though they were all of a piece, were impossible to trace consecutively to their beginning or end. The monotonous green of late summer depressed her wherever she looked; earth was hot and tired, as hot and tired as one of the women at the show yesterday. Life was not much more varied than a big turnip-field in which two or three coveys of birds were put up, some to be killed, some to be wounded, some to whir away into turnip-fields beyond.

"Which means that I'm still thoroughly exhausted," Dorothy murmured. "But I can't think of the past because he is there, and the future seems dreary because he will never be there."

When at the beginning of October the moment came to drive up to London, the problems of birth and death, of love and happiness, were overshadowed by the refusal of the car to go even as far as Exeter.

"We really must get a Lee-Lonsdale," said Tony. He made this announcement in the same tone, Dorothy reflected bitterly, as he had announced that they would have another baby.

When the butler opened the door of 129 Curzon Street, the house was full of birds' singing.

"Canaries, don't you know, and all that," Tony explained. "I thought you'd like to be reminded of the country."

Dorothy looked at him sharply to see if he was teasing her, but he was serious enough, and for the first time since that night in June when her son was born dead she was able to feel an affection for him so personal and so intimate that if they had been alone at the moment she might have flung herself into his arms. He had taken a box for the theater that night and was most eager for her to dine out with him, but she was much tired after the journey and excused herself. Since he was evidently dismayed by the prospect of an unemployed evening, she begged him to go without her, which after a short and not very stoutly contested argument he agreed to do.

Dorothy went up early to her bedroom, where for a long while she sat at the open window, listening to the traffic. How often she had sat thus at the window of her bedroom in Halfmoon Street and what promises of grandeur had then seemed implicit in the majestic sound. Only three years ago she had still been in Halfmoon Street; she could actually remember one October night like this, an October night when the still warm body of a dead summer was being pricked by wintry spears. On such a night as this Olive had called to her not to take cold, had warned her that it was bad for her voice to sit at an open window. She had been thinking about herself in Debrett and planning to be a marchioness; it was Olive's interruption which had brought home sharply to her the necessity of cutting herself off forever from the theater if she married Clarehaven. Yes, it had been a night just like this, and that other window was not five minutes away from where she was sitting now.

A taxi humming round a distant corner reminded Dorothy of an evening on the lawns at Clare when Doctor Lane had lectured her on the habits of night-jars.

"Country sights and country sounds," she exclaimed, and she shivered in a revulsion against them all, because, though she had proved her ability to share in that country life, the blind overseer Fate had withdrawn her to another environment and the overseer must always be propitiated.

The sound of the traffic was casting a spell upon Dorothy's tired nerves; she began to take pleasure in it, welcoming it as a sound familiar and cherished over many years. She looked back at herself a year ago sitting in Clarehaven church, with almost a blush for the affectation of it all, or rather for what must have seemed like affectation to other people. She had allowed herself to exaggerate everything, to dream sublimely and wake ridiculously, to be more than she was ever meant to be. Not music of wind and sea, but this dull music of London traffic was the fit accompaniment for her. She knew that now, when her own sighs absorbed in the countless sighs of the millions round her took their place in the great harmony of human sorrow. Above the castanets of hansoms and the horns of motors the omnibuses rolled like drums ... the hansoms were going back, back, the motors were going forward; but the omnibuses were going home, home, home. And was not her own journey through life like journeys she had taken as a child when the omnibus after a glittering evening went home, rumbling and rolling home?

Dorothy had nearly fallen asleep; waking to full consciousness with a start, she laughed at her fancies; quickly shutting the window, she drew the curtains and walked about the golden bedroom as if she would assure herself that the evening was not nearly spent yet, that not for her was some dim omnibus waiting to carry her home ... home. She checked the fresh impulse to dwell upon the monotonous rumble of the traffic and drove the sound from her mind. Of what could she complain, really? What other girl like herself would not envy her good fortune? What other girl would not laugh at her for thinking that life was dull because she had failed at the first attempt to produce a son? In this comfortable bedroom, amid flowers of chintz, was she not already more at home than she had ever been along the herbaceous borders of Clare? The fact was that her life at Clare had been a part sustained with infinite verve and accomplishment through many months, but always a part. Yes, it had been a part which she had sustained so brilliantly that she had nearly ruined the well-mounted but not very brilliant play in which she had been performing. The dowager had been right when she had expressed her fears for the effect upon Tony of his wife's behavior. She had considered her warning as kindly, but quite unnecessary; she had even pitied the poor little beaver-like dowager for likening her own position with that rake of a husband to that which Dorothy occupied in respect of the son. But the dowager had been right. Herself had risked the substance for the shadow, and in her lust for personal success she might abruptly have found that the play had stopped running. Luckily, it was not too late to remedy the mistake. Here was the scene set for a new act in which Tony must be allowed his chance. Poor old boy, he was not asking for much, and he was still so dependent upon her that it would be a pleasure to spoil him a little now. Should she not really be flattered that he loved her more than an heir to his name, his rank, and his fortune? What would it signify if the house of Clare became extinct? Would those ladies in the long gallery, those ladies simpering eternally at sea and sky, be a whit less immobile if children laughed on the lawns below? Would they blink their eyes or move a muscle of their rosy lips? Not they. And if strangers held their beauty in captivity, would they care? Not they. And if the earth fell into the sun so that nothing of poor mortality, not even Shakespeare, endured, would they simper less serenely in the moment before their painted lips blistered and were consumed? Not a whit less serenely. None of the people on other planets would care if the fifth Earl of Clarehaven was the last; even if the people of Mars had a telescope big enough to see what was happening on earth, they would only watch us with less compassion than we watch ants on a burning log.

"And if by chance they have got such a telescope," Dorothy murmured, "how absurd we must look."

Earth shrank to nothing even as she spoke, for on that thought she fell asleep where she was sitting and did not wake until Tony came back.

"Hullo, Doodles! Why do you go to sleep in your chair?" he asked.

"Did you enjoy the theater?"

"Well, as a matter of fact," he admitted, "I didn't use the box. I thought, as you wouldn't come, I'd drop in and have a look at the new show at the Vanity. Pretty good, really. Your friend Olive Fanshawe was in a quintet. She has a few lines to speak, too, and looks very jolly. I wish you'd come with me one night. I think you'd enjoy it."

"I will if you like," said Dorothy.

"No, really?" he exclaimed, his eyes lighting up. "Now, isn't that splendid! I'll tell you what we'll do. We'll have a party for my birthday next week. Dine at the Carlton. Two boxes at the Vanity, and supper afterward at the Savoy. I say I shall enjoy it, Doodles!"

"How old will you be?" she asked, with a smile.

"Twenty-six. Aging fast. Have to hurry up and enjoy ourselves while we can."

"I shall be twenty-five in March," she said.

Then suddenly she seemed able to throw off all her fatigue and to forget all her disappointment.

"Sorry I've been so dull these last few weeks," she murmured. "Tony, do you still love me?"

"You never need ask me that," he said. "But do you love me?"

She nodded.

"Couldn't you say it? You never have, you know. Couldn't you just whisper 'yes'?"

"Yes."

"Cleared it," he shouted, and while he was in his dressing-room she heard him singing:

"For Dolly's out and about again,
She doesn't give a damn for a shower of rain.
Here's Dolly with her collie!
And London, dear old London,
London is itself again."

This outburst was followed by a silence which was presently broken by a sound of torn paper.

"What are you tearing up, Tony?"

"Oh, nothing," he called back, in accents of elaborate indifference. "Only an old program."

In the morning Dorothy looked in the paper-basket, the bottom of which was lightly powdered by the fragments of a letter. She stooped to pick up the pieces; then she stopped.

"What does it matter who it was for? It was never sent. But I was only just in time."

On October 15th a party of eight visited "The Belle of Belgravia" at the Vanity. Besides Tony and Dorothy, there were Arthur Lonsdale, who had long forgotten all about Queenie Molyneux and could now watch a musical comedy as coldly as a dramatic critic whose paper did not depend on the theatrical advertisements. He brought his partner, Adrian Lee, whose pretty little wife, all cheeks and hair, looked much more like an actress than Dorothy, though she was really the daughter of a bishop. People used to wonder how a bishop came to have such a daughter; they forgot that while he was a vicar he had written a commentary on the Song of Solomon, with foot-notes as luscious as the plums that sink to the bottom of a cake. Harry Tufton came, and a Mrs. Foster-ffrench who went everywhere except where she most wanted to go and was always a little resentful that even with her two "f's" she could not hook herself up to some altitudes. However, that was Mrs. Foster-ffrench's private sorrow, and she did not let it mar a jolly evening. The other guests were Capt. Archibald Keith, late of the 16th Hussars, who had abandoned the cavalry in order to write the librettos of musical comedies, and a Mrs. Mainwaring, who kept a fashionable hat-shop in Bruton Street and was the widow of poor Dick Mainwaring, a brother of Lord Hughenden.

Everybody always spoke about him as poor Dick Mainwaring, but whether because he had been killed at Paardeburg or because he had married Rita Daubeny was uncertain; it probably varied with the point of view of the speaker. The friends of Mrs. Mainwaring put down any oddness in her behavior to French creole blood and a childhood in Martinique; to the former was also attributable her chic in hats; to the latter the dryness and pallor of her complexion; French blood or French brandy, Martinique or Martell, the Hon. Mrs. Richard Mainwaring certainly did stimulate conversation just as paprika stimulates the appetite. But however jocund her life, her hats were chaste, and however sharp her play, her name was honorable. Moreover, so many people owed her money that they had to be pleasant to her. Mrs. Foster-ffrench, in spite of her name, had no French blood to excuse her odd behavior; in fact, she had nothing except a hyphen and those two "f's." Mr. Foster-ffrench was a younger son who, having failed to grow sisal profitably in the Bahamas, was now experimenting in Mozambique with the jikungo or Inhambane nut, and liable at any moment to experiment with vanila in Tahiti or pearls on the Great Barrier Reef; the only experiment he was never likely to make was going back to Mrs. Foster-ffrench. Dorothy wondered what Tony found to attract him in such a gathering; yet he was in tremendous spirits, obviously delighted that Archie Keith should have met the Vanity comedian that afternoon and warned him who would be in front. He was proud that all the girls on the stage kept their eyes on Dorothy throughout the evening, proud that the comedian inserted two special gags for the benefit of the jolly party, which were rewarded by a loud burst of laughter; and when the alarmed audience trained their opera-glasses upon the boxes as a beleagured garrison might train their guns upon the wild yell of savages he was radiant. After the performance they sat round a large circular table in the Savoy, and when the orchestra played "Dolly and her Collie" there was so much applause from the tables all round that Dorothy could not help feeling rather proud of the pleasure her return to town had given and was touched to think that her memory was still green. The evening wound up at the Lees' flat in Berkeley Street, when Adrian Lee and Clarehaven hospitably lost a good deal of money to their guests in the course of three hours' baccarat.

Now that Dorothy had broken her rule and had visited the Vanity for the first time since she had left the boards, she felt that she could not maintain her policy of isolation any longer; she told Clarehaven as much when they were strolling back down Curzon Street and breathing in the air of night after those feverish rooms.

"Doodles, my dear thing, I'm delighted! I never wanted you to give up any of your old friends. It was you who insisted on cutting them out like that."

"And if," she went on, "we can sit in a box with Rita Mainwaring, I don't think I can keep up this pretense of not being able to meet Olive."

"I quite agree with you. I should love to meet Olive again."

"Then what about asking her to lunch?" Dorothy suggested.

"The sooner the better," he assented, enthusiastically.

A note was sent round to the Vanity, in which Dorothy, without making the least allusion to anything that had happened in the past, most cordially invited Olive to lunch with them two days later. Olive replied, thanking Dorothy for the invitation, but mentioned that she was now living with Sylvia Scarlett, and, since she did not like to go without her and since she knew Dorothy and Sylvia were no longer on good terms, was afraid she must decline lunch, though she promised to come and see her old friend some afternoon.

"Living with Sylvia Scarlett, eh?" commented Tony, with raised eyebrows.

They were sitting in the smoking-room, where in the silence that ensued the red arm-chairs seemed to be commenting upon this problem raised so suddenly, seemed, like wise and rubicund ministers of state, to be bringing their minds to bear silently upon things in general. "Sylvia Scarlett!" Dorothy kept saying to herself, while the scarlet leather answered her. She was perplexed. For one reason she should like to meet Sylvia again, because she felt that better, perhaps, than anybody Sylvia would appreciate her point of view. Could she but bring herself to be frank with Sylvia, she could think of no one who would respond with a more intelligent sympathy to the tale of her disappointment. Moreover, if she showed the least disinclination to exclude Sylvia she might give Tony the impression that she was still resenting that week-end at Brighton, a notion which her pride was not sufficiently subdued to contemplate with equanimity. Yet to make friends again with Sylvia openly would be to penetrate rather more deeply into the hinterland of the bohemian seacoast than she had intended, even after going to the Vanity with Mrs. Mainwaring and Mrs. Foster-ffrench.

"I suppose you wouldn't care to have Sylvia here," Tony said at last; "though of course...."

Dorothy interrupted him sharply. "Why not?" she asked. "Why should I object to have Sylvia here any more than I should object to being seen at the theater with Rita Mainwaring?"

"I thought that perhaps...." he began again.

She told him to ring for a messenger-boy and immediately wrote to invite Sylvia to lunch as well.

It was difficult, considering the circumstances in which Dorothy had parted from Sylvia and Olive, for any of the girls to avoid a feeling of constraint when they met again; Dorothy, for her part, had to make a great effort not to let her nervousness give an impression that she was being reserved with her old friends. Lonsdale, however, who had fortunately been invited, was very talkative, and Tony was in boisterous spirits, so boisterous, indeed, that once or twice Dorothy looked at him in surprise. When he returned her glance defiantly she wondered if she had not made a mistake in her policy; if before consenting to come down to her husband's level she had properly safeguarded herself. No doubt in spite of her disapproval he would have gambled and drunk and made an ass of himself with the Mainwarings and the Foster-ffrenches, but by withholding herself she would have retained, at any rate, as much power over him as would have kept him outwardly deferential to his wife. Now he was no longer afraid of her.

Dorothy was roused from her abstraction by hearing herself addressed as Cousin Dorothy by Lonsdale. He was in a corner with Sylvia, and they were amusing themselves, presumably at her expense; Dorothy darted an angry look at Sylvia, who shook her head with so mocking a disclaimer that Dorothy gave up the notion of confiding in her old friend. Sylvia evidently still regarded her with hostility and contempt, and was as ready to pour ridicule upon her now as she used to be in the dressing-room on tour. On tour! The days on tour crowded upon her memory. From the corner where Sylvia and Lonsdale were chatting she heard Lily's name mentioned. What was that? Lily had married a croupier in Rio de Janeiro? But how unimportant it was who married what in this world. After so short a time, life lost its tender hues of sunrise or sunset and became garish or dim. On tour! The funny old life trickled confusedly past her vision like a runaway film, and she took Olive's hand affectionately. Olive was as sympathetic as if she had never been treated so heartlessly that day in Brighton, as eager to hear that Dorothy was happy, as eager to accept her assurances that she was. Tears stood in her eyes when she was told about the baby; but somehow her sympathy was not enough for Dorothy, who only awarded her a half-hearted sort of confidence that was sentimentalized to suit the listener. If she could have confided in Sylvia she would have told the story without sparing herself, but Sylvia had snubbed her; and, anyway, the past was not to be recaptured by talking about it.

Notwithstanding Sylvia's indifference, Dorothy went out of her way to invite her often to Curzon Street that autumn and early winter. She was fascinated by her play at baccarat and *chemin de fer*; she wondered upon what mysterious capital she was drawing, for, though her name was not coupled with any man who would pay her debts, she was apparently able to lose as much money as she chose. It seemed impossible that it should be her own money; but so many things about Sylvia seemed impossible. In January Olive showed symptoms of a tendency to consumption; Sylvia, without waiting an instant to win back any of her losses, took her off to Italy for a long rest.

"*I* despise Tony, and *she* despises me," Dorothy thought. "But isn't she right?"

She looked round her at the drawing-room of 129 Curzon Street, where in a foliage of tobacco smoke the faces of the gamblers stared out like fruit, and upon the green tablecloth the cards lay like fallen petals. Was not Sylvia right to despise her for encouraging Mrs. Mainwaring and Captain Keith and Mrs. Foster-ffrench and half a dozen others like them? Was not Sylvia right to despise her for setting out as a countess so haughtily and coming down to this? How she must have laughed when Olive told her about the parting in Brighton, and how little she would believe her tales of rural triumphs like the meet at Five Tree Farm. Sylvia probably considered that she had found her true level in seeing that her gambling guests were kept well supplied with refreshments.

In March even Clarehaven grew tired of baccarat with Captain Keith and the rest of them, and one morning a big new six-cylinder Lee-Lonsdale was driven up to 129 Curzon Street by the junior member of the firm, who wanted to advertise his wares on the Continent. Clarehaven's man and Dorothy's maid took the heavy luggage by train; the car with Dorothy, Lonsdale, Clarehaven, and a chauffeur swept like an arpeggio the road from London to Dover, transhipped to Calais, and made a touring-car record from Paris to Monte Carlo, whence Lonsdale, after booking some orders, returned to England without it. Tony lost five thousand pounds at roulette, a small portion of which he recovered over pigeons. He would probably have lost much more had not Dorothy told him, on a rose-hung night of stars and lamplight, that she was going to have another baby and that she must go back to Clare.

The prospective father was so pleased with the news that he set out to beat the record established by Lonsdale on the way down, drove into a poplar-tree, and smashed the car. Dorothy had a miscarriage and lay ill for a month at a small village between Grenoble and Lyons. Tony was penitent; but he was obviously bored by having to spend this idle month in France, and as soon as Dorothy was well enough to travel and he had assured himself that she was not nervous after the accident, he drove northward faster than ever. They reached Clare at the end of May.

II

The bluebells were out when Dorothy came home, their pervasive sweetness sharpened by the pungency of young bracken; even as sometimes the heavenly clouds imitate the hills and valleys of earth or lie about at sunset like islands in a luminous and windless ocean, so now earth imitated heaven, and the bluebells lay along the woodland like drifts of sky. May was not gone when Dorothy came back; the cuckoo was not even yet much out of tune; the fallow deer did not yet display all their snowy summer freckles; the whitethroat still sang to his lady sitting close in the nettles by the orchard's edge; apple-blossom was still strewn upon the lengthening grass; the orange-tip still danced along the glades; the red and white candles upon the horse-chestnuts were not yet burned out. It was still May; but June like a grave young matron stood close at hand, and May like a girl grown tired of her flowers and of her finery would presently fall asleep in her arms. And like the merry month Dorothy pillowed her head upon the green lap of June. For several weeks she made no allusion to the accident on the way home from Monte Carlo; nor, beyond the perpetually manifest joy she took in the seasonable pageant, did she give any sign of her distaste for the way she and Tony had spent the past year. The problem of what was to happen next autumn was not yet ripe for discussion, and in order to enjoy fully the present peace Dorothy persuaded Clarehaven to accept an invitation to go fishing in Norway, after which he would camp with the yeomanry for three weeks; and then another year would have to be catered for so that not one minute of it should be wasted—in other words, that it should be squeezed as dry as an orange to extract from it the last drop of pleasure. Tony wanted her to come with him to Norway, but she made her health an excuse and sent him off alone.

In July the countess and the dowager were pacing the turf that ran by the edge of that famous golden border now in its prime. The rich light of the summer afternoon flattered the long line of massed hues which had been so artfully contrived. The unfamiliar beauty of the bronzed Himalayan asphodels, of citron kniphofias from Abyssinia and sulphur-lilies from the Caucasus, of ixias tawny as their own African lions, of canary-colored Mexican tigridias and primrose-hooded gladioli that bloom in the rain forest of the Victoria Falls, mingled with the familiar forms of lemon-pale hollyhocks and snapdragons, with violas apricot-stained, and with many common yellow flowers of cottage gardens to which the nurserymen had imparted a subtle and aristocratic shade.

"What a success your golden border has been," the dowager exclaimed.

Dorothy felt suddenly that she could not any longer tolerate such compliments. The life-blood of her marriage seemed to be running dry before her eyes while she was amusing herself with golden borders, and she wanted her mother-in-law to understand how critical the position was, and what disasters lurked in the future while the sun flattered the flowers, and she flattered her son's wife.

"I'm going to be very frank," Dorothy began. "I want to know more about Tony's father."

The dowager with a look of alarm leaned over the border to hide her embarrassment.

"My dear," she said, "how cleverly you've combined this little St.-John's-wort with these copper-colored rock-roses. They look delightful together."

"Why did you marry him?" Dorothy asked.

"Dorothy! Such a question, but really, I suppose—well, I don't know. I suppose really because he asked me."

"Your mother didn't insist upon it?"

"Well, of course, my mother didn't oppose it," the dowager admitted. "No, certainly not ... she didn't actually oppose it; in fact possibly ... yes ... well.... I think one might almost say that she.... Oh, aren't these trolliums gorgeous? They are trolliums, aren't they? I always get confused between trilliums and trolliums?"

"Troll*ius*. Persuaded you into it?" Dorothy supplemented. "Did you love him?"

This was altogether too intimate an inquiry, and the dowager, failing to bury her blushes in the opulent group of butter-colored flowers that she was bending over to admire, took refuge in her bringing-up.

"We were brought up differently in those days," she said. "I don't think that men depended upon their wives to quite the same extent they do now."

"I'm asking you all this," Dorothy explained, "because as far as the future is concerned Tony and I are standing now at crossroads. If I oppose or, even without opposing them, if I fail to share in his pleasures, my attitude won't have any sobering effect. But if I take part with him willingly and enjoy what he enjoys, it may be that I shall have enough influence to prevent his going too far. Frankly, he doesn't seem to have an idea that there may be something else in life besides self-indulgence, the instant and complete self-indulgence that he always allows himself. Money and rank only exist for him because they are useful to that end. The only thing he was ever denied for five minutes of his life was myself, and after a period of active sulking he got me. I suppose you spoiled him, really."

The dowager looked melancholy.

"I'm not reproaching you," said Dorothy. "I quite understand the temptation. That's why I asked if you ever loved your husband. I thought that perhaps you didn't and that you'd had to love Tony much more in consequence. I'm sorry about that son of mine, because I should have liked to prove that it is possible to devote oneself utterly to a son without spoiling him. Meanwhile, I'm afraid it's too late to do anything with Tony. You must forgive me for this attack upon illusions. I shall never make another. I only wanted you to know, because you were kind to me when I first came here, that I've done my best and that there's nothing more to be done."

"But you're so beautiful," said the dowager. "I was never beautiful."

"Oh, so far as keeping him more or less faithful is worth while, I don't suppose I shall have the least difficulty," Dorothy admitted. "But each time I tame him with a kiss I reduce my own self-respect a little bit, and I blunt his respect for me. If I were his mistress, my kisses would be bribes to make him spend money on me; as his wife my kisses are bribes to prevent his spending money on other women. Anyway, this is the last that you or any one else shall ever hear on this rather unpleasant subject. I think these tigridias that Mr. Greenish was so keen to combine with the ixias were a mistake. They are quite faded by the afternoon."

It was now Dorothy's turn to direct the conversation toward flowers, while the dowager endeavored to keep it personal.

"I've often thought," she began, "what a pity it was for you to cut yourself off so completely from your own family."

"I certainly shouldn't find them of any help to me now," said Dorothy.

"Well, I don't know. I think that a mother can always be helpful," the dowager argued. "I think it's a pity that you should have felt the necessity of eliminating your family like this. I dare say I was to blame in the first place, and I'm afraid that I gave you the impression that we were much more snobbish down here than we really are. Your impulse was natural in the circumstances, but I had hoped that I had been able to prove to you that my opposition was only directed against your profession, and you who know what Tony is will surely appreciate my alarm at the idea of his marrying merely to gratify himself at the moment. My own dear old mother was perhaps a little more sensitive than I am to old-fashioned ideas of rank. She belonged to a period when such opinions were widely spread in the society she frequented. I confess that since she died I have found myself inclining more and more every day to what would once have been called Red Radicalism. You know, I really can't help admiring some of the things that this dreadful government is trying to do." The epithet was so persistently applied by the county that for the dowager it had lost any independent significance; it was like calling a tradesman "dear sir."

Dorothy was tempted to ask the dowager if she did believe the account she had given of her family, but she felt that if she suggested even the possibility of such skepticism she should be admitting its justification. And then suddenly she had a profound regret that her mother had never seen Clare, had never trodden this ancient turf nor sat beneath those cedar-trees. If the dowager had extended the courtesy of breeding to accept those legends her daughter-in-law had spread about herself, her courtesy would certainly not be withheld from accepting that daughter-in-law's mother. The idea took shape; it positively would be jolly to invite her mother to stay for a month at Clare. Tony would not be bored; he would be away all the time.

"And not merely your family," the dowager was saying. "Oh no, it's not merely cutting yourself from them, but also from your friends. I've heard somebody called Olive alluded to once or twice, and surely she would enjoy visiting here. Though please don't think me a foolish busybody. Perhaps Olive prefers London."

"Olive has just got married. She was married last week."

"Then I've heard you talk about a Sylvia, who possibly might care to stay down here. Dear child, don't misunderstand me, I beg. I'm only trying to suggest that you are conceivably making a mistake in dividing your life into two. After all, look at this border. See how the old-fashioned favorites of us all are improved by these rarer flowers. And do notice how well the simple flowers hold their own with those exotics that have been planted out from the greenhouse. You see what I'm trying to tell you? If Tony has certain tastes, if he likes people of whom you and I might even mildly disapprove, let him see them here in another setting. However, that you must decide later on. The only thing I should like to lay stress upon is your duty toward your family...."

"To my mother only," Dorothy interrupted. "I have no duty toward my father."

"Perhaps you will think differently when you have seen your mother. I like her so much already. How could I do otherwise when she has given me a daughter-in-law for whom I have such a great admiration?"

Dorothy took the dowager's hand and looked down earnestly and affectionately into her upturned gaze.

"Why are you always so sweet to me?" she asked.

"Whatever I am, my dear child, it is only the expression of what I feel."

That evening Dorothy wrote to her mother.

CLARE COURT, DEVON,
July 8, 1909.

MY DEAR MOTHER,—Such a long time since I saw you. Don't you think you could manage a visit to Clare next week? Come for at least a month. It will do you all the good in the world and I should so much enjoy seeing you. You will find my mother-in-law very sympathetic. I had thought of suggesting that you should bring Agnes and Edna with you, but I think that perhaps for the first time you'd rather be alone. The best train leaves Paddington at eleven-twenty. Book to Cherrington Lanes and change at Exeter. On second thoughts I'll meet you at Exeter on Wednesday next. So don't make any excuses.

Your loving daughter,
DOROTHY.

The prospect of her mother's visit was paradoxically a solace for Dorothy's disappointed maternity. The relation between them was turned upside down, and her mother became a little girl who must be looked after and kept from behaving badly, and who when she behaved well would be petted and spoiled.

Heaven knows what domestic convulsions and spiritual agitations braced Mrs. Caffyn to telegraph presently:

Am bringing three brats will they be enough.

For a moment Dorothy thought that she was coming with Vincent, Gladys, and Marjorie, so invariably did she picture her family as all of the same age as when seven years ago she first left Lonsdale Road to go to the stage. A little consideration led her to suppose that *hats* not *brats* were intended, and she telegraphed back:

You will want a nice shady hat for the garden.

Dorothy went to meet Mrs. Caffyn at Exeter in order that the three hours in the slow train between there and Cherrington Lanes might give her an opportunity of recovering herself from that agitation which had made her telegram so ambiguous. It was impossible to avoid a certain amount of pomp at the station, because the station-master, on hearing that her ladyship was expecting her ladyship's mother, led the way to the platform where the express would arrive and unrolled before her a red carpet of good intentions.

"Stand aside there," he said, severely, to a boy with a basket of newspapers.

"First stop Plymouth," shouted the porters when the express came thundering in.

"Stand aside," thundered the station-master, more loudly; perhaps he was addressing the train this time.

Mrs. Caffyn looked out of a second-class compartment and popped in again like some shy burrowing animal that fears the great world.

"What name, my lady, would be on the luggage?" asked the station-master when, notwithstanding her emersion from a second-class compartment, he had seen Mrs. Caffyn embraced by her ladyship.

"Caffyn! Caffyn!" he bellowed. "Stand aside there, will you? Both vans are being dealt with, my lady," he informed her.

The luggage was identified; a porter was bidden to carry it to No. 5 platform; and the station-master, taking from Mrs. Caffyn a string-bag in which nothing was left except a paper bag of greengages, led the way to the slow train for Cherrington.

"I traveled second-class," Mrs. Caffyn whispered, nervously, while the station-master was stamping about in a first-class compartment, dusting the leather seats and arranging the small luggage upon the rack. "I hesitated whether I ought not to travel third, but father was very nice about it."

"Please change this ticket to first-class as far as Cherrington Lanes, Mr. Thatcher," said Dorothy.

"Immediately, my lady," he announced; and as he hurried away down the platform Mrs. Caffyn regarded him as the Widow Twankay may have regarded the Genie of the Lamp.

"I've brought five hats with me," Mrs. Caffyn announced when the slow train was on its way and Mr. Thatcher was left standing upon the platform and apparently wondering if he could not give it a push from behind as a final compliment to her ladyship. "And now—oh dear, I must remember to call you Dorothy, mustn't I? By the way, you know that Dorothy is going to have a baby in November? Her husband is so pleased about it. He's doing very well, you know. Oh yes, the Norbiton Urban District Council have intrusted him with—well, I'm afraid I've forgotten just what it is, but he's doing very well, and I thought you'd be interested to hear about Dorothy. But I really *must* remember not to call you Norah."

"It wouldn't very much matter, mother."

"Oh, wouldn't it?" Mrs. Caffyn exclaimed, brightening. "Well, now, I'm sure that's a great weight off my mind. All the way down I've been worrying about that. And now just tell me, because I don't want to do anything that will make you feel uncomfortable. What am I to call your sisters-in-law? I understand about your mother-in-law. She will be Lady Clarehaven. Is that right? But your sisters-in-law?"

"Bella and Connie."

"Bella and Connie?" repeated Mrs. Caffyn. "Nothing else? I see. Well, of course, in that case I don't think I shall feel at all shy."

Although Dorothy was no longer concerned whether her mother did or did not behave as if she were in the habit of visiting at great houses during the summer, she could not resist indulging her own knowledge a little, not with any idea of display, but because she enjoyed the feeling that somebody was dependent upon her superior wisdom in worldly matters. Mrs. Caffyn enjoyed her lessons, just as few women—or men, for that matter—can resist opening a book of etiquette that lies to hand. They would not buy one for themselves, because that would seem to advertise their ignorance; but if it can be read without too much publicity it will be read, for it makes the same appeal to human egoism that is made by a medical dictionary or a work on palmistry. One topic Dorothy did ask Mrs. Caffyn to avoid, which was the life of her own mother. After that conversation by the golden border she had little doubt that the dowager did not accept as genuine the tapestry she had woven of her life; but that was no reason for drawing attention to all the fabulous beasts in the background.

"Perhaps you'd better not say anything about Grandmother Doyle," Dorothy advised. "I had to give an impression that she was related to Lord Cleveden, and if you talk too much about her it would make me look rather foolish."

"But she did belong to the same family," said Mrs. Caffyn.

"Yes, but I'd rather you didn't mention it. You can talk about Roland and Cecil and Vincent, only please avoid the topic of Grandmother Doyle."

"Of course I'll avoid anything you like," Mrs. Caffyn offered. "And perhaps I'd better throw these greengages out of the window."

The dowager was much too tactful, as Dorothy had foreseen, to ask Mrs. Caffyn any questions; she, with a license to talk about her children, was never at a loss for conversation. There is no doubt that she thoroughly enjoyed herself at Clare, and with two garden hats worn alternately she sat in placid survey of her daughter's grandeur, drove with the dowager in the chaise, congratulated Mrs. Beadon and Mrs. Kingdon upon their children, patted every dog she met, and went home first-class surrounded by baskets of peaches.

Notwithstanding the dowager's advice, Dorothy sent her mother home before Tony came back, not because she was ashamed of her, but because she dreaded his geniality and cordial invitations to bring the whole family to Curzon Street. She could not bear the idea of her father's arriving at all hours, for since the revelation of his tastes that night in St. John's Wood she fancied that he would rather enjoy the excuse his son-in-law's house would offer him of forgetting that he was still secretary of the Church of England Purity Society. So long as Tony did not meet any of her family he would not bother about them; but if he did, the temptation to his uncritical hospitality would be too strong.

The partridges were very plentiful that autumn at Clare; the pheasants never gave better sport. Dorothy invited Olive and her husband, a pleasant young actor called Airdale, to visit Clare, but Olive had to decline, because she was going to have a baby. Sylvia Scarlett Dorothy did not invite; but Sylvia Lonsdale came with her brother, and late in the autumn the Clarehavens went to stay with the Clevedens in Warwickshire. Lord Cleveden talked to Tony about the need for a strong colonial policy, and Lady Cleveden talked to Dorothy about the imperative necessity of finding a wife for Arthur at once. The shooting was not so good as at Clare, and Tony decided that he required London as a tonic for the rural depopulation of his mind.

"These fellows who've been in administrative posts get too self-important," he confided to Dorothy. "Now I don't take any interest in the colonies. Except, of course, British East and the Straits. When a fellow talks to me about Queensland my mind becomes a blank. I feel as if I was being prepared for Confirmation, don't you know?"

They reached town toward the end of November, and within a week the old set was round them. Baccarat and *chemin de fer*, the Vanity and the Orient, smart little dances and rowdy little suppers, Mrs. Foster-ffrench and the Hon. Mrs. Richard Mainwaring, they were back in the middle of them all. Sylvia Scarlett turned up again, still apparently with plenty of money to waste on gambling. She and Dorothy drifted farther apart, if that were possible, and their coolness was added to by Sylvia's recommendation of a rising young painter called Walker for Dorothy's portrait, which Dorothy considered a failure, though when afterward she was painted by an artist who had already risen that was a failure, too. Sylvia seemed to misunderstand her wantonly; Dorothy armed herself against her old friend's contempt and tried to create an impression of complete self-sufficiency. Once in the spring an occasion presented itself for knocking down the barrier they had erected between themselves. Sylvia had just brought the sum of her losses at cards to over six hundred pounds, and Dorothy, on hearing of it, expressed her concern.

"I suppose you wonder where I find the money to lose?" Sylvia asked.

"Oh no, I wasn't thinking that. I'm not interested in your private affairs," said Dorothy, freezing at the other's aggressive tone.

"No?" said Sylvia. "You easily forget about your friends' private affairs, don't you? But I warned Olive that your chauffeur wouldn't be able to find the way to West Kensington."

"How can you...." the countess broke out. Then she stopped herself. If she tried to explain what had kept her from visiting Olive Airdale all these months, she should have to reveal her own intimate hopes, her own jealousy and disillusionment; she would prefer that Sylvia supposed it was nothing more than snobbery that kept her away from Olive. If once she began upon explanations she should have to explain why she so seldom visited or spoke of her family. She should have to admit that she could no longer answer for Tony, even so far as to be sure that he would not invite her father to sit down with him to baccarat. And even those explanations would not be enough; she should have to go back to the beginning of her married life and expose such rags and tatters of dreams. Her mind went back to that railway carriage on a wet January afternoon when "Miss Elsie of Chelsea" traveled from Manchester to Birmingham. She remembered the supper that was kept waiting for Sylvia and her cheeks all dabbled with tears and a joke she had made about trusting in God and keeping her powder dry. She had tried to win Sylvia's confidence then and she had been snubbed. Should she volunteer her own confidence now?

"I'm sorry you've lost so much money in my house," said the countess.

Then she blushed; the very pronoun seemed boastful.

"Never mind. I'm going down to Warwickshire to-morrow to help Olive bring an heir into the world."

"Does she want a girl or a boy?" Dorothy asked.

"My dear," said Sylvia, "she is so anxious not to show the least sign of favoritism even before birth that in order to achieve a perfect equipoise she'll either have to have twins or a hermaphrodite."

In April Dorothy heard that her friend actually had produced twins.

"It seems so easy," she sighed, "when one hears about other people."

"Cheer up, Doodles," said Tony. "I won four hundred last night. It's about time I got some of my own back from Archie Keith; he's been plucking us all for months, lucky devil. I shall chuck shimmy."

"I wish you would," said Dorothy.

"Solemn old Doodles," he laughed. "Harry Tufton wants me to take up racing. By Jove, I'm not sure I sha'n't. You'd like that better, wouldn't you?"

"I'd like anything better than these eternal cards," she declared, passionately.

At the same time she was a little nervous of the new project, and she took an early opportunity of speaking about it to Tufton, who addressed her with the accumulated wisdom of the several thousand hours he had spent in the Bachelors' Club.

"My dear Dorothy," he began, flashing her Christian name as his mother flashed her diamonds. "I'm very glad you've broached this subject. The fact is, Tony really must draw in a little bit. I don't know how much he's lost these last two years; but he has lost a good deal, and it certainly isn't worth while losing for the benefit of people like Archie Keith and Rita Mainwaring. Only the other day at the Bachelors' I was speaking to Hughenden, and he said to me, 'Harry, my boy, why don't you exercise your influence with Tony Clarehaven and get rid of that harpy who unfortunately has the right to call herself my sister-in-law?' Well, that was rather strong, don't you know? And your cousin Paignton spoke to me about him, told me his father was rather worried about Tony—the Chatfield push feel it's not dignified. As I said to him: 'My dear fellow, if you want to lose money, why don't you lose money in a gentlemanly way? There are always horses.'"

"But I don't want him to lose his money at all," Dorothy protested.

"Quite, quite," Mr. Tufton quacked. "But you'd prefer him to lose money over horses than present it free of income tax to Archie Keith and Rita Mainwaring? At this rate he'll soon lose all his old friends, as well as his money."

Dorothy looked at the speaker; she was wondering if this was the fidgeting of a more than usually apprehensive ship's rat.

III

The Clarehaven property outside the park itself did not now include more than three thousand acres; but some speculations in which the fourth earl indulged after selling the old Hopley estate had grown considerably in value during his son's minority; and when Tony came of age, in addition to his land, which, after the payment of the dowager's jointure and all taxes, brought him in a net income of about three thousand pounds a year, he had something like seventy thousand pounds invested in Malayan enterprises which paid 10 per cent, and brought up his net income to well over eight thousand pounds. He had already been forced to sell out a considerable sum for the benefit of Captain Keith, Mrs. Mainwaring, and the rest of them; but should he decide to start a racing-stable he would have plenty of capital left on which to draw. Dorothy protested that he ought not to look upon a racing-stable as a sound and safe investment for capital that was now producing a steady income and that, with rubber booming as it was, would probably be much augmented in the near future. Yet she was afraid to be too discouraging, for, whatever might be urged against horse-racing, it offered a more dignified activity to a gambler than baccarat.

Clarehaven began his career on the turf with a sobriety which contrasted with his extravagance at cards. He bought the stable of Mr. Tufton, senior, and, leaving it in the cautious hands of old William Cobbett at Newmarket, was content during his first season to compete in a few minor handicaps and selling-plates. Such betting as he did was, on the whole, lucky; he found himself toward the end of the season with a margin of profit; and triumphantly he announced to Dorothy that he was going to invest in some really first-class yearlings at Tattersall's and Doncaster. She did not dissuade him, because she had had a talk with honest old William Cobbett, who had assured her that his lordship was willing to listen to his advice, and that if he would be guided by him there was no reason why his lordship should not win some of the great classic races the year after next, fortune being favorable. He spoke of the black, white, and purple of Clarehaven as of colors once famous upon famous courses, and implied that Saturday afternoons at Windsor or Lingfield Park were hardly worthy of the time-honored combination. Dorothy could not help agreeing with the trainer; throughout this first season there had been a great deal too much of Captain Keith and Mrs. Foster-ffrench, too much of a theatrical garden-party about those Saturday afternoons, and although this year Tony had been lucky, another year he might be unlucky and fritter away his money and his reputation in the company of people who saw no difference between the green baize of a card-table and the green turf of a racecourse. Several people had talked of the fourth earl's great deeds upon the turf during the 'seventies; she, still susceptible to intimations of grandeur, viewed with dismay these degenerate week-ends and encouraged Tony to aim higher. If he would not speak in the House of Lords, he might at least win the Derby; and if he won the Derby, surely his lust for gambling would be satiated and he might retire to Clare to raise blood-stock. The idea of owning some mighty horse, the paragon of Ormonde or Eclipse or Flying Childers, obsessed her; she pictured ten years hence a small boy attired in Gainsborough blue, proudly mounted upon a race-horse that should be the sire and grandsire and great-grandsire of a hundred classic winners. She became poetical, so keen was her ambition, so vivid her hope; this mighty horse should be called Moonbeam, should be a ray from the full moon of Clare to illuminate them all—Anthony—herself, that son, who might almost be called Endymion. Why not? Disraeli had called one of his heroes Endymion. Affected? Yes, but Endymion Viscount Clare! Why should Endymion for a boy be more affected than Diana for a girl? And why not Diana, too? Lady Diana Clare! They might be twins. Why not? Mrs. Beadon had produced twins, Olive had produced twins. Moonshine suffused Dorothy's castle in Spain, and moonstruck she paced the battlements.

Tony bought a string of horses at Tattersall's, and at Doncaster paid £600 and £750, respectively, for two yearlings with which old William Cobbett expressed himself particularly well satisfied. It happened that year that a young Greek called Christides, who had lately come of age, won the Champagne Stakes and, in his elation, bought a yearling for three thousand guineas. It further happened that after a triumphal dinner he gave to several friends, among whom was Tony, he lost twice that sum at auction bridge. Though Mr. Christides was extremely rich, his native character asserted itself by an abrupt return to prudence. He had allowed himself a fixed sum to spend at Doncaster, and, having exceeded his calculations, he must sell the yearling—a black colt by Cyllene out of Maid of the Mist. There was no question that he was the pick of the yearlings; if old William Cobbett had not protested so firmly against the price, Clarehaven would have been tempted to buy him at the sale. Dorothy, with her mind still a tenant of Spanish castles, saw in the Maid of the Mist colt the horse of her dreams, and by letting her superstition play round the animal she became convinced that it held the fortunes of Clare. Was not the sire Cyllene, which easily became Selene— Dorothy was deep in moon-lore—and would not the offspring of Selene and Maid of the Mist be well called Moonbeam? Moreover, was not the colt black with one splash of white on the forehead? When, therefore, Mr. Christides offered the yearling to settle his losses with Tony, in other words for £2,722, Dorothy was anxious for him to accept. Old William Cobbett was frightened by the price, but he could urge nothing against the colt except, perhaps, the slightest tendency to a dipped back, so slight, however, that when Mr. Christides, still true to his native character, knocked off the odd £22, the small sum was enough to cure the slight depression.

Dorothy thoroughly enjoyed the winter that followed the purchase of the colt. As soon as Moonbeam—of course he was given the name at once— was safe in William Cobbett's stable the trainer admitted that there was not another yearling to touch him. In the two colts which he himself had advised his patron to buy he could hardly bring himself to take the least interest, and in fact both of them afterward did turn out disappointments, one bursting blood-vessels when called upon for the least effort, and the other a duck-hearted beast that for all his fine appearance never ran out a race. But Moonbeam was everything that a colt could be.

"The heart of a lion," said honest old William, "and as gentle as a dove with it all. Be gad! my lady, I believe you're a real judge of horseflesh, and damme—forgive the uncouth expression—but damme, if ever I go to another sale without you."

"But will he win the Derby?" Dorothy asked.

"Well now, come, come, come! This is early days to begin prophesying. But I wouldn't lay against him, no, begad! I wouldn't lay ten to one against him— not now I wouldn't. Dipped back? Not a bit. If ever I said his back was dipped I must have been dipped myself. You beauty! You love! You jewel!"

After which honest old William took out a bandana handkerchief as big and bright as the royal standard and blew his nose till the stable reverberated with the sound.

"See that? Not a blink," he chuckled. "Not a blink, begad! That colt, my lady, is the finest colt ever seen at Cobbett House. You bird! You gem!"

Tony himself was as enthusiastic as Dorothy or the trainer, and there was no talk of London for a long while. He rented a small hunting-lodge in the neighborhood to please Dorothy, and what between shooting over the Cambridgeshire turnips and hunting hard with two or three noted packs the winter went past quickly enough. Even better than the shooting and the hunting were the February days when Moonbeam was put into stronger work and, in the trainer's words, "ate it."

"He's a glutton for work," said honest old William.

Dorothy and he used to ride on the Heath and watch the horses at exercise, and if only Moonbeam was successful next season with his two-year-old engagements and if only he would win the Derby and if only next year she might have a son....

Moonbeam's first public appearance was at the Epsom Spring Meeting when he ran unplaced in the Westminster Plate, much to Dorothy's alarm.

"He wasn't intended to do anything," the trainer explained, soothingly. "This was just to see how he and Joe Flitten took to each other. Well, Joe, what do you think of him?"

"All right, Mr. Cobbett," said the young jockey, who was considered to be the most promising apprentice at headquarters.

The colt's next engagement was for the Woodcote Stakes at the Epsom Summer Meeting, when he was ridden by Harcourt, one of the leading jockeys of the day, and was backed to win a large sum. Something did go wrong this time, for, though he was running on strongly at the finish, he was again unplaced.

"Dash it!" Clarehaven exclaimed, ruefully. "I hope this isn't going to happen every time. You and her ladyship have made a mistake, I'm afraid, Cobbett. If you ask me, he pecked."

Honest old William looked very grave.

"If you ask *me*, my lord, it was his jockey. The colt was badly ridden. Still, it was a disappointment, there's no getting over it. But it's early days to begin fretting, and he was running on. No doubt about that. Tell you what, my lord, if you'll take my advice you'll give Joe Flitten the mount for Ascot, and if Joe doesn't bring out what there is in him, why then we'll have to put our heads together, that's all about it."

So Joe Flitten, the Cobbett Lodge apprentice, rode Moonbeam in the New Stakes, when the colt made most of his rivals at Epsom look like platers; although it was to be noted that Sir James Otway's unnamed colt by Desmond out of Diavola, which had won the Woodcote Stakes, did not run.

"Like common ordinary platers," honest old William avowed.

After this performance the racing-press began to pay attention to Moonbeam, and when in July he won the Hurst Park Foal Plate with ridiculous ease they admitted that his victory at Ascot was no fluke.

In August Tony rented a grouse-moor in Yorkshire. His other horses were not doing too well, but he was feeling prosperous, for Moonbeam had already repaid him several times over his losses at Epsom; and at the end of the month a jolly party drove over to York in a four-in-hand to see the colt canter away with the Gimcrack Stakes. At this meeting Dorothy really felt that Tony was what in another sense the press would have called "an ornament to the turf." There were no Mrs. Mainwarings and Captain Keiths with them at York, and she never felt less like a Vanity girl than when she heard the crowd cheering Moonbeam's victory—he was by now a popular horse—and looked round proudly at her party; at Uncle Chat with Paignton and Charlie Fanhope; at Bella and Connie, both bright red with joy; at Arthur and Sylvia Lonsdale, and at Miss Horatia Lonsdale, a delightful aunt who was helping Dorothy chaperon the girls, an easy enough task as regards Bella and Connie and not very difficult as regards her niece.

Finally in the autumn Moonbeam won the Middle Park Plate and was voted the finest two-year-old seen at Newmarket for several seasons.

"And now let him keep quiet till the Guineas," said William Cobbett, with a sigh of satisfaction.

"You wouldn't run him in the Dewhurst?"

"No, no, let him rest with what he's done."

"Cobbett is right," said Lord Stilton, one of the stewards of the Jockey Club, who came into the paddock at that moment. "You've got the Derby next year, Clarehaven, if you don't overwork him. That apprentice of yours is a treasure, Cobbett."

"A good boy, my lord."

"You don't know my wife," Tony was saying.

"My congratulations, Lady Clarehaven. I hear you picked out with my old friend William here."

Later on Dorothy was presented to Lady Stilton. She in turn presented her daughter, the beautiful and charming Lady Anne Varley, whose engagement to the young Duke of Ulster had just been announced.

"My dear Dorothy," said Harry Tufton that evening, "you must admit that my advice was good. How much better this sort of thing becomes you than

..." He waved his arms in a gesture of despair at finding any adjective sufficiently contemptuous for those evenings at Curzon Street before his lifelong friend, Tony Clarehaven, had followed his advice and sported the black, white, and purple colors so famous forty years ago.

The prospect of winning the Derby next year really did seem to have completed Tony's cure. He raised no objections when Dorothy insisted that his mother and his sisters should spend the autumn in town, and he actually went three times to the House of Lords to vote against some urgent measure of reform. He did not make a speech, but he coughed once in the middle of an oration by a newly created Radical peer, so significant and so nearly vocally expressive a cough that it deserved to be recorded in Hansard as a contribution to the debate.

Dorothy had been desirous of the dowager's help to consolidate a position in London society that now for the first time appeared tenable. Her meeting with Lady Stilton had given her a foothold on the really high cliffs, and if Tony did not spoil everything she saw no reason why she should not repeat on a larger scale in town her success in Devonshire. It was a pity that Bella and Connie were so ugly; if she could bring off brilliant matches for them, what a help that would be. Of course, it was not the season; most people were out of town notwithstanding that Parliament was sitting; but still surely somewhere in the crowded pages of Debrett could be found suitors for the hands of her sisters-in-law. The nearest approach to a match was when Lord Beccles, the lunatic heir of the Marquis of Norwich, became perfectly manageable if he was allowed to drive with Bella in Hyde Park, chaperoned by his nurse and watched by a footman who held a certificate from one of the largest private asylums in England. If Lord Beccles was a congenital idiot, there were three other sons of Lord Norwich who were sane enough, the eldest of whom, Lord Alistair Gay, agreed with Dorothy that, if Lady Arabella was willing, the marriage would be a kindness to his poor brother. Bella would not take the proposal seriously, and it was evident that she regarded her drives with the poor idiot in the light of a minor charity ranking with the care of a distempered dog or of a cottager's baby.

"You surely aren't serious, Dorothy," she laughed.

"Well, it would give you a splendid position. You would be a countess now and probably a marchioness very soon. Lady Norwich is dead. Lord Norwich is very old, and idiots often live a long time. I'm not suggesting that it would be anything more than a formal marriage, but you apparently don't mind his dribbling with excitement when he sees the Albert Memorial and.... However, I wouldn't persuade you into a match for anything. Only it doesn't seem to me that it would imply anything more than you do for him at present."

The dowager told Dorothy that she would rather dear Bella married somebody simpler than poor Lord Beccles, to which Dorothy retorted that it might be difficult to find even a commoner more simple. Moonbeam's victories as a two-year-old had restored that self-confidence which had been so shaken since her marriage; Dorothy, like most nations and most human beings, was more admirable in adversity than in triumph. The disposition she had shown to recognize her suburban family did not last; she knew that the integument with which she was so carefully wrapping up her reality could be stripped from it by her relations in a second. Only now, after she had been a countess for six years, had Dorothy discovered the narrow bridge that is swung over the center of the universe—the well-laid and lighted bridge so delicately adjusted to eternity that the least divergence from correctness by one of its frequenters might be enough to imperil its balance. That bridge Dorothy was now crossing with all her eyes for her feet, as it were, and she certainly could not afford to be distracted by a family. If Sylvia Scarlett had been in London to watch this new progress she would have made many unkind jokes about the countess; but Sylvia was away acting in America, and in any case she would have found the door of 129 Curzon Street closed against her.

The dowager worried over the way Dorothy was ignoring her mother, and, fortified with strong smelling-salts, she braved the Underground to pay a visit to West Kensington, an experience she so thoroughly enjoyed that she could not keep it a secret for long, but one day began to praise the beauty of Edna and Agnes.

"Frankly, my dear Dorothy," she told her daughter-in-law, "I must say I think that you would be likely to have much more success as a match-maker for your sisters than for dear Bella and dear Connie, who even in London seem unable to avoid that appearance of having just run up and down a very windy hill. Why not have Edna and Agnes to live with you until they're married? And when they are married invite the youngest two, who will also be very beautiful girls, I'm convinced. Really, I never saw such complexions as you and all your sisters have."

Dorothy thought the dowager's suggestion most impracticable.

"Yes, but my most impracticable suggestions nearly always turn out well."

Perhaps, so sure was she of the impression that Agnes and Edna would create in a London ballroom, the dowager would have had her way if she had remained in town for the spring, but in the month of February, anticipating St. Valentine's Day by a week, the Rev. Thomas Hemming wrote from Cherrington to say that Mrs. Paxton, his godmother, had just offered him the living of Newton Candover in Hampshire and would Lady Constantia Clare become Lady Constantia Hemming? Lady Constantia would. The trousseau was bought under the eyes of Dorothy, who, regardless of the fact that she was going to marry a parson, insisted that Connie should look beyond viyella for certain items. Soon after Easter Mr. Beadon had to find another curate and Connie's room at Clare Lodge was empty.

Tony was too much occupied with Moonbeam's chances of winning the two thousand guineas at the end of April to bother who married his sister; but he wrote her a generous check that compensated for the decline in value of the vicar's glebe at Newton Candover.

"And I suppose," said Dorothy, "that next January Connie will have a son."

"Never mind," said her husband. "Next June you and I shall have the Derby winner."

Honest William Cobbett had made no secret of his conviction that Moonbeam was going to canter away with the Guineas, and in the ring his patron's horse was favorite at five to two.

"It'll have to be something very hot and dark that can beat him," he told Clarehaven. "Has your lordship betted very plentiful?"

"I shall drop about ten thousand if the colt fails," said Clarehaven, airily. "But most of my big bets are for the Derby. I got sixes against him twice over to two thousand and fives twelve times in thousands. If he wins to-day I shall plunge a bit."

The trainer blinked his limpid blue eyes.

"Oh, then you don't consider you've done anything in the way of plunging so far?"

"Nothing," said Clarehaven, flicking his mount and calling to Dorothy to ride along with him to the Birdcage. They had taken a small house for the meeting, and they were just off to escort Moonbeam to the starting-post. Lonsdale and Tufton had also come down to Newmarket, the former mounted under protest on a hack which he rode as if he were driving a car.

"Well, so long, Cobbett," the owner cried. "Hope we shall all be feeling as happy in another half-hour as we are now."

"Never fear, my lord. As I told you, there's only the Diavola colt to be afraid of. There's not a bit of doubt he won the Dewhurst in rare fashion, and of course that made his win at Epsom in the Woodcote look good. And now Sir James has gone and sold him for seven thousand guineas with a contingency to this man Houston—somebody new to racing. Well, seven thousand guineas is a nice little price, and there's been a lot of money forthcoming from the Winsley crowd. Dick Starkey always tries to serve up something extra hot for Newmarket. There's nothing gives greater delight to a provincial stable like Starkey Lodge than to do us headquarter folk out of the Guineas, which, as you may say, is our specialty. Stupid name, though, to give such a nice-looking animal. Chimpanzee!"

Dorothy uttered an exclamation. She divined the owner's name at once, and when Lonsdale told her it was Leopold Hausberg who had been away in South Africa and returned more rich than ever with a license to call himself Lionel Houston in future, she was not at all surprised, but her heart began to beat faster.

"Come along, come along, you two. We sha'n't be in time to escort the horses from the Birdcage."

"I say, Tony," said Lonsdale, anxiously, "the bookies are shouting twenty to one bar two, and Moonbeam has gone out to eleven to four."

"Damn!" ejaculated his owner. "I wonder if there's time for me to get any more money on?"

"No, leave it alone," Lonsdale begged. "Good Heavens! It makes me feel absolutely sick when I think of having ten thousand pounds on the result of one race. Why, compared with that, flying is safer than walking."

Two Cambridge undergraduates riding by jostled his cob so roughly that for the next few moments his attention was bent on maintaining himself in the saddle.

"Flying would certainly be safer than riding for you," Clarehaven laughed.

"The horse's mechanism is primitive, that's what it is—it's primitive," said Lonsdale. "And to risk ten thousand pounds on a primitive mechanism like a horse—Shut up, you brute, *you're* not entered for the Guineas. I say, this steering-gear is very unreliable, you know."

Dorothy had wanted to ask Lonsdale more about the owner of Chimpanzee; but at this moment the sun burst forth from behind a great white April cloud full-rigged, the shadow of which floated over the glittering green of the Heath just as the horses emerged from the Birdcage, escorted on either side by horsemen and horsewomen of fame and beauty. It was a fair scene, to play a part in which Dorothy exultantly felt that it was worth while to lose even more than £10,000. The coats of the horses shimmered in the sunlight; the colors of the jockeys blended and shifted like flowers in the wind; no tournament of the Middle Ages with all its plumes and pennons could have offered a fairer scene.

Tufton joined his friends, and, turning their mounts, they rode back toward the winning-post.

"I say, Tony, Chimpanzee has shunted to three's—only a fraction's difference now between him and Moonbeam," he was murmuring.

"Tell me more about Houston," said Dorothy to Lonsdale. "I don't think I can bear to watch the race."

"Cheer-oh, Doodles! You can't feel more queasy than I do. And I've told you all I know about Houston."

"But why should he call his horse Chimpanzee?"

There was a roar from the crowd.

"They're off!"

They were off on that royal mile of Newmarket.

"Flitten was told to ride him out from the start. Damn him, why doesn't he do so?" said Tony.

"He is, old boy. He's all right. Don't get nervy," said Tufton.

"Which is Chimpanzee?"

"That bay on the outside."

"What colors?"

"Yellow. Harcourt up."

"Take him along! Take him along! Good God, he's not using the whip already, is he?"

"No, no! No, no!"

"Damnation!" cried Tony, "why didn't we keep to the inclosure? I believe my horse is beaten. Don't look round, you little blighter! It's not an egg-and-spoon race."

The spectators were roaring like the sea.

"Moonbeam! Chimpanzee! Moonbeam! Moonbeam!" was shouted in a crescendo of excitement.

There was a momentary lull.

"Moonbeam by a head," floated in a kind of unisonant sigh along the rails.

"O Lord!" Lonsdale gulped. "I'd sooner drive a six-cylinder Lee-Lonsdale at sixty miles an hour through a school treat."

The strain was over; the noble owner had led in the noble winner; the ceremonies of congratulation were done; there was a profitable settlement to expect on Monday; yet Dorothy was ill at ease. The resuscitation of Hausberg clouded her contentment. Coincidence would not explain his purchase of the Diavola colt, his naming of it Chimpanzee, and his running it to beat Moonbeam. To be sure, he had failed, but a man who had taken so much trouble to create an effect would be more eager than ever after such a failure to ... "to do what?" she asked herself. Was he aiming at revenge? Such a fancy was melodramatic, absurd ... after all these years deliberately to aim at revenge for a practical joke. Besides, she had had nothing to do with the affair in St. John's Wood. Nor had Tony except as an accessory after the fact. Yet it was strange; it was even sinister. And how odd that Lonsdale should be present at this sinister resurrection.

"Lonnie," she said, "do you remember about the monkey?"

"What monkey? Did you have a monkey on Moonbeam?"

"Not money, you silly boy—the chimpanzee you put in Hausberg's rooms."

"Of course I remember it. So does he, apparently, as he's called his horse after it."

"I know. I feel nervous. I think he's going to bring us bad luck."

"Hello, Doodles, you're looking very gloomy for the wife of the man who is going to win the Derby," said Tony, coming up at that moment, all smiles. "I've just bet fifty pounds for you on one of Cobbett's fillies, which he says is a good thing for the Wilbraham. And the stable's in luck."

Dorothy won £250 in a flash, it seemed—the race was only four furlongs— and when in the last race of the day she backed the winner of the Bretby Handicap and won another £250 Tony told her cheerfully that she ought not to gamble because she was now a monkey to the good. Dorothy was depressed. The £500, outside the ill omen of its being called a monkey in slang, assumed a larger and more portentous significance by reminding her of the £500 she had borrowed from her mother when she first went on the stage and of the way she had invested some of it afterward with Leopold Hausberg. All her delight in Moonbeam's victory had been destroyed by a dread of the unknown, and she suddenly pulled Tony's sleeve, who was busily engaged in taking bets against his horse for the Derby. He turned round rather irritably.

"What is the matter with you?"

"Give it up," she begged. "Don't bet any more."

"Give up betting when I've just won twenty-five thousand pounds over the Guineas and am going to win one hundred and twenty-five thousand pounds over the Derby? Besides, I thought you were going to live happily ever afterward if Moonbeam won?"

He turned away again with a laugh, and Tufton's grave head-shake was not much consolation to Dorothy. She was walking away a few paces in order not to overhear Tony's jovial badinage with the bookmakers, when a suave voice addressed her over the shoulder and, looking round, she saw Leopold Hausberg.

"You've forgotten me, Lady Clarehaven," he was saying. "I must explain that I—"

"Yes, yes," Dorothy interrupted, quickly, "you're Mr. Houston. I've just been told so by Mr. Lonsdale, whom no doubt you also remember."

She mentioned Lonsdale's name deliberately to see if Houston would speak about the monkey or even show a hint of displeasure at the mention of Lonsdale's name, but there was no shadow on his countenance, and he only asked her if she would not introduce him to her husband.

"I should like to congratulate him," he said, "though his win hit me pretty hard."

At this moment Tony with a laugh closed his betting-book and joined them.

"By Jove! there's not a sportsman among you," he called back to the bookmakers. "What do you think, Doodles? There's not one of them who'll give me four thousand to a thousand against Moonbeam for the Derby.... I'm sorry, I didn't see you were talking to somebody."

Dorothy made the introduction.

"I'll give you four thousand to a thousand, Lord Clarehaven," the new-comer offered. "Or more if you wish to bet. I don't think my horse showed his true form to-day. He swerved badly at the start, and my jockey says he was kicked."

Clarehaven was delighted to find somebody who would lay against Moonbeam, and he entered in his book a bet of £20,000 to £5,000.

"I had the pleasure of meeting Lady Clarehaven before her marriage," Houston was explaining. "I should have called upon you long ago, but I've been away for some years in South Africa."

"Making money, eh?" said Tony, holding in his mouth like a cigarette the pencil that was going to make money for him.

"I've not done so badly," said the other, deprecatingly.

"Look here, you must dine with us to-night," Tony declared, cheerily. "We're having a little celebration at the Blue Boar."

"Delighted, I'm sure. That's what I always like about racing," said Houston, "it brings out all our best sporting qualities as a nation."

Dorothy thought her husband was going to say something rude, but she need not have been worried. He had no intention of being rude to a man who would lay so heavily against the horse he thought was bound to win. In fact, he went out of his way to be specially friendly to Houston, and during the month of May the financier was at Curzon Street almost every day. Moreover, he brought with him others like himself who were willing to bet heavily with Clarehaven, and Dorothy began to think that even Captain Keith and Mrs. Mainwaring and those Saturday afternoons of peroxide and pink powder at Windsor or Lingfield Park were better than this nightmare of hooked noses and splay mouths.

"Well," said Lonsdale, "if anybody ever talks to me again about the 'lost' tribes or the missing link, I shall ask him if he's looked in Curzon Street. He'll find both there."

"Tony's being a little bit promiscuous," said Henry Tufton. "But of course one *must* remember that the king was very fond of Jews. And then there was Disraeli, don't you know, and the late queen."

Just before the Derby, Houston, whom, in spite of the menace he seemed to hold out against the future of Tony's career on the turf, Dorothy could not help liking in the intervals when she forgot about her premonitions of misfortune, said to her in a tone that it would have been hard to accuse of insincerity:

"Look here, I want to show you I'm a true friend, and I warn you that my horse is going to win the Derby. Nothing can beat him. Tell Clarehaven to hedge. I wish I'd not laid that bet now, for I hate taking his money. I suppose he'd be insulted if I offered to cancel the bet? But I would, if he would."

Dorothy told Tony about Houston's offer; but he laughed at her and said that, like all Jews, Houston did not relish losing his money. Nevertheless, finding that his liabilities were alarmingly high and knowing that Houston, not content with laying against Moonbeam, was backing Chimpanzee wherever he could, Tony invested some money on the second favorite and declined to lay another halfpenny against him. As a matter of fact, the money he invested thus was in comparison with the thousands for which he had backed Moonbeam a trifle; but rumor exaggerated the sum, and when Chimpanzee won the Derby, with Moonbeam just shut out of a place, there were unpleasant rumors in the clubs.

Dorothy did not go to Epsom—her nerves could not have stood the strain—and when she heard of Moonbeam's defeat she was grateful to her impulse. Nowadays her self-confidence was very easily upset, and from the moment

Houston had appeared upon the scene at Newmarket she had never in her heart expected that Moonbeam would win the great race.

It was Tony himself who brought her the bad news. In a gray tail-coat and with gray top-hat set askew upon his flushed face—flushed with more than temper and disappointment, she thought—he strode up and down the smoking-room at Curzon Street, swinging his field-glasses round and round by their straps, until she begged him not to break the chandelier.

"Break the chandelier," he laughed. "That's good, by Jove! What about breaking myself? You don't seem to understand what this means, my dear Doodles. I've lost sixty thousand pounds over that cursed animal. Sixty thousand pounds! Do you hear? And I've got four days to find the money. Do you realize I shall have to mortgage Clare in order to settle up on Monday?"

"Mortgage Clare?" Dorothy gasped; she turned white and swayed against the table. At that moment Tony let the straps escape from his hand and the glasses went crashing into a large mirror.

"Yes, mortgage Clare," he repeated, savagely.

It was only the noise of the broken glass that kept her from fainting; weakly she pointed at the mirror and with a wavering smile upon her usually firm lips she whispered something about seven years of bad luck.

"Well, it's nothing to laugh about," said Tony.

"I wasn't laughing. Oh, Tony, you can't lose Clare; you mustn't."

"Oh well, I mayn't lose it. I may have some luck late in the season. But my other horses have let me down badly so far."

"You won't go on betting?"

"How else am I to get back what I've lost? I can't make sixty thousand pounds by selling papers!"

"Oh, but you...." She put her hand up to her forehead and sank into one of those comfortable chairs upholstered in red leather. "How did Cobbett explain Moonbeam's defeat?" She felt that, however agonizing, she must have the tale of the race to give her an illusion of action, and to silence these bells that were ringing in her brain: "Clare! Clare! Clare!"

"Cobbett?" exclaimed Tony, viciously. "He's about fit to train a bus-horse to jog from Piccadilly to Sloane Street. 'The colt doesn't like the Epsom course, and that's about the size of it,' said Mr. Cobbett to me. 'Course be damned, you old plowboy!' I told him. 'If you hadn't insisted upon giving the mount to that cursed apprentice of yours my horse would have won.' 'I don't think it was the lad's fault, my lord,' said Cobbett, getting as red as a turkey-cock. 'Don't you dare to contradict me,' I said. By God! Doodles, I was in such a rage that it was all I could do not to take the obstinate old fool by the shoulders and shake the truth into him. 'I'd contradict the King of England, my lord, if I trained his horses and he told me I didn't know my business,' 'Well, I tell you that you don't know your business,' I answered. 'Why didn't you let me do as I wanted and get O'Hara over from France to ride him?' 'If you remember, my lord, in the Woodcote Stakes, we gave the mount to Harcourt, and he made a mess of the race.' I couldn't stand there shouting 'O'Hara! Not Harcourt!' It wouldn't have been dignified in the paddock, and so I just told him quietly that I should have to consider if after to-day's fiasco I could still intrust my horses to a man who wouldn't listen to reason; after that I pulled myself together with a couple of stiff brandies and drove the car home myself. By the way, I ran over a kid in Hammersmith and broke its leg or something. Altogether it's been my worst day from birth up."

Dorothy would have liked to reproach him for drinking, to have expressed her dismay at the accident to the child, to have whispered a word of hope for the future, to have taken his foolish flushed face between her hands and kissed it ... but the only speech and action she could trust herself to make or take was to ring for a footman to sweep up the broken glass from the floor of the smoking-room.

Two days later, while Tony was hard at work raising the money to pay his debts on Monday, a letter came from Newmarket:

COBBETT HOUSE., NEWMARKET,
June 7, 1912.

To the Earl of Clarehaven.

MY LORD,—After our conversation in the paddock at Epsom on Wednesday I must give your lordship notice that I must respectfully decline to train your horses any longer in my stables. I would be much obliged if your lordship will give instructions to who I must transfer them.

I am,

Yours respectfully,
W. COBBETT.

Houston, who happened to be with Tony when this letter arrived, asked him why he did not train with Richard Starkey at Winsley on the Berkshire Downs.

"Yes, that's all very well," said Clarehaven, "but what about the Leger?"

"I'm not going to run Chimpanzee for the Leger. In fact, I've sold him to an Australian syndicate for the stud. Your horse will be the only representative of the stable."

Finally Clarehaven's horses were transferred to Starkey Lodge, and Moonbeam, as the obvious choice of the stable, gave the public a good win at Doncaster. The victory did not do Clarehaven much good in narrower circles, where many people had backed Chimpanzee to win the Leger. The rumors that had gone round the clubs after the Derby sprang to life again, and with an added virulence circulated freely. Lord Stilton, as a friend of his father, warned Tony in confidence that he would not be elected to the Jockey Club and advised him to go slow for a while.

"If the Stewards wish for an explanation," said Tony, loftily, "they can have an explanation."

"It is not a question of your horse's running," said Lord Stilton. "Technically there are no grounds for criticism. But a certain amount of comment has been aroused by your change of stables and by your friendship with this man Houston. Altogether, my dear fellow, I advise you to go slow—yes, to go slow."

Tony, with the amount of money he had won back by Moonbeam's victory in the Leger, did not feel at all inclined to go slow, and with Richard Starkey at his elbow he bought several highly priced yearlings at the Doncaster sales. He would show that pompous old bore Stilton that the Derby could be won without being a member of the Jockey Club.

IV

Moonbeam's victory in the St. Leger had apparently freed Clare from mortgages, and it enabled the owner to meet a large number of bills that fell due shortly afterward. Dorothy, who was continually hearing from Tony how decently Houston was behaving to him, began to wonder if her dread of the Jew had not been hysterical; and when in October he proposed a cruise round the Mediterranean in his new yacht she did not attribute to the proposal a new and subtle form of danger. She and Houston were talking together in the drawing-room at Curzon Street while Tony was occupied with somebody who had called on business. During the summer these colloquies down in the smoking-room had kept Dorothy's nerves strung up to expect the worst when she used to hear Tony accompany the visitor to the door and come so slowly up-stairs after he was gone. But since Doncaster the interviews had been much shorter, and Tony had often run up-stairs at the end of them, leaving the visitor to be shown out by a footman. Throughout that trying time Houston had been always at hand, suave and attentive, not in the least attentive beyond the limits of an old friendship, but rather in the manner of

Tufton, though of course with greater age and experience at the back of it. His ugliness, which, when Dorothy had first beheld it again so abruptly that afternoon in the ring at Newmarket had appalled her, was by now so familiar again that she was no longer conscious of it, or if she was conscious of it she rather liked it. Such ugliness strengthened Houston's background, and when Tony's affairs seemed most desperate gave Dorothy a hope; the more rugged the cliff the more easily will the wrecked mariner scale its forbidding face. Yes, Houston had really been invaluable during an exhausting year, and when now he proposed this yachting trip she welcomed the project.

"I think it would be good for Clarehaven to get him away from England for a while—to give him a change of air and scene. We'll lure him with the promise of a few days at Monte Carlo, and something will happen to make it impossible to go near Monte Carlo, eh? A nice, quiet little party. I have cabins for eight guests. Three hundred ton gross. Nothing extravagant as a yacht goes."

"And what do you call her? *The Chimpanzee?*" asked Dorothy, with a smile.

"No, no, no," he replied. "*The Whirligig.* A good name for a small yacht, don't you think?"

"Tell me," said Dorothy, earnestly. "Why did you call your horse Chimpanzee? You know, when I first heard it, I felt you were still brooding over that stupid business in those flats. What were they called?"

"Lauriston Mansions."

"Ah, you haven't forgotten the name. I had. But what centuries ago all that seems."

"Does it?"

"To me, oh, centuries!" she exclaimed, vehemently.

Houston's eyes narrowed, as if he were seeking to bring that far-off scene into focus with the present.

"I oughtn't to have reminded you of it," said Dorothy, lightly. "It was tactless of me."

"Not at all," said Houston. "Besides, contemporary with that there are many pleasant hours to remember" ... he hesitated for a second and blew out the end of the sentence in a puff of cigarette smoke ... "with you."

"Yes, I have often wondered why you were so kind to me. I think I must have been very tiresome in those days."

"On the contrary, you were the loveliest girl in London."

"Girl," Dorothy half sighed.

"Come, my dear Lady Clarehaven." Was he mocking her with the title? "My dear Lady Clarehaven," he repeated, with the least trace of emphasis upon the conventional epithet. "You don't expect me to be so bold as to say what you are now?"

For one moment he opened wide his dark eyes, and in that moment Dorothy decided that the party on the yacht should include the dowager and Bella. Simultaneously with this decision she was saying, with a laugh of affected dismay, "Oh no, please, Mr. Houston."

Tony was not at first in favor of the proposed trip, and pleaded that he wanted to see how his yearlings wintered; but Houston insisted that Starkey would look after them better without being worried by the owner. Then Tony urged the claims of pheasants. He had neglected his pheasants of late, and it would be a pity to let the Clare coverts alone for another year.

"Besides, I ought to look after the property," he added.

Dorothy had heard this declaration of duty urged too often to be taken in by it any longer. A week in Devonshire would cure Tony of a landowner's anxiety whether about his pheasants or his peasants; after that he would discover in his bland way that London was more convenient than the country.

"You can get plenty of shooting in the Mediterranean," said Houston. "There's a desert island in the Ægean with mouflon that nobody ever succeeds in getting."

"What? I'll bet you two hundred to one in sovereigns that I bag a couple," Tony cried.

"I won't bet, because you'll lose your money. A friend of mine lay off for a week of fine weather—that's a rare occurrence in those waters—lost nearly a stone climbing the rocks, and at the end of it came away without hitting one."

"Ridiculous," Tony scoffed. "What gun did he use?"

"Don't ask me," laughed Houston. "All I know is he was a first-class shot, and if he couldn't succeed I don't believe anybody can."

"That's rot," Tony declared, angrily. "When are we going to start?"

"She's in commission and now lying at Plymouth, which will save your mother a long journey by train."

"My mother?" Tony echoed, in astonishment.

Dorothy revealed her plan for inviting the dowager and Bella, and Tony was so anxious to prove he was right about the mouflon that he made no objections.

"Then," Dorothy continued, "I thought Harry Tufton had better be asked. He'll be so good at buying souvenirs in port. Your mother is sure to want souvenirs, and you'd hate to scour round for them yourself."

"I suppose Lonnie couldn't come," Tony suggested.

Houston knitted his brows, but said hurriedly that Lonsdale would be an ideal passenger for a cruise. Dorothy did not like to oppose the suggestion; yet she was relieved when Lonsdale replied that, having luckily arrived on this earth many years after the Flood, he did not propose to slight dry land. "Sea-trips," he wrote, "beginning with the Ark's have always been crowded and unpleasant. Besides, I'm learning to fly."

"Silly ass!" said Tony, tearing up the note.

The dowager was rather fluttered by the notion of a cruise in a yacht. Her knowledge of the sea was chiefly derived from Lady Brassey's journal of a voyage in the *Sunbeam*, the continual references of which to seasickness were not encouraging. Bella, who since Connie's marriage had taken to writing short stories, was as eager for local color as a child for a box of paints, and her enthusiasm at the idea of visiting the classic sea was so loudly expressed that the dowager had not the heart to disappoint her. She did, however, make one stipulation that surprised her daughter-in-law.

"If I go," she said, "you must promise me to invite one of your sisters. Now please, Dorothy, listen to me. You owe it to them. Of course, I should like you to invite them all and your mother, who could talk to me while you were all climbing volcanoes and searching for the ruins of Carthage; but I dare say Mr. Houston won't have room. However, one of them you must invite."

And then suddenly the dowager's suggestion seemed to provide a perfect solution of a problem that had been vexing Dorothy. In thinking over Houston's attitude she had been forced to explain it by the existence of something like a tender feeling for herself. To speak of tenderness in connection with him seemed absurd; but she was beginning to fancy that perhaps in the old days he had in his heart all the time wanted her for himself. If that were so, he had certainly behaved very well both now and then. No doubt he had realized that so long as her marriage with Clarehaven was attainable he stood no chance; but if that should have definitely come to nothing, he must have intended to ask her to marry him. It was with that idea he had helped her with investments, had avoided the least hint of an ulterior motive, and had always treated her so irreproachably. If he had concealed his love so carefully in the past, it was not ridiculous to suppose that he might be in love with her now. The other day he had been on the verge of saying something much more intimate than anything in the most intimate conversation they had ever had together. Perhaps he fancied that she and Tony were nothing to each other now—alas! with gambling as his ruling passion Tony might have given Houston some reason to suppose that she no longer stood where she used to stand in his eyes—or perhaps with a real chivalry he had perceived the dangerous course that Tony was taking and wished to save her without obtruding himself too much. Poor ugly man, with all his wealth he was a pathetic figure. He would suffer when he saw how devoted she was to Tony; she had made up her mind to charm Tony back to his old adoration of herself; this cruise might be her last opportunity.

Then why not ask one of her sisters? Such a sister, reflecting if somewhat faintly her own glories, might console Houston for an eternal impossibility. In that case she must invite the eldest now at home, and with her roses and rich brown hair might serve as a substitute for herself.

"Of course she hasn't my personality," Dorothy admitted. "And she hasn't my brown eyes. But she is beautiful, and what an excellent thing it would be if Houston should marry her. Jews have such a sense of family duty."

With the inclusion of Agnes the party was complete, and in the middle of November *The Whirligig* left Plymouth for the Mediterranean. Tony's astonishment at the production of this beautiful sister-in-law was laughable; but if heavy weather in the Bay of Biscay had not blanched most of her roses, while Dorothy's own throve in the fierce Atlantic airs, that astonishment might have turned to something less laughable. Houston, indeed, did ask Dorothy once in an undertone if it was not rather imprudent of her deliberately to create a rival for herself; but by the time the yacht had rounded Cape St. Vincent and was lying at ease in the harbor of Cadiz Tony was nearly as much his wife's slave as he was in the first days of their marriage. Dorothy, who had felt a momentary qualm about the success of her project when she saw the effect of Agnes's fair form of England against this passionate beauty of the south, decided that, on the contrary, it would be this very effect that would impress Houston much more than Tony. So far as mortal women are concerned, she had never had to bother much about Tony except when she herself had been cold with him. The fickle goddess of fortune was her only rival; but on board *The Whirligig* he seemed out of reach of temptation by her. Yes, the party was well chosen. Tufton by this time had recovered sufficiently from the heavy seas to help the dowager obtain her souvenirs of the various ports at which they called, and she at last forgave him for his advice about the pergola; Bella, inspired by a visit to Fielding's tomb at Lisbon, which was the first assurance she had received that England even existed since the Lizard Light had dropped below the horizon, was much occupied with a diary of her impressions; Tony was occupied by herself; and what should Houston do except occupy himself with Agnes? At the same time Dorothy had her doubts. Whenever she was sitting quietly with Tony in some snug windless corner of the yacht their host would always find an excuse to intervene.

After Cadiz they called at Malaga, Cartagena, and Alicante, whence by Valencia and Barcelona they were to sail by the shores of France toward the lights of Monte Carlo, which Houston now wanted to visit, although in London he had said that nothing should induce him to take the yacht there. Tony unexpectedly argued against a visit to Monte Carlo, and was only eager to attack the mouflon on that inaccessible Ægean isle. So the yacht's course was set eastward from Alicante.

"Why did you change your mind about Monte Carlo?" Dorothy asked Houston.

"Isn't it fairly obvious?"

She thought he was going to seize her hand and plunge headlong into a declaration of passion; but he turned away quickly and called her attention to the view. They were passing the southern shores of Formentera, so close that upon the sandy beach flamingos preening their wings in the sunset were plainly visible. The yacht called at Cagliari and Palermo, visited the Ionian islands, and reached the Ægean by way of the Corinth canal. The bet about the mouflon had to be canceled in the end, because the sea was never sufficiently calm to allow a boat to be lowered off Antaphros, and was still less likely to remain calm long enough for a boat to leave the deserted island again. They made several attempts to land, sailing there from their headquarters at Aphros, the white houses of which, stained with the purple Bougainvillea and mirrored in the calm waters of the harbor, seemed eternally to promise fine weather. Luckily the island also offered sufficient entertainment to compensate Tony for the loss of the mouflon; there was a club of which many rich ship-owners were members, where high play at écarté was the rule, and Tony, with the good luck that often attends strangers, repaid his hosts by winning from them nearly twenty thousand drachmas. The war in the Balkans made it difficult for the yacht to visit Constantinople, which was her original destination; and it was decided to substitute Alexandria and allow the members of the party to spend a few days in Cairo; from Egypt they would cruise along the coast of Syria, turn westward again by Cyprus and Rhodes, and with luck land a boat at Antaphros on the journey home, for Tony still regretted those mouflon.

Agnes would probably have found her stay in Aphros romantic enough at any time; but now with the supreme romance of war added and with handsome young Aphriotes going north upon their country's business by every steamer, she wished no higher ecstasy from this wonderful voyage. Agnes had enjoyed a great success on the island, where she had taught the young men and maidens to dance whatever ragtime was then the mode in West Kensington; where with them, when the dancing was done, she had climbed to the ruined temple of Aphrodite on the heights above the town and sat beneath a waning semilune that emptied her silver upon the bare and rounded hills, upon the sea, and upon a necklace of sapphire islands, past which the troopship now winking in the harbor below would sail at dawn. Like father, like son, even love shoots more arrows than usual in time of war. Agnes did not think that Egypt or Palestine could offer better than this, and when the parents of her new friends Antonia and Ariadne Venieris invited her to stay with them in their ancient house until the yacht came back, she begged her sister to make it easy for her to accept this invitation. Dorothy saw no reason to refuse, and they sailed away without her.

Three weeks later, when the yacht reached Rhodes, Dorothy found a letter from Madame Venieris awaiting her arrival, in which she announced that Agnes had married a young lieutenant called Sommaripa; she did not know what Lady Clarehaven would think of her; she did not know how to make her excuses; but at least she could assure Lady Clarehaven that the bridegroom, who was now in Thrace, was an excellent young man, an orphan with plenty of money and well regarded at court. Meanwhile, the bride must be her guest until peace was signed and her husband was released from service.

Agnes herself wrote as follows:

APHROS,
January 19, 1913.

MY DEAR DOODLES,—I suppose you're awfully fed up with me; but he is such a perfect darling and so frightfully good-looking. He owns a lot of land and a castle in Aphros that belonged to the Venetians. His ancestors were Dukes of Aphros. He's an orphan and his name is—don't laugh—Phragkiskos (Francis!) Sommaripa. I shouldn't have married in such a tearing hurry if he hadn't been going to the front. I'm writing to mother and father, etc. I suppose they'll have fits; but I really don't believe there is such a place as Lonsdale Road any more. He told me I was another Aphrodite risen from the foam. Aphros is Greek for foam. I dare say it sounds rather exaggerated when written down, but when he said it with his foreign accent I collapsed in his arms. Oh, my dear, don't be cross when you come back with the yacht. Love to everybody on board.

Your loving sister,   AGNES SOMMARIPA.

The news of her sister's escapade—well, it was something more than an escapade—affected Dorothy with a jealousy that she recognized for what it was in time to prevent herself from betraying the emotion she felt; so eager, indeed, was she to hide it that she proclaimed her approval of what Agnes had done, and so emphatically that the dowager was much agitated lest Bella should follow her example; but Bella did nothing more alarming than to sit down forthwith in the saloon and begin a very passionate and romantic story founded upon fact and drenched in local color.

Meanwhile, the Italian governor of Rhodes was taking steps to assure himself that *The Whirligig* was not a Greek war-ship with evil designs upon the Turkish population, which he was petting as a nurse pets a child she has lately had the gratification of smacking. As soon as the police spies guaranteed the harmlessness of the yacht the governor was hospitable and invited the members of the party to shoot the red-legged partridges and woodcock upon the Rhodian uplands. Tony, Bella, and Tufton accepted the invitation; the dowager, fearful lest Bella should envy the repose of some fascinating Turk's harem in the interior, accompanied them in the motor-car as far as the road permitted, where she alighted and passed the time in picking the red and purple anemones that blew in myriads all around, until the sportsmen had killed enough birds and were ready for lunch.

Houston suggested to Dorothy that they should take a walk round the town while the others were away; she accepted, for she was anxious to shake off this brooding jealousy which had oppressed her since the news in Agnes's letter.

"I shouldn't worry myself about your sister," he was saying.

Dorothy frowned to think he should have read her thoughts so easily.

"I'm not worrying. I think she has done exactly right."

"Envying her, in fact," Houston added.

"Why should I envy her?"

He shrugged his shoulders.

"Don't we always rather envy the people who do things with such decision? Don't we sometimes feel that we're wasting time?"

He said this so meaningly that Dorothy pretended not to hear what he had said and looked up to admire the fortified gate of St. Catherine through which they were passing.

"It's like Oxford!" she exclaimed.

Her jealousy of Agnes was stimulated by this comparison, for when they came to the Street of the Knights she was reminded of that day when she walked down the High with Sylvia, that Sunday afternoon which had been the prelude of everything. How many years ago?

"O God!" she exclaimed, reverting in her manner, as she often used in Houston's company, to that hard Vanity manner. "O God! I shall be twenty-nine in March!"

"I'm over forty."

"But you're a man. What does your age matter?"

She was looking at him, and thinking while she spoke how ugly he was. Perhaps he realized her thought, for his face darkened with that blush of the very sallow complexion, that blush which seems more like a bruise.

"You mean I'm too hideous?"

"Don't be silly. Let's explore this gateway."

They passed under a Gothic arch and found themselves in a cloistered quadrangle, so much like a small Oxford college that only a tall palm against the blue sky above the roofs told how far they were from Oxford.

"It's uncanny," said Dorothy. "How stupid Tony was to go off shooting without first exploring the town. How stupid of him!"

Dorothy wanted her husband's presence as she had never wanted it; she wanted to help the illusion that she was back in Oxford with all the adventure of life before her. She wanted to see him here in this familiar setting and revive ... what?

"I hope Agnes will be happy," she sighed.

Close by a couple of Jews in wasp-striped gabardines were arguing about something in a mixture of Spanish and Yiddish; without thinking and anxious only to get back to the present, Dorothy asked Houston if he could understand what they were talking about. Again that dark blush showed like a bruise.

"Why should I understand them?" he asked, savagely.

"No, of course. I really don't know," she stammered, in confusion, for she was thinking how much better a gabardine would suit Houston than his yachting-suit and how exactly his pendulous under lip resembled the under lips of the two disputants. An odd fancy came into her mind that she would rather like to be carried off by Houston, to be held in captivity by him in the swarming ghetto through which they had picked their way a few minutes ago, to sit peering mysteriously through the lattice of some crazy balcony ... to surrender to some one strong and Eastern and.... Oh, but this was absurd! The sun was hot in this quadrangle; she was in an odd state; it must be that the news about Agnes had upset her more than she had thought. At that moment her eyes rested upon the broken headpiece of a tomb that was leaning against the cloister, and she found herself reading in a dream: "Gilbert Clare of Clarehaven. With God. 1501." The palm still swayed against the blue sky; the Jews still chattered at one another. Dorothy looked round her with a dazed expression, and then impulsively knelt down among the rubble that surrounded the tombstone and read the words again: "Gilbert Clare of Clarehaven. With God. 1501." The Italian curator of the museum that was being formed in the old hospital drew near and explained to Dorothy in French that this was the tombstone of an English knight.

"An ancestor of mine," Dorothy told him.

The curator smiled politely; being a Latin, he certainly did not believe her.

"I've never seen you so much interested by anything," said Houston.

"I never have been so thrilled by anything," she declared. "Gilbert Clare of Clarehaven! Clarehaven! And when he left it he must have often thought of our little church on the headland; and when he died here, how he must have longed to be at home."

"Does Clare mean very much to you?" Houston asked.

"*You* could never imagine how much. For Clare I would do anything!"

"Anything? That's a rash statement."

"Anything," she repeated.

Houston tried to persuade the curator to let him have the tombstone for Dorothy to take away with her; but the curator was shocked at such a suggestion and explained that it was an unusual inscription—the earliest of the kind in English that he knew; he should have expected Latin at such a date.

The countess failed to rouse much enthusiasm in the earl about the tomb of his ancestor, but the dowager was glad he was with God; Bella had a subject for another story; and Tufton photographed it. The next day the wind seemed likely to shift round into the north, and *The Whirligig* left the exposed harbor, traveling past the mighty limestone cliffs of the Dorian promontory, past Cos and many other islands, until once more her anchor was dropped in the sheltered blue waters of Aphros.

There were interminable discussions at the house of Monsieur and Madame Venieris; but there was no doubt whatever that Agnes was married.

"And do you know, my dear Doodles," her sister added, when they were alone, "do you know I believe I'm already going to have a baby?"

Dorothy could stand no more; but when she begged that all speed should be made for England there came a series of breathless days during which Tony stalked the mouflon on the heights of Antaphros. In the end he actually did hit one, and though it fell at the foot of a difficult precipice he scrambled down somehow, raised the carcass with ropes, and rowed triumphantly away with it to the yacht. Houston tossed him double or quits for the sovereign he had won; Tony won five tosses in succession and thirty-two pounds.

"My luck's in," he shouted, gleefully. "Come on, Houston, full speed ahead. I want to see my horses again."

When the yacht reached Plymouth the whole party went ashore and traveled up to Clare.

"Yes," Houston admitted to Dorothy, "I can understand the appeal this sort of thing must have for anybody. It must be glorious here in summer. I suppose the deer look after themselves? Yes, it's a wonderful old place."

A week after their guests had left Tony and Dorothy followed them to London.

"Oh, by the way, Doodles," said Tony at Paddington, "I ought to have explained before, but I've got a little surprise for you. I had to sell one hundred and twenty-nine. I was offered a nailing good price."

"And where are we going to live?" she asked.

"Well, that's the surprise. You'll never guess. I've taken your old flat in Halfmoon Street."

Dorothy looked at Tony.

"You're not angry?" he asked.

"I think I'm past anger," she said, dully.

While they were driving to their new abode Dorothy decided that it would be easy to convince her family that such a romantic marriage was the right thing for Agnes, because her arguments would come from the depths of her heart.

"And *I* shall be twenty-nine in March," she kept thinking.

"Of course I kept all your favorite things," Tony was saying. "I sold the rest. The pictures fetched a deuced poor price. I hope that if the Clare pictures ever have to go I shall have more luck with them."

"I wonder you don't offer to sell me," said Dorothy, bitterly.

He squeezed her arm affectionately.

"Sha'n't have to do that just yet awhile. I'm going to have a lucky year. I felt that when I pipped that mouflon. Ever since I broke the glass at one hundred and twenty-nine I've been deuced uneasy. As soon as the house was sold I began winning at écarté, and then I pipped that mouflon."

V

The sale of the house in Curzon Street revived all Dorothy's worst fears. If Tony could successfully hide from her knowledge such a transaction he was capable of announcing one day that Clare itself was gone. Life had not offered much stability since that fatal June except for the brief period when Tony's career upon the turf had accorded with the traditions of his order and had seemed to possess the dignity that confers itself automatically upon those who put forth their hands to claim their due, her existence had been periodically shaken like a town in the shadow of a volcano. Was not his marriage judged from the outside a contribution to failure similar to the running of Moonbeam in the Derby? Was she herself much more than a disappointing race-horse? She had failed to keep her classic engagements at Clare; she had failed to carry her weight in the big handicap at Curzon Street. Was the flat in Halfmoon Street a selling-plate? Oh, this flat, how it was haunted with the ghosts of old ambitions! The color schemes and patterns of the chintz might be different, but how familiarly the bells rang, how familiar was the sound of the doors opening and shutting, and the light upon her dressing-table ... and the rumble of the traffic ... leading whither?

"Tony, what *do* you want?" she asked, passionately, one morning when the sparrows were maddening her with their monotonous chirping praise of the sunshine.

"I want to win the Derby," he said.

"And lose everything else, even me?" she asked.

"And lose nothing," he maintained, obstinately. "Starkey fears nothing."

Starkey feared nothing! Starkey with his long, thin nose and red hair!

By now two of Tony's yearlings stood out well above the rest. Of these a bay colt by Cyllene out of Midsummer Night and, therefore, a half-brother of Moonbeam, had run well in the Brocklesby Stakes at Lincoln, still better in the Westminster Plate at the Epsom Spring Meeting, and had cantered away with the Spring Two-year-old Stakes at Newmarket. He was considered to be a certainty for the Woodcote Stakes; but on Starkey's advice Tony ran instead a chestnut filly by Spearmint out of Blushrose, who won with considerable ease, beating horses that had shown up well in the previous races. Clarehaven was jubilant; Starkey feared nothing; they had next year's Derby in their hands. It had been just after this last victory that Tony had affirmed his only ambition in life to be the Derby. At Ascot, still running unnamed, the filly won the Coventry Stakes; half an hour afterward Moonbeam took the Ascot

Stakes by five lengths, and two days later, starting as an odds on favorite, he won the Gold Cup without being extended; finally on the same day the Midsummer Night colt won the New Stakes and was named Full Moon, for certainly the fortunes of Clare seemed in their complement.

"There's never been such an Ascot," said Tony to his wife.

Houston had had to go to South Africa soon after he returned from the Mediterranean cruise; while he was still away, Tony's luck touched its zenith when Moonbeam won the Eclipse Stakes at Sandown Park.

"Though it's lucky Mr. Houston sold Chimpanzee to that Australian syndicate," said Starkey. "Because I give you my word, my lord, that Chimpanzee was a better horse than Moonbeam, just as the filly is better than the colt."

"I think you're wrong about Moonbeam," Tony argued, "though you may be right about the filly."

When Houston reached England in July he motored down to Winsley with the Clarehavens to discuss future plans with the trainer, and when the old argument about the respective merits of Chimpanzee and Moonbeam began, as usual, he laughed, saying that for him the discussion was a barren one, because after this Derby victory he did not intend to tempt fortune any more.

"I wish you could persuade Tony to follow your example," said Dorothy.

"Don't be silly, old thing. I haven't won the Derby yet," Tony proclaimed, in a hurt voice.

"Don't be afraid, my lord; you can't lose it next year, not if you tried. Of course I'm not going to say yet for certain whether it'll be with the colt or with the filly; but I think it'll be with the filly."

"Which reminds me," said Tony. "We haven't given the lady a name yet."

"Why not Vanity Girl?" Houston suggested.

"Of course," Tony shouted, gleefully. "Vanity Girl she is."

Dorothy protested that the name would bring bad luck and begged for Mignonette instead.

"Mignonette won a race at Liverpool only yesterday," said the trainer.

"But there must be plenty of other names that haven't been used," Dorothy insisted. "As we've got the Full Moon of Clare, why shouldn't we call the filly Supporting Angel?"

"Well," said Mr. Starkey, "with her ladyship's permission, I prefer Vanity Girl. It sounds like a winner."

Tony and Houston were emphatically in favor of Vanity Girl, and the filly was named accordingly. Dorothy stayed behind to contemplate the beautiful creature in her box, the fair, shimmering creature lately anonymous and now burdened with what was surely a title of ill omen.

"But you have no ambitions," said Dorothy. "If you fail you won't mind. What do you care about your purple clothing with its black border and its silver coronet?"

Dorothy left the dim, cool stable and emerged into the glare of the July noon. She felt sad about the filly's name, and, unwilling to meet the others until she had recovered from her depression, she walked away from Starkey Lodge, walked up the sloping single street of the little village of Winsley, the houses of which seemed to have drifted like leaves into this cranny of the bare downs. At the top of the street the village ended abruptly where a white road ran like a line of foam between a sea of grass that stretched skyward to right and left until the horizon faded into the summer haze.

"Thirty next March," said Dorothy, aloud. "And what have I done with my life?"

She envied the thistledown that floated by, envied its busy air and effect of traveling whither it would; compared with those winged seeds the blue butterflies seemed as irresolute and timorous of the future as herself ... herself.... A voice shouted that lunch was waiting, and there was Tony waving to her from the road. Lunch was waiting for herself; but for that thistledown what was waiting? Dorothy's clear-cut personality was becoming blurred; she never used to speculate about thistledown in cloud cuckoo land. Everybody noticed the change. Some had heard that there really was something between Dorothy Clarehaven and that fellow Houston; others knew for a positive fact that Tony Clarehaven neglected his wife; and all the women decided that she must be well over thirty by now.

Tony began to bet recklessly as soon as Houston returned, and by the autumn he was again in difficulties. Moonbeam failed to give two stone to a smart three-year-old in the Jockey Club Stakes, and he lost much more than Full Moon had made for him by winning the Boscawen Stakes the day before. But there had been no purchase at Tattersall's, no ambitious yearlings from Doncaster, for Tony had given his word to Dorothy that after next year's Derby he would retire from racing. In fact, to show that this time he was in earnest he sold all his horses except the two sons of Cyllene and Vanity Girl. The filly had just won a severe trial and on Starkey's advice was preferred to Full Moon for the Middle Park Plate. She was heavily backed, started a hot favorite, and was not placed. Tony declined to accept her running as true and backed her heavily to win the Dewhurst Plate. O'Hara was brought over from France to ride her, and she was again unplaced. Some people declared she was no stayer, some that her victories at Epsom and Ascot had been flukes; others spoke of coughing in the Starkey Lodge Stables; a few murmured that a coup for next year's Derby was being carefully engineered.

"I knew it would bring bad luck to call her Vanity Girl," Dorothy lamented. "Sell her. Get rid of her. Get rid of them all."

"Sell the Derby winner?" Tony ejaculated. "My dear Doodles, you surely must realize that her form at Newmarket was too bad to be true. If she can beat Full Moon at home, and if Full Moon can beat the winner of the Middle Park as he did in the Boscawen Stakes, one or other of them *must* win the Derby. We'll see how they winter. Meanwhile I've sold Moonbeam to Houston. He paid me twenty-six thousand pounds. He intends to start a stud; I'm bound to say he got my horse cheap; whatever Starkey says, Chimpanzee would never have beaten him again; but I wanted the money."

"I'm sorry you've had to sell Moonbeam, but do sell Vanity Girl, too. Don't bet any more on any of them. Run Full Moon for the Derby, and if he wins be content with that. Then we could start a stud at Clare ourselves. But do get rid of Vanity Girl."

She felt as the dowager must have felt when she was trying to dissuade Tony from marrying an actress; she instanced every disadvantage she could think of for the filly; but Tony was obstinate.

They were going out that afternoon to the Pierian Hall. Sylvia Scarlett, after over two years' absence in America, had returned to England and suddenly taken the fancy of the public with a new form of entertainment that was considered very futurist. Dorothy did not think that her performance deserved all the praise it had received, but she felt jealous of Sylvia's success and, turning to Tony in the interval, said, fiercely, that sometimes she wished she had never married him.

"I should have done better to stick to the stage," she vowed.

"If you're wishing you hadn't married me because you'd like to be doing this sort of thing," said Tony, "you can spare your regrets. This, my dear Doodles, is the rottenest show I ever saw in my life."

"But it's a success."

"Only because it's so devilish peculiar. If I walked down Bond Street in pajamas I should attract a certain amount of attention the first time I did it, but people would get used to it, and I should soon be forgotten. By the way, would you like to send round a card?"

"No, no," said Dorothy. "I've seen quite enough of her from where we are."

"Don't get bitter, Doodles. I don't know what's come over you lately. You seem to hate everything and everybody."

That winter was a miserable one, because Tony took to baccarat again, and, having been accustomed to bet on the turf in large sums, he carried his methods to the tables with such recklessness that Dorothy, unable to stand the strain, left him in London and went down to Clare. She had a notion to kill herself out hunting, but even in this she was unsuccessful, for in February all the hunters, including Mignonette, were sold. Moreover, at the end of the month a valuer arrived with an authorization from Tony to complete the details for a forthcoming auction of the whole property as it stood, pictures and all. Dorothy hastened up to London and demanded what was the matter.

"The matter is that I've got to sell Clare."

"Sell Clare?" she repeated. "I suppose you mean mortgage it?"

"Mortgage it? It's mortgaged already."

"But you paid that off."

"Yes, once. But you don't suppose that I've always got money handy?" he asked, petulantly. "Some damned firm has bought up all my bills; I'm being pressed all round; and the Jews won't lend me another farthing."

"Then you must sell the horses."

"The Derby winner? They're my only chance of keeping out of the bankruptcy court. They're all we have, Doodles."

"You have Clare."

"How can I pay the interest on the mortgages and live at Clare? Try to be a little reasonable. I've got a good offer, and the money will come in very handy for the final plunge."

"You're mad."

"All right. I'm mad."

"But your mother?"

"I've given Greenish notice to leave Cherrington Cottage and I'm reserving that from the sale."

"But what will your mother live on?"

"Oh, of course her jointure will be paid. Besides, I tell you that this season with Full Moon and Vanity Girl I simply can't go wrong. The mistake I made was playing baccarat with my ready cash."

"Won't Houston help you?"

"My dear Doodles, it's Houston who's going to buy Clare."

She was silent before the revelation of what for long she had surmised. The quadrangle of the hospital in Rhodes where she had admitted openly that for Clare she would do anything flashed upon her vision, and the thought of that Oriental patience practised for so long terrified her. His desire for her must have been kindled years ago, a desire that, once kindled, had been fed by the will to revenge himself for being what he was upon Clarehaven for being what *he* was. It was Houston who had subtly helped his rival along the road to ruin, taking him by the arm as it were to the edge of the precipice and toppling him over. Now it was her place to interview this enemy, plead with him, entreat him to be content with what he had done already ... but of what use would entreaties be? Of no use except to stimulate the lust of victory.

"You can't sell Clare to Houston," she was saying, mechanically, lest her silence should be noticed. "You can't sell Clare to Houston," she was repeating; and then she was off again, chasing the excited, restless ideas in her brain until she should have driven them like poultry into a corner and be able to pick the victim that should serve her best. Yes, yes, if Houston really did covet her, she still had a chance to preserve Clare. There was no weaker adversary for a woman whose heart was untouched than a man who was madly in love ... no weaker adversary.... Should she write to Houston and give him the idea that by pressing her hard he could win? In the past she had known how to cook a dozen geese in fierce ovens without cooking her own by mistake, without even burning her fingers. If Houston had waited years, he would surely be willing to risk a few more weeks.

"You can't sell Clare to Houston," she said, once more.

"For God's sake, don't go on repeating that like a parrot," said Tony. "I'm going round to settle the matter now."

A few moments later the door of the flat slammed behind him. Houston lived in Albany, not five minutes away, and Dorothy went across to the telephone.

"Yes? Who's speaking?"

"Dorothy Clarehaven. Listen," she said, hurriedly. "Once you lent me money, or at any rate you helped me make money, and you were always very decent about it. Won't you do the same thing again? You know that Tony is putting everything on the ability of one of our two horses to win the Derby. Tell me—there's every reason to suppose he will win the Derby—why shouldn't you lend him enough to prevent his selling Clare?"

"Why not, indeed?" said Mr. Houston. "But what's the security?"

"Aren't the horses a security?"

"Horses are very capricious, almost as capricious as women."

"Would you prefer a woman as security?" she asked, trying to rake up from nine years ago a coquetry that had once been so profitable. It was easier by telephone. "Supposing I offered myself as security?"

So much was she playing a part of long ago that instinctively she had used her old invincible gesture of lightly touching a man's sleeve. That also was easier by telephone.

"I could lend a good deal," twanged the voice of the buyer along the wires. "I could lend a good deal."

"Very well then," said Dorothy. "Lend *me* the money."

"By telephone? Not good enough. Come, come, let's be frank, let's be brutally frank. You know you're worth twenty Derby winners to me; but, as I said, women are more capricious than horses. I'm no longer a schoolboy. Are you in earnest or not?"

"Of course I'm in earnest," she said. "Why should you think I wasn't?"

"So much in earnest that you'll come to my rooms this afternoon and tell me so?"

"Yes, if you like," she replied, without hesitating. "But you must prove to me that you're in earnest too. Send me something on account."

"How much do you want?"

"Oh, I don't know," she said. "About fifty thousand pounds I suppose."

Dorothy's sense of proportion about large sums of money had been destroyed by her husband's extravagant betting. When one lives with a man who will win £50,000 at Ascot and lose it all and more the following week, it is difficult to preserve a table of comparative values. She supposed that £50,000 would represent about half the price of Clare, and the importance she attributed to Clare gave money such a relative unimportance that she saw nothing even faintly ridiculous in demanding a sum of this magnitude from Houston. Perhaps he was impressed by the size of her demand into believing that she really was in earnest about accepting his proposals; even a financier like himself might be excused for supposing that a woman, one of the most beautiful women in England and a countess to boot, does not ask for £50,000 without being in earnest. At the same time it appealed to his sense of humor that any woman, even England's most beautiful countess, should ask for £50,000 by telephone.

"Why, it's not even a note of hand," he chuckled, and his laugh, traveling from Albany to Halfmoon Street along the wires, lost its mirth on the way and reached Dorothy with the sound of a dropped banjo.

"Well, I must have something to prove you're in earnest," she argued, fiercely. "Tony is on his way to see you now. He'll be with you in another minute. Tell him that as a friend you can't let him sell Clare. Offer him enough to tide him over the Derby. I'm willing to risk everything on that."

"Are you trying to tell me that if Clarehaven pulls off the Derby our arrangement is canceled? Ring off. Nothing doing, dear lady."

Away in Albany she heard a bell shrill; it was like a prompter's warning of the play's ending.

"That's Tony now," she cried. "Do what I ask. Give him enough. He'll say how much is necessary for the moment. Lend it to him on the security of Clare. Buy up his mortgages. Do what you like, and if Tony comes back with Clare still his, at any rate until he has lost all or saved all on the Derby, I'll come to Albany this afternoon and thank you."

"Tangibly?" murmured Houston.

"Tangibly."

Her agitated breath had so bedewed the mouthpiece that when with trembling hands she replaced the holder it was like being released from a kiss.

VI

Tony came back from his visit to Houston in a temper of serene optimism.

"Well, Doodles," he cried, gaily, "I've saved Clare for you."

"Oh, you've saved Clare, have you?" She could not resist a slight accentuation of the pronoun, but he did not notice it.

"Yes, Houston was very decent. I told him how much I hated getting rid of the old place, and he was very decent. Of course he knows from Starkey that the Derby is a certainty and that in Full Moon and Vanity Girl I've got the two best three-year-olds in England."

"You're still infatuated with the filly?"

"Now wait a minute. Don't begin arguing till you hear what's been decided. Houston is going to lend me enough cash to pay off the present mortgages of Clare, and when that is done I'm going to mortgage the place to him on the understanding that if I don't settle up on the Monday after the Derby he takes immediate possession. I told him that I should want some ready money, and he offers to buy whichever horse I don't run in the Derby."

"Then sell him Vanity Girl," said Dorothy, quickly. She could hardly refrain from adding, "One of us he must have."

"Don't be in such a hurry. At present Full Moon has engagements in the Two Thousand Guineas and the Derby, also in the Grand Prix and the Leger. Vanity Girl is entered for the Thousand Guineas, the Derby, and the Oaks. I shall run Full Moon for the Guineas; if he wins he will be the Derby favorite. In that case I shall scratch Vanity Girl for the Thousand Guineas, and we'll have a secret trial at Winsley. Houston hasn't taken Moonbeam away yet, and Starkey is to put him into strong work for this trial. If Full Moon shows up best in the trial I shall sell Vanity Girl to Houston, who will run her in the Oaks; then I shall back Full Moon for the Derby till the cows come home. But if, as Starkey thinks and as I think, Vanity Girl is the goods, Houston is to have Full Moon for ten thousand pounds as soon as I've scratched him for the Derby. I don't want to scratch him until I've got my money out on the filly, but I shall get busy quickly, and the public will have plenty of time to know which horse I think is going to win. Then you and I, Doodles dear, will retire from the turf and live ever afterward at Clare."

"And if Full Moon doesn't win the Guineas?"

"Oh, I've thought of that. In that case I shall run Vanity Girl in the Thousand Guineas, declare to win with either in the Derby, and Houston is to have his pick after the race for ten thousand pounds."

"And you've thought out all this wonderful and complicated plan of campaign?"

"Not entirely," Tony admitted.

"Not at all," said Dorothy, sharply. "You know perfectly well that Houston thought out every detail of it."

She wondered if a man who could juggle like this with the future of horses might not be equally expert with women. But no, he wanted the woman; he did not want the horses. She sent a note round to Albany saying that a bad headache kept her at home that afternoon, but that she fully appreciated the good will he had just shown and that she hoped to see him at dinner to-morrow. She knew that she could not keep Houston at arm's-length indefinitely, but if she could keep him there until, at any rate, Clare was temporarily safe she should have a breathing-space until June. Then if Tony lost the Derby, she should have to offer herself to preserve Clare; but if he won, she and Clare would both be saved.

"God!" she cried to her soul, "with me it always seems that June is to decide everything."

When the following night Houston reproached her for breaking the appointment of yesterday she reminded him that he, too, had only made promises so far; but when Houston kept his word and freed Clare until the settling day after Epsom, she still held back.

"You'll appreciate me all the more for being kept waiting."

"I've waited years," he said.

"I'll go for a drive with you to-morrow."

So it went on until the week before the Guineas.

"You're trying to fool me. You think you can get something for nothing as easily now as you could when you were at the Vanity."

"Be reasonable, my dear man," she begged. "Your money is perfectly safe. What are you risking? If Tony loses the Derby you win me the moment you put in my hands the title-deeds of Clare. If Tony wins the Derby...." She let her deep-brown eyes gaze into his.

"Kiss me," said Houston. "Kiss me once and I'll believe you."

A good lady's maid is bound to enjoy a considerable amount of intimacy in her relationship with her mistress; no lover is allowed as much. Dorothy from youth had trained her kisses to be her servants; they had always served her well, and if a degree of intimacy was unavoidable it was always the intimacy of a servant, which does not count. One of these kisses she summoned to her aid now.

Tony proposed that Lonsdale should drive them down to Newmarket for the Guineas, but Lonsdale said he was booked to fly on that day.

"You never come near us now," said Dorothy, reproachfully.

"I can't stand that fellow Houston. I can't think how you can bear him around all the time."

"He's very amusing," said Dorothy.

"So's a bishop in a bathing-dress. If you want amusement you can get plenty of it," Lonsdale growled, "without having to depend on a fellow like that."

Tufton, who was as sensitive as a tress of seaweed to the atmosphere, had also neglected his old friends recently, and Dorothy knew by his manner that people must now be talking very hard about herself and Houston.

Tony kept his promise not to bet heavily on the result of the Guineas, and Full Moon's win did not do more than keep quiet a certain number of low-class creditors who had for some time been supplying Lord and Lady Clarehaven with such trifles as wine, food, and clothes. However, the win did seem to make the Derby a certainty for the stable; Full Moon and Vanity Girl, unlike Moonbeam, had both won at Epsom as two-year-olds, and if Vanity Girl could beat Full Moon, surely no horse in England could beat her on a course to which she had already shown her partiality. When the filly did not appear in the Thousand Guineas the quidnuncs, the how-nows, and the what-nots of the turf said she had wintered disappointingly and that she would never be seen in the Oaks. There was scarcely a sporting paper that did not assure its readers that they would soon hear of Vanity Girl's having been scratched for both the Derby and the Oaks. She was a flier, but a non-stayer, and the Stewards' Cup at Goodwood was her journey.

At the same time the quidnuncs, the how-nows, and the what-nots of the turf were puzzled to find that after Full Moon's victory in the Guineas no money from Starkey Lodge seemed to be going on the colt's chances for the Derby. All the touts set hard to work to solve what was called the Starkey Lodge Puzzle; Winsley and the hamlets round were frequented by inquisitive men whose pockets were bulging with sheaves of telegraph forms.

"They think we've got something up our sleeves," said the trainer to the owner. It was half past four o'clock of a morning early in May; Tony, Dorothy, Houston, and Starkey had just taken up their positions to watch the trial that was to decide which horse should carry the Clarehaven colors a month hence. They had motored down to Winsley the night before; and under a cold sky of turquoise scattered with pearls and amethysts they had ridden up here at dawn; but when their clothing had been taken off the horses, heads had popped up like rabbits from behind every hillock along the course.

"No good running it this morning," said the trainer, shouting some abuse at the touts and galloping his hack in the direction of the horses.

The sun was now well about the rounded edge of the downs; the air of the morning was lustrous and scented with young grass upon which the dew lay like golden wine.

"You can't get up too early for these touts," Starkey told them at breakfast, "and if we want to know where we are for the Derby a bit before any one else, we'll have to run the trial by moonlight. I'll keep 'em on the hop all the day before and tire some of these Nosey Parkers into staying at home for once in their lives."

Dorothy was never sorry of an excuse to spend a few days with the horses. They had caused her so much misery; but she had no ill will when she saw them.

"Yes," said the trainer. "A moonlight trial. That's the ticket. What with Full Moon and Moonbeam you can't say it isn't highly suitable. I'm not going to pretend that Moonbeam is up to his best form. Thinking Mr. Houston was going to take him to the stud, I only began putting him into strong work a month ago. So I thought we'd run them at weights for sex, and put in a couple of good handicappers belonging to Mr. Ginsberg to make a bit of a field."

At two o'clock there was the clank of a pail in the stable-yard, followed by a low murmur of voices and the grumble of the big yard gates being cautiously opened. Presently the team emerged and walked slowly up the village street, where half a dozen touts were fast asleep, because they must be up at dawn to haunt the entrance to the Starkey Lodge Stables. By the magic of the moon the horses in their clothing were turned into the caparisoned steeds of knights-at-arms setting forth upon a romantic quest. Dorothy, Houston, Tony, and the trainer followed on hacks; and even when far out of hearing of the most vigilant tout they continued to talk in half-tones. So breathless was the night that the thundering of the hoofs coming nearer and nearer over the turf seemed to vibrate the stars, and Dorothy had a fancy that presently all the people in the little villages below the rim of the downs would wake and run with lanterns up here to know if the moon had fallen down upon the great world.

Vanity Girl won the trial; Moonbeam was second; the winner of the Guineas was third.

"Well, I hope that's decisive enough," said Tony, gleefully. "Starkey, you were right!"

He and the trainer moved off in excited conversation. Houston took Dorothy's hand, and she did not try to withdraw it from his grasp; Vanity Girl was going to win the Derby; Clare would be safe in June; she should be safe in June. The benevolent moon, quite undisturbed by all this mad nocturnal galloping, gazed blandly at Dorothy's complaisance; she would not have put a cloud up to her face for much more than that, the unscrupulous old bawd.

A week later the following paragraph appeared in one of the sporting weeklies:

THE STARKEY LODGE PUZZLE

Rumor says that the young Earl of Clarehaven, who has recently had very heavy losses on the turf, positively intends to capture the Derby this year. It was only a few months ago that we had to condole with the gallant young nobleman on the sad necessity which forced him to sell that great horse Moonbeam last year to the well-known South African capitalist, Mr. Lionel Houston, who indorsed the public view that Moonbeam's defeat in the Derby by his own horse Chimpanzee was not true form when he sold Chimpanzee to an Australian syndicate of breeders and bought Moonbeam for the stud he is now forming, and which we have no doubt will give many famous new names to the history of English racing. But our readers' present concern is what is popularly known as the Starkey Lodge Puzzle. We have the highest authority for saying that this is no longer a puzzle. At an important trial held in great secrecy on the Starkey Lodge training-grounds it was conclusively established that Vanity Girl is more than likely to give the Blue Riband of the turf to Lord Clarehaven and console him for the failure of Moonbeam. It will interest our readers from the smallest punter upward to hear that Full Moon, the victor of the Two Thousand Guineas and the present Derby favorite, will not run at Epsom, having been sold like his half-brother to Mr. Lionel Houston, who no doubt intends to keep him for the St. Leger, a race which he is ambitious of winning. We need scarcely point out to our readers the obvious tip for this year's Derby, and we do not hesitate to plump right out for Vanity Girl as the winner. We were the only paper to advise our readers not to back Full Moon until the intentions of the stable were a little plainer, and to all those who failed to follow our advice we can only say, "I told you so." Lord Clarehaven has done well to scratch the winner of the Guineas, for there is no doubt that if both the colt and his stable companion had faced the starter at Epsom the public would have followed the son of Cyllene. As it is, we confidently expect to see Vanity Girl a raging favorite before the week is out, and we may remind our readers that Lord Clarehaven's beautiful chestnut has already shown that she likes the Epsom course by winning the Woodcote Stakes last year. Her running at Newmarket last autumn may be discounted. We happened to know that the stable was coughing; as we have hinted, the gallant young nobleman who sports the black, white, and purple was very hard hit by her defeats, and this expression of renewed confidence in the chestnut daughter of Spearmint cannot be disregarded.

The people who had hurried to put their money on Full Moon grumbled loudly; but the public appreciated the clear lead that Tony had given them. He had put his own money on Vanity Girl before the result of the trial leaked out, and though he had obtained tens against the first two thousand he wagered, the news ran round the clubs so quickly that even before the public was warned by the scratching of Full Moon that Vanity Girl was the hope of Clare, he was finding it hard to get fours against the filly; after that her price shortened to five to two; in the week before the race it was only six to four; in the ring on the day itself not a bookmaker was risking more than eleven to ten, and with money still pouring in faster than ever she seemed likely to start at odds on, an unprecedented price for a horse that had not been seen in public since two consecutive defeats in the autumn of the year before. The public could not be blamed for their eagerness to back the filly. It was generally known that Clarehaven either had to win the Derby or be ruined, and if he preferred Vanity Girl to the winner of the Guineas at such a crisis in his affair she must indeed be sure of her success. If the public had known that even his wife's honor was in pawn besides his house and his lands they could not have been more confident.

"If Vanity Girl fails," Dorothy asked, on the morning of the race, "you won't have a halfpenny left?"

"I might have an odd hundred pounds," Tony reckoned.

"And your mother—and Bella?"

He shrugged his shoulders.

"I suppose Uncle Chat will look after them."

"And us?"

"Oh, we'll emigrate or something. Rather fun, don't you know. I shall wangle something. The going will be hardish," he said, looking at the sky, "and that's always in her favor. She hated that Newmarket mud last autumn. Come on, Doodles, the car's waiting."

They walked down the steps of the flat, and the porter who had hurried out to shut the door of the car touched his cap.

"Good luck, my lady! Good luck, my lord! Shepherd's Market is on Vanity Girl to the last copper."

"Put on a sovereign for yourself, Galloway," said his lordship, grandly proffering the coin.

Several loafers who had sometimes run for his lordship's cabs shouted, "Hurrah for the Derby favorite!" and Tony flung them some silver to back his filly. The road to Epsom was thronged; Tony, who was obviously feeling nervous, had left the driving to the chauffeur, and was sitting back with Dorothy in the body of the car.

"I think Lonnie might have come with us," he said, fretfully.

"Does it bore you so much driving with me alone?" she asked.

"Don't be silly! Of course not. But I'm nervy and.... Oh, but what rot! Nothing can go wrong."

They were passing a four-in-hand with loud toots upon their Gabriel horn, which were being answered by the guard of the coach, when he suddenly recognized the occupants of the car. Standing up, he blew a dear "Viewhalloo!" and shouted: "Berkshire's on the filly, my lord, to the last baby! Hurrah for Vanity Girl!" There was a block in the traffic; the occupants of every vehicle in earshot, from the gray hats and laces of the four-in-hand to the pearlies and plumes of a coster's cart, applauded the earl and countess, each after his own fashion.

"Don't forget the Mile End Road, Mr. Hearl of Clarehaven," bawled one of the costers, "if that's who you are. Hoobeeluddiray!" he went on, and caught his moke an ecstatic thwack on the crupper.

In the ring friends and acquaintances crowded round them, eager to say how they had backed Vanity Girl and how fervently they hoped for her victory. There was no doubt that if the filly was beaten a groan of disappointment would resound through England.

"I think it's so sweet that Lord Clarehaven's horse should be called Vanity Girl," some foolish woman was babbling. "So sweet and romantic," she twittered on.

"Yes, what devotion," chirped another as foolish.

Tony wanted to go round to the paddock to have a few last words with Starkey and the jockey O'Hara, but Dorothy did not think she could bear to see the filly before the race.

"I'm so nervous," she said, "that I feel I should communicate my nerves to her. But don't you bother about me. I'll wait for you in the inclosure."

"Where's Houston?" said Tony, irritably. "I thought he was going to meet us."

At that moment a messenger-boy came up. "Are you the Earl of Clarehaven?" he asked, perkily, and handed Tony a note, which the latter read out:

"DEAR CLAREHAVEN,—To what will I'm sure be my lifelong regret, important business prevents me from being at Epsom to see your triumph. Believe me, my dear fellow, that there is no one who hopes more cordially than I do for your success to-day. My kindest regards to your wife and tell her from me that I'm looking forward to our Derby dinner at the Carlton to-night.

Yours ever sincerely,
LIONEL HOUSTON."

"Funny chap! But I believe he's sincere," Tony muttered, "though it would be all to his interest if I lost."

But how much to his interest, Dorothy thought, how little did Tony know.

She waited for him in the company of the twittering women until he returned from the paddock.

"They're going down now," he told her.

"Everything all right?" she asked.

"Yes, yes." He was biting his nails and cursing the focusing arrangements of his field-glasses.

"They're off!"

The roar of the crowd was like a mighty storm within which isolated remarks were heard like the spars of a ship going one by one.

"She isn't finding it so easy."

"He's taking her into the rails too soon."

"My God! I wouldn't lay sixpence there won't be an objection for crossing. Did you see that?"

"Go on, Vanity Girl! Go on!"

"Go on, you blasted favorite!"

"She's swishing her tail."

"No, she's not. That's ... yes, it's her. Vanity Girl! Vanity Girl!"

"Go on, Vanity Girl!"

The roaring died down to a suppressed murmur of agitation.

"What's the matter with the favorite?"

"O'Hara's flogging her along."

The horses flashed past the stand with the black, white and purple of Clarehaven twinkling in the ruck like a setting star.

"Tony!" Dorothy screamed. "She's beaten!"

"Oh well," said the owner, "don't make such a noise about it."

He was smiling a foolish, fixed smile, but he let his glasses drop from his hands on the toes of a lady close by.

"I'm very sorry, ma'am," said Tony, raising his hat. "I hope I didn't hurt you."

The injured lady glared at him; it was her first Derby, and perhaps she did not realize that it mattered who won or lost.

"Come on, Doodles," said Tony. "Home. For God's sake, let's get home."

He would not wait to hear any explanation of the filly's defeat, but pushed his way savagely through the crowd to find the car.

"Gorblime!" a ragged vender of unauthorized race-cards was ejaculating near the garage. "Gor strike me blurry well pink! She'd make a blurry tortoise crick his blurry neck looking round to see why she was dawdling behind. Race-horse? Why, I reckon a keb-horse could give her three stone and win in a blurry canter, I do. Vanity Girl? Vanity Bitch, that's what she ought to have been called."

VII

The news of the defeat had already reached Halfmoon Street, and Galloway inclined his head when they passed quickly from the car into the hall of the flats, as if his patrons were returning from a funeral.

"We must telephone round to the Carlton to say that the dinner is off," said Tony; even that small action he left to his wife, himself sitting for the rest of the evening mute of speech, but drumming upon the table with his fingers or sometimes tambourinating upon an ash-tray. His dinner consisted of anchovy sandwiches washed down by brandy. There was no word from Houston, and Dorothy supposed that he was waiting to hear from her. "Going! Going! Clare! Clare! Clare!" The auctioneer's hammer seemed to be striking her temples, and, passing her hand over her forehead, she realized that it was only Tony who was drumming upon the table or tambourinating upon the ash-tray. She went to bed before he did and, lying awake in the rosy light of the reading-lamp, she wondered if, perhaps, he would try to forget this day in her arms, half hoped he would, and picked up the hand-mirror beside her bed to see how she was looking. He must have sat up drinking till very late—she had fallen asleep and did not hear him come to bed—and in the morning his eyes were bloodshot, his razor tremulous.

The letter-box was choked with bills; but there were several letters of condolence, and a reminder of the Day of Judgment from an enthusiastic enemy of the turf who, with ill-concealed relish, advised his lordship to observe the hand of God in the retribution which had been meted out to him and to turn away from his wickedness. Finally there were letters from O'Hara, the jockey, and Houston.

EPSOM SUMMER MEETING 1914.
Wednesday evening.

MY LORD,—I had hoped to have a few words with your lordship after the race, but was told you already left the course. I was intending to say that I could not go through what I suffered to-day on Friday, and would be obliged if your lordship wouldn't insist I would ride Vanity Girl in the Oaks. My lord, the filly is tired, and I wouldn't say another race mightn't kill her dead. It's not for me to give advice to your lordship, but how you ever come to run her in the Derby I don't know. She never was a stayer. I saw that plainly enough last autumn at Newmarket. I'm going back to France as soon as I hear from your lordship you won't run her in the Oaks. I'm engaged to ride Full Moon in the Grand Prix by Mr. Houston, and I hope I won't have to suffer what I suffered this afternoon. It's enough to make a jockey chuck riding for good and all.

I am,

Your lordship's obedient servant,
PATRICK O'HARA.

Pardon me if I've written a bit unfeelingly. It wasn't the filly's fault. She was tired. She didn't seem to know where she was, somehow, and when I flogged her along it near broke my heart to do it. She couldn't seem to understand what she was wanted to do. Poor little lady, I was so savage I could have shot her. But afterward I went and had a look at her, and had a few words with Mr. Starkey when he was abusing her.

QZI ALBANY, W.
Wednesday.

DEAR CLAREHAVEN,—I'm not going to worry you with sympathy at such a moment. But I'm writing as soon as possible to let you know that last week, owing to circumstances which would not interest anybody except a business man, I was compelled to part with my Clare mortgages for ready money, and I'm afraid that without doubt Reinhardt and Co. will foreclose on Monday. I wish I could offer to lend you the money to put yourself straight again, but I have been speculating myself and for the moment am a little short. By the way, I think Full Moon is a good thing for the Grand Prix. Perhaps you might get a bit on. Kindest regards to Lady Clarehaven.

Sincerely,
LIONEL HOUSTON.

Tony telegraphed to scratch Vanity Girl for the Oaks and ordered that she should be sold outright for what she would fetch; £200 was the figure, a tenth of what she had cost as a yearling and an insignificant fraction of what she had cost in ruinous disappointment, to which, perhaps, dishonor was soon to be added.

Houston's letter showed plainly that nothing was to be hoped for in that quarter.

"Reinhardt and Co.," scoffed Tony. "In my opinion Reinhardt and Co. includes Houston."

Dorothy wondered if the communication was intended to bring her quickly to heel, to show her brutally that unless she kept her bargain Clare was lost.

She supposed that somehow Houston would be ingenious enough to keep Tony from being suspicious when he found his house and lands restored to him, and she even wondered if under the demoralizing effect of gambling he would much mind if he did know. She looked at him with a feeling half compassionate, half contemptuous while he was calculating, with an optimism rapidly rising, every knickknack in the flat at four times its value in the sale-room. She persuaded him to go out and forget his troubles at the theater, and telephoned to the Albany that she was coming to see Mr. Houston after dinner.

Dorothy dressed herself in a frock of champagne silk and wore no jewelry except a drop pendant of black pearls, thinking ironically, when she fastened it round her neck, how premature Tony had been in estimating that it would fetch £500 at auction. She flung over her shoulders a diaphanous black opera-cloak stenciled in gold and, covering her face with a heavy veil of black Maltese lace, she passed out of Halfmoon Street and walked slowly up Piccadilly in the June starlight. On second thought she decided to enter Albany from Burlington Street instead of through the courtyard, and, turning into Bond Street, moved like a ghost along the pavements where on thronged mornings in old Vanity days her radiance and roses used to compete for the public regard with the luxurious shops on either side. Burlington Street at this hour was deserted, and the porter of Albany with his appearance of an antique coachman, and his manner between a butler's and a beadle's, dared not hesitate to admit such an empress, and perhaps marveled, when he watched her walk imperiously along the glass-roofed cloister that smelled of freshly watered geraniums toward QZI, with what honey the ugly tenant of it was able to attract this proud-pied moth.

Lady Clarehaven might have been excused for feeling a heroine, a Monna Vanna in the tent of the conqueror, when she found herself in the big square room which she now visited for the first time. She did not indulge herself with heroics, however; it seemed to her so natural for her to save Clare that the adventure was as commonplace as when once in early days on the stage she had pawned a piece of jewelry she did not like in order to save a set of furs to which she attached a great importance. She threw back the opera-cloak and sat down in an arm-chair to wait for Houston with as little perturbation as if she were waiting for a dinner guest in her own drawing-room.

Suddenly he appeared from an inner doorway and, turning on several more lights, looked at her. He was in evening dress, and the sudden glare gave the impression that he was going to perform; he looked more like an intelligent ape than ever when he was in evening dress.

"Well, here I am," she said.

Her coolness seemed to confuse him, and he began to ask her how she liked his rooms, to say that he had been lucky enough to take them on as they stood from a man called Prescott who had killed himself here. One had the impression that he had bought the furniture for a song on account of the unpleasant associations with a suicide.

"I'm rather tired of values," said Dorothy. "Clarehaven has been valuing the flat at Halfmoon Street."

"Will you have something to drink?"

"Do you think that I require stimulating? Thanks, I don't."

It was curious that this man, who in Rhodes had appeared so sinister and powerful and almost irresistible, should here in this decorous room with only a background of good-breeding appear fussy and ineffective.

"But let me recommend you to have a drink," Dorothy laughed. "For, now that you've got me, you're as awkward as a baboon with a porcelain teacup."

Her instinct told her that she must dispel this atmosphere of embarrassment unless she wanted to be bowed out of the chambers as from those of a money-lender who had been compelled most respectfully and without offense to refuse a loan to her ladyship. The allusion to the baboon was sufficient. The decorum of Albany was shattered and Houston held her in his arms.

At that moment the servant tapped at the door and announced that Lord Clarehaven was in the anteroom; before Houston could hustle his quaking servant outside and lock the door Tony appeared in the entrance, a riding-crop in his hands.

"My God! you rascal," he was saying, "I've just found out all about you. I've been fooled by you and that scoundrel of a trainer you recommended. I've been ... That trial.... I've seen.... I've understood ... you blackguard!" Without noticing Dorothy he had forced Houston across a chair and was thumping him with the crop. "Yes, I've heard all about you.... Of course people tell me afterward ... damned cowards.... You damned sneaking hound ... I.D.B.... hound.., you dog ... and there's nothing to be done because you were too clever ... curse you ... but I'll have you booted off every racecourse in England...."

By this time he had beaten Houston insensible, and, looking up, perceived his wife.

"Tony," she cried, "you really are rather an old darling."

"What are you doing here?" he panted.

"I was pleading for Clare."

"You oughtn't to have done that," he said, roughly. "You might get yourself talked about, don't you know. Come along. It's rather lucky I blew in. I met old Cobbett, who talked to me like a father. Too late, of course, and nothing can be done. Besides.... However, come along. As you're dressed we might see the last act."

"We've seen that already," said Dorothy. So brilliant and gay was she that Tony forgot about everything. So did she, and they walked home arm in arm along the deserted streets of Mayfair like lovers.

The scene in Albany was not made public property; Houston came to himself in time to prevent that. Dorothy accepted Tony's interruption as a sign that fortune did not intend her to preserve Clare, and she now watched almost with equanimity the fabric of a great family crumble daily to irreparable ruin. Then Full Moon, the winner of the Guineas, scratched ignominiously for the Derby, won the Grand Prix in a canter, and the following letter from the Earl of Stilton, K.G., appeared in the *Times*:

SIR,—In the interests of our national sport, which all Englishmen rightly regard as our most cherished possession, I call upon Lord Clarehaven to give a public explanation of his recent behavior. The facts are probably only too painfully known to many of your readers. In May Lord Clarehaven's horse, Full Moon, won the Two Thousand Guineas; two years ago his horse Moonbeam won the same race. Moonbeam ran fourth in the Derby and was transferred to the same stable as the winner, Chimpanzee. This horse, owned by Mr. Lionel Houston, was scratched for the St. Leger, and the race was won by Moonbeam. This was explicable; but when two years later another of Lord Clarehaven's horses wins the Two Thousand Guineas and finds his stable companion preferred to him to carry Lord Clarehaven's colors in the Derby, when, furthermore, the chosen filly runs like a plater, and when this morning we read that Full Moon, now in the ownership of Mr. Lionel Houston, has won the Grand Prix in a canter at a price which the totalizator puts at sixty-three to one, a proof that nobody in Paris considered the chances of this animal, the public may, perhaps, demand what it all means. They will ask still more when I inform them that I have absolute authority for saying that this horse was heavily backed in England, which proves that by some his chance was considered excellent. I have no wish to accuse his lordship of having deliberately deceived the public for his own advantage; but I do accuse him of folly that can only be characterized as criminal. Perhaps he has been the victim of his friend and of his trainer; at any rate, if his lordship was deceived about the chance of Vanity Girl, and if it is true that the defeat of Vanity Girl in the Derby represented to his lordship a loss of thousands of pounds in bets, he should make this clear. In that case I have no hesitation in accusing Mr. Lionel Houston, formerly known as Leopold Hausberg, of having deliberately conspired with the Starkey Lodge trainer to perpetrate a fraud not only upon their friend and patron, but also upon the public.

I have the honor to be, sir,

Your obedient servant,   STILTON.

Although Lord Stilton's letter hit the nail on the head, Tony was so furious at being called a fool in public that he sent the following letter to the paper:

SIR,—If Lord Stilton had not been my father's friend and a much older man than myself, I would pull his nose for the impudent letter he has written about me. The running of my filly in the Derby is an instance of the uncertainty of fortune, by which I am the greatest loser. I was convinced by a trial which I saw with my own eyes between Full Moon and Vanity Girl that the former did not stand a chance against the filly. It was I who insisted upon scratching him for the Derby so that the public might be spared the unpleasant doubt that always exists when an owner runs two horses in the same race. I sold the colt shortly after this trial to Mr. Houston, because I wished to put every halfpenny I could raise upon Vanity Girl. When I say that Mr. Houston is so little a friend of mine that I was unfortunately compelled to horsewhip him in his rooms on the day after the Derby, it will be understood even by Lord Stilton that there can be no possible suggestion of any collusion between myself and Mr. Houston. I do not know if Lord Stilton seriously means to insinuate that I have benefited by Full Moon's victory in the Grand Prix. If he does, the insinuation is cowardly and unjust. If Lord Stilton is so much concerned for the future of English sport, let him think twice before he hits a man who is down. Full Moon did not carry a halfpenny of my money.

I am, sir, etc.,   CLAREHAVEN.

This letter, with the reference to Lord Stilton's nose excised by a judicious editor, rehabilitated Tony in the eyes of the public and earned him a gracious apology from Lord Stilton, who also had to apologize much less graciously to Houston and Starkey, being threatened with legal proceedings unless he did so. Had there been the least chance of substantiating the ugly rumors, both earls might have gone to law; unfortunately legal advice said that neither of them stood a chance with the astute pair, and public opinion contented itself with compassion for the gallant young nobleman who had been thus victimized.

It may have been the victory of Full Moon in the Grand Prix with its suggestion of what might have been, or it may have been only the invincible optimism of the gambler, that started Tony off again upon his vice. When by the middle of July he and Dorothy found themselves with the rent of the flat paid up to Michaelmas, with enough furniture and enough clothes for present needs and with £250 in ready money, he told Dorothy that their only chance was for him to make money at cards. It was in vain that she argued with him; he seemed to have learned nothing from this disastrous summer, and with £100 in his pocket he went out one night, to return at six o'clock the next morning with £1,000.

"My luck's in again," he declared, "and I've got a thundering good system. You shall come with me every night, and I will give you two hundred pounds, which I must not exceed. Nothing that I say must induce you to give me another halfpenny. If I lose the two hundred pounds I must go away. It'll be all right, you'll see. I'm playing at Arrowsmith's place in Albemarle Street. Arrowsmith himself has promised not to advance me anything above two hundred pounds, so it'll be all right."

Dorothy begged him to be satisfied with the £1,000; but it was useless, and the following night she accompanied him. He won another £1,000, and when they had walked back under a primrose morning sky to Halfmoon Street Tony was so elated that he handed over all his winnings to Dorothy. The next night he lost the stipulated £200, but he came away still optimistic.

"I'm not going to touch that two thousand" he assured her. "I've got fifty left of my own, and one always wins when one's down to nothing; but on no account are you to offer me a halfpenny from your money. It's absolutely essential that you should bank everything I make."

The next evening Tony took the keeper of the hell aside and told him that he was to be sure not to let him exceed £50; if he should lose that, Arrowsmith was not to accept his I.O.U. and on no condition to allow him to go on. They were playing *chemin de fer* and Tony's luck had been poor; when his turn came to take the bank and he was stretching out his hand for the box of cards Arrowsmith told him he had already reached his limit.

"Oh, that's all right, Arrowsmith. I only meant that to count if I'd already had a bank."

"Excuse me, Lord Clarehaven, but I never go back on my word. The agreement we came to was...."

"That's all right," Tony interrupted, impatiently. "Dorothy, lend me some money."

"No, no. You made a promise, and really you must stick to it."

"Dash it! I haven't had a single bank this evening."

"You should have thought of that before."

"But, my dear girl, our agreement was that I shouldn't lose more than two hundred pounds at a sitting. I've only lost fifty pounds to-night."

"If I lend you any more," she said, "I must break into the two thousand pounds, which you told me I was not to do on any account."

The other players, with heavy, doll-like faces, sat round the table, waiting until the argument stopped and the game could be resumed. The keeper of the hell was firm; so was Dorothy; and Clarehaven had to yield his turn to his neighbor.

"I'll just stay and watch the play for a bit," he said. "It's only three o'clock." He took a banana from the sideboard and sat down behind the player who held the bank.

"No, no, come away," Dorothy begged him. "What is the good of tormenting yourself by watching other people play when you can't play yourself?"

"Damn it, Dorothy," he exclaimed, turning round angrily. "I wish to God I'd never brought you here. You always interfere with everything I want to do."

It happened that the bank which Tony had missed won steadily, and while the heavy-jowled man who held it raked in money from everybody, Tony watched him like a dog that watches his master eating. At last the bank was finished, and with a heavy sigh of satisfaction the owner of it passed on the box to his neighbor.

"How much did you make?" asked Tony, enviously.

"About two thousand five hundred. I'm not sure. I never count my winnings."

Tears of rage stood in Tony's eyes.

"God! Do you see what you've done for me by your confounded obstinacy?" he exclaimed to his wife.

All the way home he raged at her, and when they were in the flat he demanded that she should give him back all his £2,000.

"So you've reached the point," she said, bitterly, "when not even promises count?"

"If you don't give it back to me," Tony vowed, "I'll sell up the whole flat. Damn it, I'll even sell my boots," he swore, as he tripped over some outposts for which there was no place in the line that extended along the wall of his dressing-room.

Dorothy thought of that lunch-party in Christ Church and of the first time she had beheld those boots. She remembered that then she had beheld in them a symbol of boundless wealth. Now they represented a few shillings in a gambler's pocket. And actually next morning, in order to show that he had been serious the night before, Tony summoned two buyers of old clothes to make an offer for them.

"Don't be so childish," Dorothy exclaimed. "You can't sell your boots! Aren't you going down to camp this year?"

"To camp?" he echoed. "How the deuce do you think I'm going to camp without a halfpenny? No, my dear girl, a week ago I wrote to resign my commission in the N.D.D. You might make a slight effort to realize that we are paupers. And if you won't let me have any of that two thousand pounds we shall remain paupers."

At that moment a telegram was handed in:

All officers of North Devon Dragoons to report at depot immediately.

"Hasn't that fool of an adjutant got my letter?" Tony exclaimed.

Another telegram arrived:

Thought under circumstances you would want to cancel letter holding it till I see you.

"Circumstances? What circumstances?"

In the street outside a newspaper-boy was crying, "Austrian hultimatum! Austrian hultimatum!"

"My God!" Tony cried, a light coming into his eyes. "It can't really mean war? How perfectly glorious! Wonderful! Get out, you rascals!" and he hustled the old-clothes men out of the flat.

Three weeks later Dorothy received the following letter from Flanders:

DEAREST DOODLES,—You'd simply love this. I never enjoyed myself so much in all my life. Can't write you a decent letter because I'm just off chivvying Uhlans. It's got fox-hunting beat a thousand times. Sorry we had that row when I made such an ass of myself at Arrowsmith's that night. It's a lucky thing you were firm, because you've got just enough to go on with until I get back. Mustn't say too much in a letter; but I suppose we shall have chivvied these bounders back to Berlin in two or three months. Then I shall really have to settle down and do something in earnest. A man in ours says that Queensland isn't such a bad sort of hole. Old Cleveden put me against it by cracking it up so. It's suddenly struck me that Houston is probably a spy. If he is, you might make it rather unpleasant for him. I feel I haven't explained properly how sorry I am, but it's so deuced hard in a letter. By the way, Uncle Chat has just written rather a stupid letter about my mother's jointure. Perhaps you'd go down and talk to him about it. He ought to understand I'm too busy to bother about domestic finance at present. I had another notion—rather a bright one—that when I get back you and I could appear on the stage together. Rather a rag, eh? The captain of my troop was pipped last week. Awful good egg. I'm acting captain now. Paignton sends his love. Dear old thing, I wish you were out here with me.

Yours ever,
TONY.

A week later the fifth Earl of Clarehaven was killed in action.

CHAPTER VI

I

DOROTHY was at Little Cherrington when the news of Tony's death reached her. The dowager had already vacated Clare Lodge, and with a few of her dearest possessions was now established in Cherrington Cottage. Only extreme necessity could have driven her into that particular abode, because in order for her to go into it, Mr. Greenish had to go out of it, which upset Mr. Greenish so much that he went out of Cherrington altogether, out of Devonshire, even, and as far away as Hampshire. His choice of a county was the dowager's only consolation; Connie lived in Hampshire; the world was small; Mr. Greenish and Bella might even yet come together. Bella, absorbed in her short stories—one of which had been accepted, but not published, and another of which had been published but not paid for—found that the chief objection to being in Cherrington Cottage was the noise that the children made going to and from school. It was strange to find Bella, who in her youth had made as much noise even as Connie, so dependent now upon quiet; but in whatever divine hands mortals fall, their behavior usually changes radically afterward. We all know what love can do for anybody; we all know what the Salvation Army can do for anybody; and if Virgil's account of the Cumæan Sibyl may be trusted, the transforming influence of Apollo is second to none.

Tony's consideration in securing Cherrington Cottage to his mother could only have been bettered if he had made some provision for a sum of money to maintain it, or, for that matter, herself; delicious as the exterior of it undoubtedly was, the walls were not edible. The sudden stoppage in the payment of her jointure put the dowager in the humiliating position of having to ask her brother, Lord Chatfield, to pay the weekly bills, and it was with the intention of dealing with this matter that Dorothy had gone down much against her will to the scene that was consecrated to her greatest triumph and her greatest failure. Perhaps the nerves of the usually so genial Uncle Chat had been too much wrought upon by the outbreak of war. As deputy lieutenant of the county he had been harried by a series of telegrams from the War Office, each of which had contradicted its predecessor. He had had to lend not merely all his own horses to England, but to arrange to lend most of his neighbors', some of whom were not quite such willing lenders as his lordship. His eldest son, Paignton, was already at the front in the North Devon Dragoons, and his second son was assisting an elderly gentleman who had lived in obscurity since Tel-el-Kebir—where he had been jabbed in the liver by a dervish—to command, drill, and generally produce for their country's need the two hundred and ten rustics that at present constituted the Seventh Service Battalion of the King's Own Devon Light Infantry. His daughters, Lady Maud and Lady Mary, had given him no rest till they were allowed to do something or other; though before he understood what exactly this was the war had lasted many months longer than the greatest pessimist had believed possible. His sister, Lady Jane, in despair of finding anything else to do, was collecting mittens for the soldiers, a hobby which made the ground floor of Chatfield Hall look like a congested wool-warehouse in the city.

At such a moment the problem of his younger sister's financial future struck poor Uncle Chat as much more hopelessly insoluble than it would have seemed in those happy days when he had nothing to talk about except cigars and pigs. Bella immediately after the outbreak of war put down the pen and took up the sword, or in other words yearned to join the V.A.D., and it was the imperative need of finding money for Bella to gratify her patriotism in London that drove the dowager into discussing her finances with her brother. Dorothy, who could not bear the suggestion that Tony had heartlessly left for France without any heed of his family obligations, a suggestion that reflected upon herself, at once turned over to the dowager half of the £2,000 in the bank. Actually, she only left herself with something over £600, for extra money had had to be found for Tony's equipment and for the payment of bills he had overlooked. There was no reason to suppose that Uncle Chat was really criticizing her behavior in the least; but his air of general irritation gave her the impression that he was, which preyed upon her mind so much that she began to feel almost on a level with her unfortunate namesake who had lost the Derby. She fancied that everybody was ascribing Tony's mad career to his marriage, and thinking that if he had only married a nice girl in his own class none of these disasters would have happened. She fancied that the disapproval of the family which had been carefully concealed all these years out of deference to Tony's feelings was now making itself known, she was embittered by the imagined atmosphere of hostility, and she made up her mind that as soon as possible she would cut herself off from the Fanhopes and from what was left of the Clares.

Tony in his last letter had proposed that he and she should go on the stage when he came home, which of course would have been ridiculous; but, now that Tony was dead, there was surely nothing to prevent her return to the stage. When she got back to town she might go and ask Sir John Richards if he could not find a part in the autumn production at the Vanity Theater. Whatever was now lacking to her voice, whatever the years had added to her appearance, and notwithstanding the wear and tear that had added very little, would be counterbalanced in the eyes of the British public by the privilege of reading upon the program the name of the Countess of Clarehaven. Nothing was any longer owing to the family name; no, indeed, except Bella still bore it, and if third-rate stories were to appear in third-rate magazines under the signature of Arabella Clare, there was no reason why a bill of the play should not advertise the Countess of Clare. It happened that Harry Tufton had come down to Cherrington to assist at the memorial service which was to be held in Clarehaven church. Dorothy supposed that he was anxious to keep in with the Chatfields, and in speaking to him about her project she was not actuated by any desire for the sympathy of an old friend. She asked his advice in a practical spirit, because he was connected with the theater, and when he tried to discourage her by hinting at the fickleness of public affection, she discerned in his opposition to her plan nothing except the tired anxiety of one who was being importuned by an old friend to give the best advice compatible with the minimum of trouble to himself. Tufton's doubtfulness of her capacity still to attract the favor of an audience had the effect of strengthening her resolve to test his opinion; she asked him with that indifferent smile of hers, which had lost none of its magic of provocation, if he really thought that the British public was as fickle as himself. Tufton protested against the imputation, and excused himself for the evasion of friendship implicit in his attitude by pleading that the War Office kept him so very busy nowadays.

"Of course it was an awful blow when they wouldn't accept me for active service," he said, earnestly. "Heart, don't you know."

"Oh, your heart is weak," she inquired, with a mocking air of concern. "I suppose the very idea of war produced palpitations. Don't strain it going up-stairs in Whitehall."

"Somebody must do the work at home," he said, irritably.

"Yes, I feel so sorry for you poor Cinderellas," she murmured. "But never mind, you'll always be able to feel that if it wasn't for you the poor fellows at the front, don't you know, wouldn't be able to get along. I suppose you call yourselves the noble army of martyrs?"

It had been fun to twist the tail of that ship's rat, Dorothy thought, when she saw him hurry away from Cherrington to catch the first train back to town after the service.

The news of Tony's death had reached Cherrington on the morning of the day that Dorothy was going back to the flat. When she had made over half of her money to the dowager and was clear of the fancied atmosphere of hostility at Chatfield, she had begun to feel penitently that she had misjudged her mother-in-law and sister-in-law. It had seemed dreadful to leave them here in this cottage almost within sight and sound of the changes at Clare Court, and she had invited them to come and stay with her in Halfmoon Street until the flat was given up. The dowager had been unwilling to leave the country, and when the news of her son's death arrived was firm in her determination to remain in Cherrington.

"He was born here," she said, "and it is here that I shall always think of him best. I don't think I can afford to put up a window to his memory; he must just have a simple stone slab. I should like to copy that inscription at Rhodes. Do you remember it? 'Anthony, Fifth Earl of Clarehaven. With God. 1914.'"

Dorothy's grief at the death of Tony had for the moment been kept in control by the tremendous effort she had been called upon to make in facing the future; it was the future which had occupied her mind to the exclusion of any contemplation of the past. Now when her mother-in-law spoke these simple words she burst into tears. They linked Tony with so many generations of his house; and they brought home to her almost as a visible fact his death. She had spent so many years perpetually on the verge, as it were, of broken promises, of resolutions never carried out, of little optimisms and extenuations, that when the announcement of his death arrived it was more than usually true in her case that she did not at first realize it. The telegraphic form in which the news had been conveyed to her involuntarily merged itself with so many telegrams in the past which had turned out false, and only when the dowager stated his death like this in terms that admitted of no doubt did Dorothy suddenly confront the reality. She remembered that once a telegram had arrived almost on this very date to say that Tony could not get away from camp in time to be present at the annual show. There was no annual show this year—war had obliterated it—but on the afternoon of this day on which she had meant to return to town she walked, instead, about the field where the show had customarily been held, and so vivid was the familiar scene of hot women and blazing dahlias that she was transported back in imagination and found herself excusing on the ground of his military duties her husband's absence from this spectral exhibition. A farmer, one of her late tenants, passed her while she was wandering over the field, touched his cap, and begged to express his sorrow at the news.

"'Tis going to be a handsome year for partridges, too," he said. "But there, my lady, his lordship of late never seemed to care for partridges so much as he belonged. I remember when he was a youngster he'd regular walk me off my feet, as the saying is, after they birds. And he was uncommon fond of land-rails. Yes, it always seemed to give him a sort of extra pleasure, as you might say, when he could get a shot at a land-rail."

The reproach that was implied in the farmer's first words was mitigated by these reminiscences of Tony as a boy, and Dorothy thought that if her son had lived he would already be over six years old and within measurable distance of shooting his first land-rail in the company of the burly farmer beside her. Her son! Would it have made any difference to Tony if he had had an heir? Ought she to thank God or reproach Him for her childlessness?

Three days later Mr. Beadon sang for the late earl a requiem at Clarehaven church. Whoever should be the new owner of Clare—nobody had materialized from that mysterious firm of Reinhardt & Co.—he was not yet flaunting his proprietorship. The mourners passed slowly through the somber groves of pines and looked back at the empty house across the short herbage burnished by the drought of August, and the house empty and solemn, perhaps more solemn because it had not been dressed for grief, eyed with all its windows their progress seaward.

It would be cynical to say that at such a moment Mr. Beadon derived a positive pleasure from conducting a mass of requiem for the dead earl, and if for a moment he regarded with a kind of gloomy triumph Squire Kingdon's inevitable conformity to the majestic ritual of woe expressed by the catafalque from which depended the dead earl's hatchment, he made up by the grave eloquence of his funeral oration for any fleeting pettiness. The windows of the little church on the cliff were wide open to the serene air, and if ever the preacher fell mute for a space to recover from his emotion the plaint of the tide was heard in a monody above the mourners' tears; but above the preacher's voice, above all the sounds of nature in communion with human grief, there was continuously audible a gay chattering of birds among the tombs, of whinchats and stonechats that were mobilizing along these cliffs, unaware that there was anything very admirable or very adventurous about their impending migration. A cynic listening to those birds might have criticized the rector's sermon for its exaggeration of the spirit in which the young earl had set out to Flanders; a cynic might have given himself leave to doubt if the fifth Earl of Clarehaven was inspired by the same spirit as inspired Sir Gilbert Clare to defend Rhodes against the Moslem; but, whatever the spirit in which he had set forth, no cynic could impugn the spirit in which he had died; no living man, indeed, had any longer the right to sneer at his frailties and follies or to condemn his vices and his extravagance. Besides, a cynic contemporary with Sir Gilbert Clare may have questioned the spirit in which the Hospitaller had watched the cliffs of Devon fade out in the sunset. Who knows? There were stonechats and whinchats then as now.

On the morning after the requiem Dorothy was confronted with the possibility of an event that in its significance, should it come to fruition, would obliterate all that had happened in the past and would provide her in the future with a task so tremendous that she almost fell on her knees then and there to pray for strength and wisdom to sustain it. This was the possibility that she was going to have a child.

Such a prospect changed every plan for the future that she had been making and destroyed her freedom in the very moment it had been given back to her by the death of her husband. Her intention of proving to Harry Tufton that she could again be a favorite of the public must now be relinquished; her ambition to withdraw haughtily from the protection of Lord Chatfield must presumably be abandoned. Yet need they? She should not be too impulsive. Who now except herself had the right to say a word about her child's future? Who else could claim to be the guardian of its destiny? If she was right about her condition, she should rejoice that Tony was dead. If he had been alive and in that mood he was in before the outbreak of war solved his future so rapidly and so completely, this wonderful prospect would only have led to recriminations, even to open hatred. It would have been he who had robbed their child of its inheritance, and she could never have refrained from taunting him with his egotism. Nor was it likely that he would have been reformed by the prospect of being a father; he had not shown much inclination that way in the early years of their marriage; and even if for a while he had changed his habits, he would gradually have relapsed, and, moreover, with his genial and indulgent character he would have held out not merely a bad, but also an attractive, example, which would doubtless have been eagerly and assiduously imitated by any child of his. Yes, but now the future lay in her hands ... and meanwhile she must not be too sure that she was going to have a child at all, nor, even if it were established that she was, must she make too many plans in advance, because everything would be ruled by whether it was a boy or a girl. If it should be a girl, she might go back to the stage next year; she would only be thirty-one next March. It was odd how much younger thirty-one seemed than thirty. But if it should be a boy ... well, even if it should be a boy, why should she not go back to the stage and by her own exertions keep him, educate him, prepare him to be what he must be— landless, houseless, moneyless, but still the sixth Earl of Clarehaven? Stoic, indeed, should be his training, and his nobility should be won as well as conferred.

Several days of uncertainty went by, and finally Dorothy decided to ask Doctor Lane his opinion of her condition. He was a very old man now and no longer in practice, but at least he would know how to keep a secret, and a secret she intended his opinion to remain at present. Already plans were seething in her head for the immediate future, and when Doctor Lane assured her that she was going to have a baby, without saying a word even to the dowager she left next day for London.

Dorothy, who had been fancying that Tony's family wanted to be rid of her, soon found that, on the contrary, they would not let her alone, and when the lease expired at Michaelmas and while she was still wondering where she was going to live next, she received an invitation to join the dowager, Bella, and Lady Jane at the Chatfield town mansion in Grosvenor Square. It appeared that Lady Jane had by this time become so inextricably entangled in unknitted wool that the only way she could disentangle herself was by coming up to town to continue there with proper help the preparation of mittens against the winter cold.

"Not that it will be necessary," everybody said, "but it's as well to be prepared, and of course it *might* drag on till the spring."

The dowager, who had been worked up by her sister to feel that even though she had given a son to England she was still in debt, and Bella were among the twenty ladies collected by Lady Jane to make mittens, and the spinster was anxious to add Dorothy to her flock, for what between wool and ladies she was become very pastoral. So great pressure was put on Dorothy to make mittens, too. Uncle Chat was very penitent for his behavior over the jointure, and he now insisted that the money Dorothy had shared with her mother-in-law should be returned to her. Had it not been for her condition, she would have taken pleasure in refusing this; in the circumstances she accepted it, but she still did not say a word about her pregnancy, for reasons compounded of superstition and pride. Her experience of child-bearing had destroyed her self-confidence and she felt that she could not bear to have a great fuss made about her and to be installed in state at Chatfield Hall to wait there doing nothing through all this anxious winter of war. Nor did the manufacture of mittens in Grosvenor Square appeal to her. Moreover, it was possible that the news would not be welcome. She could not have borne to see Uncle Chat's face fall again at the prospect of having to support a grandnephew of the same rank as himself, and though she did not think that the dowager would attempt to interfere, or that she would be anything but delighted and tactful, there was the chance that after her son's death she might arrogate to herself a right to spoil her grandson. If Dorothy accepted for him the charity of his grandmother's family, she could not avoid admitting the dowager to the privilege of maternity; but if during the months of expectation she kept close her secret and if it were a boy, untrammeled by any obligations she should be at liberty to make her own decision about his up-bringing. More and more she was forming all her plans to fit the future of a boy, and one of her chief reasons for not relying upon the good will of the family was her desire to spare this son prenatal coddling by coddling herself.

Dorothy might have found it hard to analyze justly all the motives that inspired her to take the step she did; but whatever they were, a hot morning in late September found her sitting at the window of her old room in Lonsdale Road.

II

If outwardly Lonsdale Road presented the same appearance as it had presented on that September morning twelve years ago when Dorothy, after washing her hair, made up her mind to be engaged to Wilfred Curlew, the standpoint from which she now looked out of her window was so profoundly changed that the road itself was transmuted by the alchemy of her mind to achieve the significant and incommunicable landscape of a dream. It was as if in looking at Lonsdale Road she were looking at herself, and a much truer self than she ever used to see portrayed in that old mirror upon her dressing-table.

In an upper room of the house opposite a servant was dusting. Down below, amid that immemorial acrid smell of privet, two little girls were busily digging in the front garden. These were the daughters of her second sister, the rightful Dorothy, who was staying with her parents because her husband, Claude Savage, had left Norbiton for France with his regiment of territorials. Mrs. Savage, a dark, neat little woman, as capable a housewife as she had promised to become, and at twenty-eight not quite so annoying as formerly, came into the room from time to time and glanced out of the window to see that her little girls were not making themselves too dirty.

"Hope they're not disturbing you with their chattering."

"No, no," said the countess. "I like listening to them."

Ah, there was Edna down below, not as twelve years ago giggling back from school with Agnes, but wheeling a perambulator and from time to time bending cautiously over to arrange the coverlet over her sleeping baby. Edna was a dull edition of Agnes, and already at twenty-six much more like Mrs. Caffyn than any of her sisters. Her chin was rather furry; she was indefinite, not so indefinite as her mother because modern education had not permitted to her what was formerly considered a prerogative of woman. Edna had been married for about three years to Walter Hume, a young doctor in Golders Green, who was stationed at some northern camp with the R.A.M.C. She, too, was staying with her parents.

"Edna keeps on fussing with the coverlet," said Mrs. Savage, critically. "But she ought not to be walking along the sunny side of the pavement."

The countess did not pay much attention to the practical sister looking over her shoulders; she was thinking of Agnes and wondering what she was doing, and how her baby was getting on.

"Have you heard from Agnes lately?" she asked.

"Yes. Her husband has gone in for politics. But of course politics out there must be very different from what they are in England. You can't imagine Agnes as the wife of a politician. Tut-tut! Ridiculous!"

"What did she call her little boy?"

"Oh, gracious, don't ask me! Some perfectly absurd name. Could it be Xenophon? I know Claude laughed muchly when he heard it. Thank goodness, he wouldn't have let me choose such names for Mary and Ethel. I suppose Agnes is happy. She seems to be. I sometimes wonder where some of the members of our family get their taste for adventure."

"But you've no idea what a lovely place Aphros is ... it lies in the middle of a circle of islands and...."

"Yes, yes," Mrs. Savage interrupted, "but it's a long way from England, and the idea of living abroad doesn't appeal to me."

"Don't you ever want to travel?"

"Well, Claude and I had planned to go to Switzerland with a party this August, but of course the war put a stop to that."

"By the way, isn't the war rather an adventure for Claude?" the countess asked, with a smile.

"An adventure?" Mrs. Savage echoed. "It's a great inconvenience."

She bustled out of the room to look after her own daughters and give Edna some advice about hers; soon after she was gone Gladys and Marjorie, the prototypes of those little girls in the front garden, strolled in to gossip with their eldest sister. Although it was nearly noon, they were only just out of bed, because they had been up late at a dance on the night before. Gladys, a girl of twenty, was very like her eldest sister at the same age. She was not quite so tall and perhaps she lacked her air of having been born to grandeur, but she was sufficiently like to make Dorothy wonder if her career would at all resemble her own. On the whole, she thought that probably herself and Agnes had exhausted the right of the Caffyns to astonish their neighbors. Gladys and Marjorie, the latter a charming new edition of the original Dorothy, with flashing deep-blue eyes, dark hair, and an Irish complexion, were already, at twenty and nineteen, too free to be ambitious. Twelve years had made a great difference to the liberty of girls in West Kensington, and Mr. Caffyn no longer objected to the young men who came to his house, mostly in uniform nowadays, which provided one more excuse for emancipation. Gladys and Marjorie frequently arrived home unchaperoned from dances at three o'clock in the morning, and their father did not turn a hair; perhaps he was already so white that he was incapable of showing any more marks of life's fitful fever. No doubt he had long ago given up the ladies of Lauriston Mansions, and probably at no period in his career was he more qualified to be the secretary of the Church of England Purity Society than upon the eve of his retirement from the post. Dorothy had not seen her father since that night she drove him back in her car from the Vanity. Tacitly they had been friends at once when the countess came to live at home for a while; indeed, she fancied that she could grow quite fond of him, and she was even compelled to warn herself against a slight inclination to accept his flattery a little too complacently. Mrs. Caffyn, with a perversity that is often shown by blondes upon the verge of sixty, would not go white, and her hair was of so indefinite a shade as to be quite indescribably the very expression of her own indefinite personality.

Of the boys—it was odd to hear of the boys again—Roland had long been married and already had four children. At this rate he was likely to surpass his father, whom on a larger scale he was beginning to resemble. Roland was continually in a state of being expected to come and look the family up. He was so long in doing so that he became almost a myth to his eldest sister, and when at last, one afternoon, he did materialize with the largest mustache she had ever seen, his appearance gave her the same kind of thrill that she used to get at the Zoo, when at short intervals the sea-lion would emerge from the water and flap about among the rocks of his cage. It was obvious that Roland regarded her with a mixture of suspicion, jealousy, and disapproval, for he had not brought his wife with him, and when the countess asked him if he had also left his pipe at home, he growled out that he supposed she was far too grand for pipes. Dorothy remembered that sometimes when they were children he and she had seemed upon the path of mutual understanding, and, feeling penitent for her share in the way they had for twelve years been walking away from each other, she tried to be specially affectionate with Roland; but he was already out of earshot. He evidently was thinking that her abrupt re-entry into the family circle would probably mean a reduction in his share of any money left by their parents, because he was continually alluding to her financial state and his own. She tried to ascribe this to his position as the manager of a branch bank; but she knew in her heart that he was dividing £500 a year first by eight and then by nine and thinking what a difference to his holiday that extra £7 would make. Of Dorothy's other brothers, Cecil was in camp somewhere, and hoping to get to France soon with the R.A.M.C.; he had been married only a few months, and his wife was living in the nearest town to his quarters. Vincent, who had won a scholarship at Sydney Sussex College, Cambridge, had already enlisted and wrote home as confidently of promotion in the near future as twelve years ago he had boasted that he would soon be in the eleven of St. James's Preparatory School.

Perhaps the most striking result of the countess's return was the impetus it gave to Mrs. Caffyn's Wednesday afternoons. The punctilious ladies came as they had been coming steadily for twelve years; but a quantity of less punctilious ladies also came and were so much over-awed by meeting a countess in a West Kensington drawing-room that they had no appetite for cakes, which was just as well because otherwise the strain put upon the normal provision by so many extra visitors might have been too much for it. In addition to the Wednesday ladies, several friends of Dorothy's youth visited No. 17 in the evenings, and though by now the billiard-table was more like a neglected tennis-lawn, she played one or two games to remind her of old times, thinking how scornful she would have been twelve years ago if any one had prophesied to her such indulgence in sentiment. Among these friends of youth came Wilfred Curlew, who in outward appearance was the least changed of all. His career had been successful, if the editorship of a society paper can be considered success. Being a journalist, he rightly considered himself indispensable at home, and it is unlikely that his inaccurate and cheery paragraphs in *The Way of the World* did any more to make the war ridiculous than some of the inaccurate and cheery despatches sent home from the front by generals. A slight tendency which he had formerly had toward a cockney accent had been checked by an elocutionist who had imprisoned his voice in his throat, whence it was never allowed to stray. If Lady Clarehaven had once been a Vanity girl, Mr. Wilfred Curlew, the editor of *The Way of the World*, had once written fierce revolutionary articles about Society in *The Red Lamp*; and whereas Lady Clarehaven had long been indifferent to her past, Mr. Curlew was still sensitive about his, as sensitive as a man who oils the wheels of railway-coaches in termini would be if it were known that he had once been a train-wrecker.

After the first awkwardness of such a rencounter had worn off Dorothy found Wilfred entertaining. It was astonishing to learn how accurately the failings and follies of so many of her friends and acquaintances were known to the editor, who had never met one of them. At first he pretended that he had met them; but as gradually he saw more of the countess he gave up this pretense, and finally he revealed the existence in his mind of a perpetual and abominable dread that soon or late in one of his cheery paragraphs he should make a mistake, not, of course, a mistake of fact or even an unjust imputation—that would be nothing—but a mistake of form. He was really haunted day and night by such bogies as referring to a maid of honor after marriage without her prefix, though to have suggested that her behavior with somebody else's husband was less honorable than that would no more have troubled him than to state positively that her main hobby was breeding Sealyham terriers, when it was really communicating every Sunday at St. Paul's, Knightsbridge. If in Lonsdale Road Dorothy beheld her present self, in Wilfred Curlew she saw the reflection of what she was twelve years ago, enough of which old self still existed to make her feel proud that never in her most anxious moments had she revealed to another person her own dread of making a mistake.

One day after a long talk about well-known people in society, Curlew exclaimed from the depths of his inmost being, "If only I had you always!"

"Is this a proposal?" she laughed.

He rose and walked about the room in his agitated fashion; then supporting with one arm the small of his back as he used, and wrenching his voice back into his throat whence in his emotion it had nearly escaped, he paused to mutter:

"Presumptuous, I know, but sincere."

This phrase remained in Dorothy's mind for long afterward, and in her gloomiest hours she could always smile when she repeated gently to herself, "Presumptuous, I know, but sincere."

Naturally, she told Curlew as kindly as she could that his proposal was far outside the remotest bounds of possibility.

"Besides," she added, "you'd really be much better off without my help. Readers of your paper will always greatly prefer your view of society to my view. My view would pull your circulation down to nothing in less than no time."

"It's true," Curlew groaned. "How wise you are!"

Only that morning he had received a sharp reminder from the great brain of which *The Way of the World* was merely an inquisitive and insignificant tentacle, to say that the last three or four numbers of the paper had shown a marked falling off in their ability to provide what the public required.

"You have to admit that I am right," Dorothy pointed out kindly.

"Yes, but if you'd marry me, in a year or two I would give up journalism and write novels. I've got a theory about the form of the English novel which I should like to put into practice."

"I'm afraid," said Dorothy, "I have heard too many theories about the form of race-horses to believe much in theories of form about anything. Form is a capricious quality."

"It's an awful thing," poor Wilfred groaned, "for a man who knows he can write good stuff never to have an opportunity of doing so. I'm afraid I've sold my soul," he murmured, in a transport of remorse.

"We all of us do that sooner or later," she said. "And it's only when we don't get a good price for it that we repent."

Dorothy's faculty for aphorisms had no doubt been fostered by the respect which was accorded to her at Lonsdale Road, but she was far from talking merely for the sake of talking, and her inspiration was really the fruit of experience, not the mere flowering of words. She had, perhaps, been wiser than she had realized in coming home for a while. Notwithstanding those two younger sisters nearly as beautiful as herself, notwithstanding the knowledge generally diffused that she was without money, her beauty and rank were still sufficiently remarkable in West Kensington to preserve her dignity. Here she ran no risks of acquiring a deeper cynicism from the behavior of old friends like Tufton, and inasmuch as misfortune had made her more truly the equal of those around her she had no temptation now to lord it over her sisters, as no doubt they had expected she would; in the homage of West Kensington she let the pleasant side of herself develop and, by a strong effort resisting an inclination to worry about the future, she resigned herself to whatever fortune had in store for her.

Dorothy was not content with waiting for all her old friends to visit her; there was one whom she herself sought out soon after she reached West Kensington. She had not seen Olive Airdale since her marriage, and she was glad she was visiting her for the first time humbly and on foot, even if Olive should think that it was only in adversity that she cared to seek out the companions of her early days. What rubbish! As if Olive would think anything except that she was glad to see her old friend. It was an opalescent afternoon in mid-October when Dorothy rang the bell of the little red house in Gresley Road, and Olive's welcome of her was as if the mist over London had suddenly melted to reveal that very paradise which for the fanciful wayfarer existed somewhere behind these enchanting and transfigurative autumnal airs.

"My dearest Dorothy," she exclaimed. "But why do you reproach yourself? As if I hadn't always perfectly understood! I've been so worried about you. And I wish you could have met Jack—but of course he enlisted at once. You don't know him or you'd realize that of course he had to."

They talked away as if there had never been the smallest break in their association; Rose and Sylvius, those nice fat twins who would be five years old next April, interested the countess immensely now that she would soon be a mother herself.

"And Sylvia?" Dorothy asked.

"Oh, my dear, we don't know. Isn't it dreadful? None of us knows. She was engaged to be married to Arthur Madden—you remember him, perhaps at the Frivolity last year—and suddenly he married another girl and Sylvia vanished—utterly and completely. She went abroad, that's all we know."

So Sylvia with all her self-assurance had not been able to escape a fall. In Dorothy's present mood it would have been unfair to say that she was glad to find that Sylvia was vulnerable, but she did feel that if she ever met Sylvia again she should perhaps get back her old affection for her more easily. And while she was thinking this about Sylvia she suddenly realized that all these other people must be feeling the same about herself.

The revival of her intimacy with Olive made a great difference to Dorothy's stay in West Kensington, and she might even have stayed on at Lonsdale Road until her baby was born had not her two married sisters turned out to be going to have babies also. Though Dorothy had never possessed a very keen sense of humor, her sense of the ridiculous had been sufficiently developed to make her feel that the sight of three young women in an interesting condition round the dining-room table of No. 17 would be a little too much of a good thing. She therefore wrote to Doctor Lane to say that she wanted her child to be born in Devonshire, and asked for his advice. He suggested that she should go to a nursing-home he knew of in Ilfracombe. Thither she went in the month of January, taking with her from Lonsdale Road that old colored supplement inscribed "Yoicks! Tally-Ho"; and there, without any of those raptures that marked her first pregnancy, but with abundant health and serenity of purpose, she waited for her time to come, and at the end of April bore a posthumous son to Clarehaven.

III

Not until her son was actually born did Dorothy apprise the dowager of the event. It was lucky that spring was already warm over France and that the sudden famine of mittens did not inconvenience the troops at this season, because the instant withdrawal of the dowager, Lady Jane, and Lady Arabella from the house in Grosvenor Square left the twenty ladies they had gathered together with neither wool to continue their good work nor with addresses to which it could be sent. The dowager in a state of perfect happiness began to trace in the lineaments of the baby a strong likeness to her dead son, and, as Dorothy had expected, to lament loudly his disinheritance; Lady Jane insisted that he must be taken at once to Chatfield, where Uncle Chat would be more than delighted to look after him entirely; Bella, who had been working herself up into a state of great excitement over a baby that Connie expected to bring into the world at the end of May, ceased to take the least interest in Connie or her child and celebrated the advent of her nephew, the sixth earl, by abandoning prose for a pæan of rhapsodic verse. As for Dorothy, she who during the months of waiting had supposed that she had at last reached that high summit of complete indifference to the world, lost nearly all her superiority, and with her strength renewed and increasing every day was on fire to secure somehow or other to her son the material prosperity that his rank demanded. She was still averse to taking him to Chatfield, because even if at such an early age it was improbable that the externals of Chatfield would make the least impression upon his character, she did not like to surrender all her fine schemes of independence at once. She compromised by consenting to take the baby to Cherrington Cottage, where his arrival elicited from their former tenants a most moving demonstration of affection for the family.

Clare Court was still vacant, and during that summer Dorothy used to wheel the perambulator of her baby round and round the domains of which he had been robbed. For his name she had gone back to her old choice of Lucius, and she felt that by doing so she was conferring upon this posthumous son the greatest compliment in her capacity. The dowager was at first a little distressed that he was not christened Anthony, but when Dorothy read to her, out of a volume of Clarendon she borrowed from the rector, that this namesake was "'a person of such prodigious parts of learning and knowledge, of that inimitable sweetness and delight in conversation, of so flowing and obliging a humanity and goodness to mankind, and of that primitive simplicity and integrity of life, that if there were no other brand upon this odious and accursed civil war than that single loss, it must be most infamous and execrable to all posterity.' 'Thus,'" Dorothy read on, "'fell that incomparable young man, in the four-and-thirtieth year of his age, having so much despatched the true business of life that the eldest rarely attain to that immense knowledge, and the youngest enter not into the world with more innocency.'"

"Yes, yes," sighed the dowager. "Dear old Tony! He was in his thirty-second year. Dear old boy!"

Dorothy looked at her mother-in-law to see if she were serious; when she saw that indeed she was she had not the heart to say that the eulogy might as a description of Tony's life be considered somewhat elevated. After all, Tony had died for his king and his country; Lord Falkland had died for his king only.

On the anniversary of the fifth earl's death, when the wind at dusk was cooing round Cherrington Cottage like a mighty dove, Dorothy was seized with a sudden restlessness and a desire to encounter the mysterious and uneasy air of this gusty twilight of late summer. Her son was fast asleep, with both his grandmother and his aunt Arabella ready to minister to his most incomprehensible baby wish and serve him, were it possible, with the paradisal milk of which he dreamed. He had been restless all day, and now that he was sleeping so calmly Dorothy felt that she could allow herself to take air and exercise. Owing to the continued emptiness of the Court, she had grown into the habit of walking about the park whenever she felt inclined, and except for the solemnity and silence of the house itself she was hardly conscious that she was no longer the mistress of Clare, because the lodge-keepers and various servants of the estate were familiar to her and always showed how glad they were to see her among them.

The park that evening was haunted by strange noises; but Dorothy's mind never ran on the supernatural, and neither swooping owl, nor flitting bat, nor weasel swiftly jigging across her path, nor sudden scurry of deer startled at their drinking-pool alarmed her. She walked on until the dusk had deepened to a wind-blown starlight, and she found herself in the gardens, where on the curved seat of the pergola she sat until the moon rose and the statues shivered like ghosts in a light changing from silver to gray, from gray to silver, as the scud traveled over the moon's face. But Dorothy had no eyes that night for shadows. She was keeping the anniversary of the fifth earl's death by concentrating upon one supreme problem—the restoration of all these moonlit acres, of all these surging yews and cedars, of every stone and statue, to the rightful heir. If any ghost had walked in Clare that night she would have thought of nothing but the best way to retain him for her son's service. Each extravagant idea that came into her head seemed to stay there but for an instant before it was caught by the wind and blown out of reach forever. Restlessly she left the pergola and wandered round the empty house where the wind in the pines on either side was like a sea and the scent of the magnolias in bloom against the walls swirled upon the air with an extraordinary sweetness. She entered one of the groves and passed through to the lawn behind, where a wild notion came into her head, inspired by the wild night and this mad close of summer, to find an ax and deface the escutcheon of Clare, to mutilate the angelic supporters, to eclipse forever that stone moon in her complement, and so spoil for the intruding owner at least one of his trophies. The unheraldic moon was not yet above the pine-trees on the eastern side of the house, and such was the force of the wind blowing straight off the sea from the northwest—blowing here with redoubled force on account of the gap in the cliffs through which it had to travel—that when a cloud passed over the still invisible moon on the far side, Dorothy had the impression that the luminary was being blown out like a lamp, so dark did it then become here in the shadow of the house. She had an impulse to defy this wind, to walk down to the headland's edge and watch the waves leaping like angry, foaming dogs against the face of the cliff; but half-way to the sea she had to turn round, exhausted, and surrender to the will of the wind. Her hair blown all about her shoulders, spindrift and spume racing at her side, she let herself sail back along the lea toward the house, looking to any one who should see her like a mermaid cast up by the tempest upon a haunted island. Haunted it was, indeed, for just as the moon shining down a gorge of clouds rose above the pines she met the Caliban of this island.

"You!" she cried. "I knew it was you the whole time."

Houston was unable to speak for a minute, so frightened had he been by this apparition from the sea, so frightened was he to be wandering round this stolen house and in his wanderings to have provoked this spirit of the place, and in the end more frightened than ever, perhaps, to find who the spirit really was. Dorothy did not realize how strange she looked, how magical and debonair, how perilous, how wild; she whose brain was throbbing with one thought perceived in Houston's expression only the shame he should naturally feel for having robbed her son.

"You look tremendously blown about," he managed to say, finally. "Won't you come inside for a minute?"

Then suddenly as if the wind had got into his brain he said to her, "Dorothy, why don't you marry me and take all this back for yourself?"

"Could I?"

She had appealed to herself, not to him; but he, misunderstanding her question, began like a true Oriental to praise the gifts he would offer her.

"Stop," she commanded. "All these things that you want to give to me, will you give them to my son? Don't be so bewildered. You knew I had a son? I can't stop here to argue about myself and what I can give you or you can give me. If you will make over Clare as it stands with all its land—oh yes, and buy back the Hopley estate which Tony's father sold—to my son, I'll marry you."

"If you'll marry me I'll do anything," he vowed.

There was a momentary lull in the wind, and as if in the silence that followed he was able to grasp how much he had undertaken, he stammered, nervously:

"And you and I? Suppose you and I have children?"

"Well," said Dorothy, "they'll be half brothers and sisters of the sixth Earl of Clarehaven, which will be quite enough for *them*, won't it?"

And that night, while the wind still cooed round Cherrington Cottage, Dorothy, Countess of Clarehaven, wrote out for Debrett and read to Augusta, Countess of Clarehaven:

"Clarehaven, Earl of (Clare.) (Earl. U.K. 1816. Bt. 1660.) Lucius Clare; 6th Earl and 11th Baronet; *b.* April 25, 1915; *s.* 1915; is patron of one living.

"*Arms*—Purpure, two flanches ermine, on a chief sable a moon in her complement argent. *Crest*—A moon in her complement argent, arising from a cloud proper. *Supporters*—Two angels, vested purpure, winged and crined, or, each holding in the exterior hand a key or.

"*Seat*—Clare Court, Devonshire."

THE END